Praise for *Bear Hunting with the Politburo*

"The best book ever on the Soviet wasteland . . . the first Soviet business narrative; it sets a high benchmark.

—*The Financial Times*

"Entertaining . . . infuriating . . . some of the most riveting stuff to emerge from *perestroika*.

—*The Los Angeles Times*

"Fresh and important. Copetas' slick writing is deadeye reporting."

—*Business Week*

"Fine, hard-ball, pure deadline-style journalism. You might as well call *Bear Hunting with the Politburo, Fear and Loathing in Moscow*."

—Dr. Hunter S. Thompson

"Timely and good reading for anyone who wants to know what's going on in the Soviet Union . . . must reading for someone daring to contemplate a business venture there."

—*The San Francisco Chronicle*

"Read *Bear Hunting* and weep—but read it nonetheless . . . a blistering portrayal."

—*Time Out*

"An extremely powerful and important book . . . you will not be able to put it down."

—CBS Radio Network

"No one has ever written about the Soviet Union and *perestroika* like Copetas. One of the best ever written about our country by an American . . . destined to become a best-seller."

—*Izvestia*

"Story-telling at its best."

—*The Pittsburgh Press*

"A gritty, absorbing tale of dreams and greed. Copetas has succeeded in putting his finger on the most daunting obstacle in the way of Russia's transition to a free market."

—*Newsday*

A. Craig Copetas

BEAR HUNTING
WITH
THE POLITBURO

A TOUCHSTONE BOOK
Published by Simon & Schuster
NEW YORK / LONDON / TORONTO
SYDNEY / TOKYO / SINGAPORE

TOUCHSTONE
Simon & Schuster Building
Rockefeller Center
1230 Avenue of the Americas
New York, New York 10020

Copyright © 1991 by A. Craig Copetas

First Touchstone Edition 1993
TOUCHSTONE and colophon are registered trademarks
of Simon & Schuster Inc.
Designed by Edith Fowler
Manufactured in the United States of America

10 9 8 7 6 5 4 3 2

10 9 8 7 6 5 4 3 2 1 (pbk.)

Library of Congress Cataloging in Publication Data

Copetas, A. Craig.
   Bear hunting with the Politburo : a gritty first-hand account of Russia's young
entrepreneurs—and why soviet-style capitalism can't work / A. Craig Copetas.—
1st Touchstone ed.
        p.   cm.
   Includes index.
   1. Entrepreneurship—Soviet Union. 2. Capitalism—Soviet Union. 3. Political corruption—Soviet Union. 4. Soviet Union—Economic conditions—
1985–1991.   I. Title.
HB615.C648   1993
338.947—dc20   92-34762
                                                                    CIP

ISBN: 0-671-70313-7
ISBN: 0-671-79721-2 (pbk.)

To the *troika:*
MARIE-CÉLINE GIRARD, for her love.
WILLIAM A. REGARDIE, for his moxie.
SABIT ATAIEVICH ORUDJEV, for his courage.

Author's Note

THIS IS THE STORY of the young men and women of *perestroika*, and how and why their attempt to create a democratic, free-market economy in the Soviet Union helped spark the military coup d'état against Mikhail Sergeyevich Gorbachev on August 19, 1991, which backflamed to immolate the Communist Party five days later, after seventy-four years of Bolshevik rule.

All episodes and conversations in *Bear Hunting with the Politburo* took place between 1987 and 1991, and the names of all individuals and official groups participating in the actions described are real. However, the reader should be aware that I have altered the names of two characters: "Thomas H. Billington" of the "Race Group," and "Trusishka," a senior Soviet official, are pseudonyms requested by each man to furnish, respectively, post-publication anonymity from publicity and protection from possible political retribution. The real names of both men may appear to be evident to readers acquainted with the characters and events in the story through previous press accounts; nonetheless I have honored the requests for anonymity for the purpose of this book and kindly ask the reader to appreciate Billington's and Trusishka's decision to remain anonymous through the unorthodox use of two pseudonyms in a work of nonfiction.

I use the term "liberal" in its European sense throughout the book. In the United States, a liberal is generally understood to be a leftist who on principle would oppose a free market. A liberal in Europe, and in the Soviet political sense, is someone who is in favor of the liberal loosening of government control.

I began covering the Soviet Union out of London in 1984 for *Regardie's* magazine and *The Village Voice.* In 1988 *Regardie's* editor Brian Kelly wanted the magazine to expand beyond monthly feature roundups of *perestroika,* and so he asked me to move to Moscow. Kelly directed me to delve into the daily realities confronted by the new Soviet freemarketeers, known as cooperators, in their attempt to shape the country into a society that rewarded democratic enterprise. Although *Bear Hunting with the Politburo* describes my relations with and perceptions of a specific group of cooperators during the *perestroika* revolution, their predicament was duplicated almost exactly, with greater or less intensity, at different intervals of time, all over the U.S.S.R. during the Gorbachev years.

Prologue

A RUSSIAN BEAR (*Ursus arctos*) is the world's largest terrestrial carnivore. Cannibalism occurs more frequently among this species than among any other animal group. Born with an incessantly antagonistic disposition and an innate ability to camouflage that fact, the bear uses his viciousness as a weapon. With stocky feet, small eyes, a broad head, and twenty highly curved claws that are impossible to retract, the Russian bear—*medved*—will strike without notice and eat his victim completely. Those who professionally hunt the bear within the Soviet Union's fifteen republics assert that he is far more preoccupied with wielding ultimate power over his domain than with developing strategy; amateurs who confront wild bear are warned not to pay attention to his facial expression. A bear's facial muscles are so poorly developed that it is impossible for him to make the expressions that other animals normally use to telegraph their intentions in the wild. In ancient times, the ancestors of the peoples now inhabiting the Soviet Union's politically and economically fractured southern republics of Georgia, Armenia, and Azerbaijan worshiped the bear as a totem animal; he was the object of mystery cults, which sometimes included ritual sacrifice. The bear, through religious creed and deity and the heavenly configuration of Kallisto (the constellation Ursa Major, the Great Bear), enjoyed exalted status.

The Russian language has a word for bears that become extremely savage and ruthless: *shatoon*. Ivan the Terrible was fond of setting *shatooni* on humans for the sheer pleasure of seeing how they would destroy their victims. Later tsars had the teeth of captured *shatooni* filed down into stumps; dogs were then released upon them, with spectators gambling on the outcome of tooth versus claw. Boyars, the noblemen of old Muscovy, indulged in the practice of pouring alcohol into muzzled *shatooni* to observe the outcome. A special breed of dog, nicknamed the *shatoon laika*, was later developed to hunt the animal in the wild depths of Russia's northern winter. Today, *shatooni* are not pursued for sport or by sportsmen. They are stalked and executed at great risk by professional hunters to ensure the survival of the people they would destroy. *Shatoon*—a bear of such dementia that it is unwilling to hibernate in winter—was an expression unique to the Russian vocabulary; a word now used by northern Russian villagers and hunters as a cautionary noun to describe the Soviet civilians, bureaucrats, and Communist Party officials who seem to have been displaced by *perestroika*. In the great taiga, Russia's vast subarctic forest, tales abound of *shatooni* rising up from apparent death to devour their executioners.

They were thorns in the flesh of the godly.

JOHN DOS PASSOS

T HE EXACT METHOD the Immortalization Commission used to transform the corpse of Vladimir Ilyich Lenin into the mummy on display beneath Moscow's Red Square is probably lost. A grisly and rather partial account of the events that took place between January 24 and January 26, 1924, has rumored its way down the years, however. The process began with syphoning the blood, and removing the brain and internal organs through various body orifices and a long abdominal incision. Cleansed and sterilized with palm wine, Lenin was packed by Immortalization Commission embalmers with spices, chemically treated cloths, and sawdust from birch trees. His flesh was dehydrated by covering the body with salt, after which it was restuffed and padded with linen bags full of chemicals and natural ingredients.

The brain was delicately sliced into seven sections and handed over to a team of Immortalization Commission scientists, with the peculiar mandate to ascertain why Lenin's intellect was superior to those of other mortals. The research still goes on, say the rumors, in sealed and secret basement laboratories of the Lenin Museum, a few hundred yards away from where the mummified remains of the founder of all that is the Soviet Union lie in a glass cage, an eerie and permanent reminder of Bolshevik horror.

The peculiarities and crimes that pockmark Russia's barbaric history are over, as every Soviet spokesman who haunted the concrete-dappled foreign press center on Moscow's Zubovsky Boulevard explained endlessly when I first walked into the place in 1985. It is *pravda*, they asserted, that the foulness of the past is at an end, liberty is at hand, and Lenin's shriveled limbic area is no longer being whacked with electrical implants for clues to his genius. Like so much in the Soviet Union, that is only half of it. In street parlance *pravda* is the state's truth, not the truth at all. The word for real, unvarnished truth is *istina*. In a land whose rulers have mastered the art of refracting reality, *pravda* is a reflection in the state's funhouse mirror. In the same way successive Kremlin regimes have advertised Lenin and the warped and oppressive top-level villains that his brain created, the Soviet government now promotes *perestroika* (the restructuring of the Soviet communist system) and *glasnost* (the openness to express one's opinions and beliefs without fear of reprisal) as *pravda*. The people want to know whether they are *istina*.

Istina is the Russian Zen, a higher plateau of consciousness extremely difficult and dangerous to reach, that has absolutely no connection to anything in the West. Reaching *istina* implies having secret knowledge. Anthropologists explain that information and experience are the beginning of individuality and consciousness. Yet information and experience have historically been state monopolies in Russia. The result of the Communist Party's control over consciousness is a nation of people whose collective sensibilities have been launched and navigated by the state.

During the turbulent Gorbachev era, a group of quite differently motivated young men and women known as cooperators came to share a belief in something far greater than *perestroika*.* Risking their lives and reputations, sometimes alone in anguish and sometimes together in hostility, the cooperators walked a treacherous

---

*Paradoxically, a Soviet cooperative is the structural equivalent of a privately owned "capitalistic" company that charges whatever price the market will bear for its goods and services. This is just the opposite of the Western notion of a cooperative, which is a "socialistic" production and/or distribution organization designed to slash free-market prices and share the profits among its members.

line between nuisance and enemy to push *perestroika*'s back up against the wall in an economic war of attrition. For these uneasy allies, *perestroika* was a point of convergence, a place where the menace of the past was destined to meet the promise of the future and, it was hoped, *istina* would be discovered.

"The cooperator's job is to legitimize a black market which the corrupt bureaucracy doesn't want to see legitimized, and to destroy the prejudices the communist power structure doesn't want to see destroyed," explained Vladimir "Volodya" Yakovlev, the chairman of Cooperative Fact, the Soviet Union's first privately owned news and information service. "The entire bureaucracy within the state distribution system channeled the best and most wanted goods to the black market in return for money and favors. The occasional black marketeers arrested for show are invariably Jews, Muslims, or members of other ethnic minority groups. The black market is so big, I think bigger than any foreigner is willing to accept, that very little goes to the shops.

"Consumers are forced to pay high prices because the black market always has been the real market in Russia," said Yakovlev, whose cooperative grew into one of the Soviet Union's richest and most powerful businesses. "So the cooperators get together with the few less-greedy individuals who exist in the state production and distribution system and buy raw materials from them to sell through privately owned businesses. The state shops are empty anyway, but then the Soviet people see the co-ops selling goods that socialism promised would be on state shelves for cheap prices. Of course, every item a co-op sells is being sold on the black market without complaint and for a much higher price than at a co-op. 'Why legalize the black market?' they ask. 'Just deliver these goods and services to the state stores and sell them at cheap, subsidized prices.'

"The public sector is dead and the cooperative sector very much alive and in constant trouble," Yakovlev explained. "The manager of a factory that made T-shirts complained to me that cooperators had bought all his T-shirts, painted pictures on them, and sold them for more money. He was amazed and angry at this. So I asked him why the factory didn't paint the pictures on the T-shirts and sell them instead. He said he didn't want to do it. This is why the public sector is dead and the cooperators face trouble."

Nobody knew the limits to which the Party and the government would allow the cooperative movement to grow, even though the officially manifested faith in the cooperative credo, "Shatter the black market with the free market," was written between the lines of *perestroika*. Whatever confidence Volodya Yakovlev had in changing the system through entrepreneurship and the application of free-market principles was snared in the petty jealousies and power scrambles of old Party hacks and newly converted democrats. Moreover, always facing him was the danger that ultraconservative political cliques would band together with the army to psychologically and economically harass the freemarketeers under the banner of fervid anti-Jewish, anti-intellectual Russian nationalism. Out of fear or genuine sympathy with the spirits of the past, the Russian people were loath to embrace cooperators with the drive and emotion necessary to suture an industrious free-market system together. On one hand, Gorbachev introduced the cooperative movement to the nation in 1988 with deliberately grand words that alluded to past Communist Party achievements; on the other hand, such moves toward freedom in the past had been mere cosmetic manipulations with a nasty history as precursors to persecution and disaster. Lubricating the entire *perestroika* system of economic restructure and free expression was the incapacitating corruption of traditional communism, a system in which graft, theft, greed, prejudice, and political blackmail were too rapacious to permit the long-term self-sacrifice necessary for any lasting economic restructuring. Moreover, no one knew *how* to privatize a centralized economy because it had never been done. This left the door wide open for Communist Party officials to usurp *perestroika's* opportunities for quick personal gain.

"Ahhh, the good old days," recalled Leonid Evenko, an aging high-level official at the Institute of the U.S.A. and Canada. Protected by his powerful state position, he was able to take sweeping and discriminatory advantage of *perestroika* to net himself thousands of dollars through a number of newly legalized cooperative business ventures that lesser-heeled Russians dared not attempt because of the obtrusive sway of the bureaucracy.*

"We lived in a bureaucratic paradise when I was young," Evenko said fondly, sucking on his third tumbler of expensive whiskey at the hard-currency bar in Moscow's Savoy Hotel. "Now, the best thing is to live in the Soviet Union with the dollars we make from cooperative ventures with America. This is life . . . leave the country every now and then for a steak and shrimp cocktail in New York City. You Americans will never understand the reality of *perestroika* because you don't really know or care what's going on in the world. This is the big difference between us."

The Russian language is rich in puns and double entendres that reflect the great Soviet gulf between dreams of what might be and the reality of what is.

There are five words that define the traits required to weather the system created by the Communist Party:

POKAZUKA, the need to show off though there is nothing to display.

TUFTA, the creative misrepresentation of Soviet achievement.

BLAT, the manipulation of an elaborate system based on bribes, blackmail, graft, and corruption to get things done.

ZLORADSTVO, the taking of delight in the misfortune of others because it brightens your own future.

VZYATKA, the unofficial payment needed if one wants to receive necessary goods and services.

These five words characterize the Russian reality that faced the cooperators—the furtive, arrogant, coercive, and above all else, contradictory nature of Gorbachev's newly advertised Soviet Union.

"I remember reading Superman comic books in America as a

---

*Evenko's cooperative was made up of staffers at the Soviet Academy of Sciences' Institute of the U.S.A. and Canada. The group used its pull to organize rooms, meals, and meetings with Soviet officials for visiting American politicians and governmental groups who came to Moscow to witness the massive social change in the Soviet Union and left, none the wiser, unaware that they had experienced a manufactured view.

child," recalled Artyom Borovik, who spent much of his youth in America. He is the gutsy Russian journalist who reported the lid off the war in Afghanistan for the Soviet weekly magazine *Ogonyok*, endangering both himself and his family for criticizing the Soviets' ten-year occupation of the country. "Superman was often transported to another dimension called Bizarro Land. It was a place exactly like Earth, except that everyone there did things in an opposite manner to that on Earth. That's the Soviet Union and that's what we are trying to change."

Bizarro Land is what Gorbachev inherited, what he came to power vowing to destroy. But the spasms of hatred and distrust that have lacerated the Russian psyche since 1917 seem not to subside. The relatively smooth overthrow of the corrupt Marxist mind-set in Eastern Europe, although ironically sparked by Gorbachev, could not occur in the Soviet Union. The human factor was different. Gorbachev's noble attempts to atone for the blood of the past obfuscated the reality that he was elevated to the leadership of the Communist Party for the sole purpose of preserving the system that created him. Lenin's mummy on display in its Red Square crypt and Gorbachev's uncompromising 1990 decree that ordered security forces to protect and preserve monuments to the Bolshevik leader who seized power two hundred forty days after parliamentary democracy had replaced the tsarist monarchy in 1917 are testaments to his charge, as were the piqued cries of the Party faithful when Mark Zakharov, the liberal director of the Leninsky Komsomol Theater, suggested to the nationwide audience of the popular and provocative late-night television show *Vzglyad* that the corpse be removed. "What Zakharov said about the most sacred thing, about Lenin," roared Central Committee member Aleksey Myasnikov, "is worse than incomprehensible!" Added Ratmir Bobovikov, a Central Committee candidate member during the 1989 flap, "Lingering over such issues is simply immoral."

Early in my stay in the U.S.S.R., Artyom Borovik—for whom I worked for four months as a guest editor at *Ogonyok*—introduced me to Sabina Orudjeva, the granddaughter of one of Leonid Brezhnev's most powerful and popular ministers. It was Sabina who served as my guide, translator, and sounding board for news from Moscow to Vladivostok; and it was she who told me in a grave voice to make sure my documents were in order as we headed out into Moscow's streets on a snowy Sunday in November 1988. Sabina, a lovely twenty-eight-year-old *alionushka,* a tender term taken from Russian folklore to describe a woman with long, fair hair, was never one to joke about serious matters such as documents. Something big was up.

But then something big was always up in Moscow. Charting Soviet destiny under Gorbachev was full-time work during my stretch in the Soviet Union. Following the announcements of change to be made in the communist system was the new international sport, and the Kremlin's declarations of change came fast and furious, followed by weeks of unspeakable boredom and the oceanic tedium that went along with trying to isolate what was different, particularly in the "Russian soul"—that fantastic and sentimental centerpiece of all that is Russia.

On this early winter evening Moscow had stopped. Throughout the day people rushed about in the never-ending search for food and drink, as if in preparation for a national celebration. A few people I passed in the street and around the office of *Ogonyok* magazine barked at each other like dogs and then laughed. Nikolai, the kindly old doorman at the Hotel Peking, where I had my apartment, warned me to hide the cat that roamed the third floor.

Sabina led me through a bitterly cold blizzard along an alley to a small, privately owned cooperative restaurant in the basement of an apartment building off Prospekt Mira. Location for many of the modern but drab and dirty apartment buildings that house both favored Communist Party officials and the government factotums who legislate and run the machinery of state at the Party's whim, it slices into the heart of Moscow like an old rusty sword. During daylight, Prospekt Mira is one of the capital's most traffic-clogged streets. The lamp posts are hung with clusters of red shooting stars—street decorations of the socialist state that remain unlit because of electrical power cutbacks. The lines of people waiting to enter the shops along Prospekt Mira are long, and they wind down the dark side streets into the huge Sadovaya road, originally a circle of fortifications built in the sixteenth century to protect Moscow from foreign invaders.

The ten tables at the Meeting Place Café were crowded with

customers whose eyes were glued to a fuzzy color television mounted haphazardly on the wall. The stench of automobile exhaust seeping through the window mingled with the acrid aroma of relit cigarette stubs and bowls of pickled garlic. The cooks and waitresses, who were leaning over the tiny bar for a better view, had huge smiles on their faces. The place was boisterous: and, for the first time in my experience of living alongside Russians, the feeling of exceptional awkwardness that comes with being in their world for long stretches of time disappeared.

Then I was introduced to Polygraph Polygraphovich Sharikov, the noblest and most famous communist bureaucrat of all—the Russian metaphor and mascot.

Sharikov was a dog, the star of *The Heart of a Dog*, a popular film adapted from the great satirical novel of the same name by Mikhail Bulgakov on the day-to-day realities inflicted by the system of Lenin, Stalin, Brezhnev, and all the other players in the Soviet tragedy. A professor who wears tweeds and a cracked pince-nez succeeds in transplanting the testicles of a freshly dead human into a little spotted dog named Sharik. The result is Sharikov, an uncontrollable bureaucrat whose lying, cheating, and stealing make the professor's life unbearable. The professor cannot reverse the process because the state committee, which at first refused to acknowledge that Sharikov even existed, has issued documents certifying the dog as a functioning citizen of the state.

"But I never made a man out of him," pleaded the professor, who is forced by the state to house, clothe, and feed the dog.

Sharikov takes a job as a vice-commissar in the Department of Cleaning the City of Homeless Cats. His rise to the top of the Communist Party is swift. The canine communist becomes a state hero for killing alley cats, using their pelts to provide "genuine" Siberian fur hats for the masses, and pocketing a tidy sum on the side from the sale of his ersatz fox. The cinema newsreels are full of Sharikov looking altogether splendid in his leather Lenin cap as he strokes his dog-whiskered beard and passionately denounces the country's cat population. Crowds roar, women swoon, and men point to Polygraph Polygraphovich as a true revolutionary.

"Look what I did," laments the professor near the end of the film. "I took a perfectly nice dog and made a son of a bitch out of him."

Like Sharikov, Russia and its people are the result of a political eugenics experiment gone bad. Seventy years of botched social tinkering by the Communist Party created a nation mired in ir- rationality and ineptitude. Facts are ignored in Russia, and the Communist Party still has the foul habit of reshaping truth to suit its interests, whether based on the Kremlin's scumbled version of democracy or the political requirements of the powers that intend to remain omnipotent. According to Cooperative Fact chairman Volodya Yakovlev, the Russian people understood the necessity of recasting truth to survive their dehumanized existence, and mas- tered the technique with the verve of acrobats walking a highwire two hundred feet above a Big Top full of Sharikovs. Sabina put it a bit differently: she taught me that every rumor in the Soviet Union contains at least a kernel of truth.

A Russian will never tell you the truth. He will also never lie to you. He will tell you what you want to hear. Russians do this to live. Operating entirely on a principle of coercion that recognizes no limitations or inhibitions, Russian people grab as grab can. Floating over the entire country are the ghosts of twenty million people butchered by Josef Stalin in his twisted pursuit of ultimate power. Stalin's spirit remains profoundly alive, and the evil, greed, and treachery of his hideous rule percolate throughout every level of Soviet society. The Russians even have a word to describe what Stalin did: *meshchanstvo*—a multipurpose noun that encompasses all of the undesirable traits in the Stalin gene pool, including av- arice, stupidity, treachery, and anti-intellectualism. *Meshchani* have two consuming ambitions: to maintain the power of the bu- reaucracy and to maintain their access to the things that the *narod* (people) only dream of. Power, not *perestroika*, is the most coveted currency in the Soviet Union, and the *meschani* have a monopoly on it. A *menshanik* need not be a communist, but he knows every slippery political rung on the bureaucratic ladder. He studies the habits of those who can help him climb and then files them away in his memory to be used in trade at a later date.

"We are a system that must steal, speculate, and keep chickens in bathrooms so that envious neighbors won't see them," said Valentin Berzhkov, Stalin's former English translator. "This is a nation constantly trying to escape catastrophe. There's no food, no desire, no imagination, no self-esteem. What can you expect from such a society?"

Perestroika represented Russia's last chance to destroy the *menshinstvo* mind-set and join the twentieth century before the twenty-first arrived. But the political and social obstacles were formidable, perhaps even insurmountable. The Communist Party's eighteen million elite members and seventy-six million drone bureaucrats, who do the Apparat's bidding, were structurally unable to provide the leadership that would enable the Soviet Union to make the leap from a controlled feudal system to the democratic free market advocated by Volodya Yakovlev and the other cooperators.* Despite elections, the people had no choice because one legacy of Stalin was that they forgot how to speak. Local district commissions, the engulfing wave of the omnipotent communist bureaucracy, were apprehensive about lending support to cooperators who would strip them of power and perk. The *menshaniki* historically has had the privilege of doing whatever it chose to do. This reality was written in blood, as history aptly revealed.

When Stalin grabbed control of the Communist Party in 1925, its ranks boasted a little over one million members, of whom, however, only eight thousand five hundred had joined before the October Revolution. Stalin, who before becoming a politician made a living by armed robbery, extortion, and giving information to the tsar's secret police, ripped the old guard apart limb by limb. Bodies piled up, so many bodies and so much fear over becoming just another corpse, that people actually committed suicide to prevent anonymous death. During the endless horror of farmland collec-

---

*The Communist Party lost 785,000 members in 1990, but 370,000 of those who quit the Party aligned themselves with various splinter factions. Nearly 20,000 of those who left were from Moscow's Party rolls. Some 125,000 Party members were expelled, 120,000 died, and 150,000 stopped paying their membership dues. Nearly 150,000 new members signed up, however. "The figures are not large enough to speak about a catastrophe or even an extraordinary situation," said Boris Pugo, the chairman of the Party's Central Control Committee. "The departure of members is not large enough to cause great concern."

tivization, entire families, in grim mimic of Tolstoy's character Anna Karenina, threw themselves under speeding trains, according to eyewitness accounts. Finding food became a full-time job. Mobs of emaciated Russians seeking grain wandered the country like characters in a George Romero movie. Cannibalism was commonly practiced. Children who died from starvation were taken not to the cemetery but to the cook. The Party tried to stop the horror by shooting the cannibalists. Those who survived adopted the dour, mummy-like expressions that have made pedestrians on Moscow's streets look like members of a funeral procession. The pose was a defense against the capricious brutality of the state. Anyone who enjoyed a degree of influence (and even a smile returned to a friend on the street implied prestige) represented a challenge to communist authority and was shot. People dared not express any feeling in public. If you did, you were shot; so much flesh fell that almost the only ones who survived were the butchers. Those who avoided death spent their lives teaching their children how to dodge the knife. As insurance against any deviation on the part of those who managed to live, the state made no secret of how it dealt with dissent: eyes were gouged out, women were raped and then chopped apart, men were rolled around in barrels lined with spikes, farmers were scalped, writers had sealing wax poured into their mouths, and hungry rats were shoved into pipes pressed against human stomachs and forced to exit by chewing their way into the intestinal cavity.

The word among *nouveau* Soviet watchers like Phil Donahue and Oprah Winfrey was that "The Gorb" was genuine, one of those rare Russian types who could actually snap the spine of this Thing called Russia. Under Gorbachev, the Soviet Union would shed its dogmatism and learn to be creative. But the smiles of Kremlin-sponsored Russian guests on afternoon talk-show television never revealed the plague left by Stalin's heavy hand. It was a disease of spirit and soul and mind and heart, and mad principles of punishment that boiled down, once again, to the Orwellian notion that "some animals are more equal than others." This was the Soviet inheritance, a heritage bereft of any "old-fashioned" values of industriousness.

Of course, in speech after speech, Gorbachev said this was no longer the case. *Perestroika*, although not proceeding smoothly, was proceeding according to plan. But nobody knew what the economic and political blueprint was or, more important, what it might do. Seasoned communists, new-age democrats, and average Soviet citizens all prided themselves on being self-made and tough survivors of the old system. For, no matter how much a Russian taxi driver or a Georgian cooperative farmer railed against and groused about the Soviet bureaucracy, the institutional superiority of the system was essentially unassailable because individuals had learned how to survive and profit from the elaborately packaged hoax. This was vintage Russia. In economic terms, *perestroika* operated under the conviction that the global marketplace had arrived and the Soviet Union had to become a part of it. But there was no Soviet market; moreover, there were no economists. As Columbia University's Soviet economics expert Richard Ericson pointed out in an address to Moscow's Western journalists in May 1990: "Not one of [Russia's] economists would receive tenure at an American university." Western market systems were more than alien concepts for Russians accustomed to subsidization of everything; they were extravagant invaders who threatened to take away what few amenities the Russian people had eked out of the system. Bread was a wonderful example of the conundrum.

In 1990 a loaf of Moscow's most expensive bread at a city bakery stall cost fifty kopecks (about seventy-five cents at the official exchange rate or about .04 cents at the black market rate). Estimates of how much a nonsubsidized, *perestroika* loaf would cost went as high as five dollars, a figure that made any communist or democratic leader vulnerable to a lot worse than public ill-will and irreverence. The Soviet Union had grown into a powerful country essentially by repeating the same act time after time: state subsidy. Political revisionism caused problems. Economic revisionism spelled calamity: blood revolution.

The business world had changed. The global marketplace in the closing decade of the twentieth century was high-profile, high-tech, and high-priced. Democracy, too, demanded more hard cash than dramatic speeches from Kremlin leaders, and the cost of economic freedom was not available at any bargain-basement price.

The Soviet Union not only had reached the bottom of the barrel, it had sold the barrel to pay for the weapons of the Cold War. The only currency left was anger.

Thanks in part to the ten-year Afghanistan war, by the end of the 1980s, the black market had spiraled beyond control, with rubles that officially sold at sixty-seven kopecks to the dollar fetching thirty rubles to the dollar.* On the street, amid widespread shortages of staples and consumer goods, the ruble was replaced by barter for Western items. Transactions were conducted in foreign currencies. The Soviet Union, transformed into an economic netherworld far removed from the U.S.S.R. Lenin had created on December 22, 1922, suffered a raging national debate over changing the country's name. "At the same time," said Gennadi Gerasimov, the Soviet Foreign Ministry spokesman during my years in Moscow, "Philip Morris is sending us billions of cigarettes, so some people suggest our new name should be Marlboro Country." The dreams of Lenin, the horrors of Stalin, the entertainment of Khrushchev, and the stagnation of Brezhnev, Andropov, and Chernenko had finally caught up with the Russian people with a vengeance under Gorbachev. The action that began on Thursday morning, February 23, 1917, when seven thousand female textile workers in Petrograd went into the streets to protest the high bread prices of the tsarist government of Nicholas II and ignited the Bolshevik Revolution that exploded eight months later, had turned into what Russian Republic President Boris Yeltsin described as "a disorganized, confused gathering of dunderheads."

Boris Yeltsin, the first man to make it both on and off the Politburo alive and without teeth marks, knew the pendulum Len-

---

*The Soviet Union's state-controlled Gosbank opened a currency exchange on January 1, 1991, at which the ailing ruble would be bought and sold against other currencies at market rates. This cautious first step toward convertibility of the ruble would be backed by the "currency resources of the Soviet government and the governments of union republics as well as funds drawn from foreign banks." Private individuals and foreign firms with no registered legal presence in the Soviet Union would not be allowed to trade on the exchanges, while on the street the ruble/dollar ratio fluctuated between fifteen to thirty rubles to the dollar, the rate linked to the amount of dollars that a seller wished to unload. The currency auction experiment was abandoned in August 1991, when Gosbank realized they could not compete with the black market.

in's heirs put into motion just kept swinging. The only way to change direction was to apply external force, like friction, or in Russia's case, *perestroika*. And it all made sense when *perestroika* began in 1985, unless, that is, you happened to be born into the system. Russians still needed to know someone deep into bribery and embezzlement if they wanted decent food, even nauseating tomatoes that looked like maroon support stockings stuffed with pus and costing thirty rubles a kilogram. The sides of beef that hung in the freezer of the Sophia restaurant on Mayakovsky Square still had "1963" stamped in red on their skin, as observed when burst plumbing flooded the freezer in 1988; and the only way to kill the taste of that rancid flesh was to buy some antifreeze posing as "concentrated alcohol" sold by the Lithuanian grandmother who hung out with the old men peddling fragrance-bereft flowers at the Byelorussian train station. The street skinny on *perestroika* was very clear right from the beginning: nobody knows what it means, but it will certainly be no different from what went before.

"*Perestroika*." Sabina Orudjeva laughed the first time she saw the word plastered over the American press to describe all the wonderful changes taking place in her life, "you mean *perestrelka*— the crossfire of bullets that will come trying to create a better life for Russia."

Gorbachev's *perestroika* barrage left the average Russian shell-shocked and shivering with the conflicting emotions of dread and hope. At no time in Russian history since Stalin had the country's future hinged on the conjuring tricks of one leader, on whether or not his vodka war would be successful, on what the KGB had in mind if the poetic voices of *glasnost* really began to usurp their moral vandalism, on what the Politburo ideologists intended to do with Gorbachev's corpse if he failed in his mission to save the Communist Party through the introduction of free-market democracy. For the cooperators committed to changing the system, *perestroika* was a case of too many questions and not enough answers.

The smart money said that over the long haul the new Russia of Gorbachev, as such, was doomed—not only because he continued to buck heavy totalitarian odds, but because the two hundred forty million Soviets who did not belong to the Communist Party were frightened witless that the dream of creating a democratic free market would ignite hostility among a power clique that had stopped at nothing to achieve and sustain its own cushy lifestyle at the moral and economic expense of the country. Although Gorbachev was a shrewdly tough leader, with an infinite capacity to surprise and astound critics and supporters alike with controversial political programs and ideas, his essence in the minds of most Soviets was pure public relations. More than any other Soviet boss he realized the value of orchestrating the media, of showing himself on camera, of driving a bandwagon that paraded myths the Soviet people could get behind. Gorbachev's merchandising of a free-market system struck the country, as the Russian proverb cautioned, as selling the bear's skin before the bear had been caught. Alexander Pushkin observed that his country preferred an elevating falsehood to dozens of unpleasant truths. Russians, Pushkin noted, loved falsehoods for the extra dimension they provided and the infinite possibilities prevarication held as a means of alleviating disenchantment. But *perestroika* brought a more final solution to erasing distasteful reality, as a visit to Moscow's suicide hospital, the Sklifosovsky Institute, revealed in graphic terms. "People kill themselves when they return from the local soviet office, or the shops, or the endless queues, because of the utter frustration and humiliation of it all," lamented Dr. Alexander Polyev, a suicide-hospital psychiatrist. "This is the gray, mindless, unendurable routine of our everyday lives, from which the more sensitive and emotional of us can see no escape."

But this is only part of the U.S.S.R.'s living dead. World Health Organization statistics published in 1989 revealed that over thirty million abortions were performed in the world every year, and that Soviet abortions accounted for over eight million of them. Although the Soviet Union made up only 6 percent of the world's population, it accounted for one in every four abortions performed on the planet. "Why does that amaze you?" asked Veronica Khelchevskaya, a twenty-five-year-old writer for the weekly Soviet news magazine *Novoye Vremya* and mother of a young son for whom food and medicine must be smuggled in from the West or purchased by friends at exclusive hard-currency shops that cater to the needs of Russia's foreign community. "There is no future here for a child, so why have one?"

Those unable to find solace in poetry or self-slaughter used alcohol to bring illusion to the feverish reality of life, but since wine and liquor were tough and expensive to come by, drinking gangs burgled shops and chemists for cheap Bulgarian eau-de-cologne, Ukrainian hair tonic, Polish varnish, Hungarian window cleaning liquid, and Latvian mouthwash. So much alcohol was stolen and diverted into the *blat* system of bribery or bottled and sold to the West as real Russian vodka that there was no alcohol solution with which doctors could swab a patient's arm before an injection—if the medicine, which could be purchased only for hard currency or in return for a favor, existed at all. "To be drunk was a common feature of Russian hospitality," explained the Russian historian Robert K. Massie. "Unless guests were sent home dead drunk, the evening was considered a failure."

"There is massive drunkenness because people are tired of muddle and dishonesty, and of not having anything to which to apply their hand or brain," *Ogonyok* writer Lev Miroshnichenko complained shortly after researching a story on Russian alcoholics. In response to Gorbachev's failed anti-booze campaign, the Party apparatus created the Temperance Society, a bureaucratic monster that included four hundred fifty thousand branches across the country. Above the local branches were three thousand "higher bodies" whose job it was to take orders from three more layers of command at the provincial, state, and republic levels. At the top in Moscow was the Central Temperance Society, manned with presidents, vice-presidents, secretaries, administrators, and officials. All told, the Temperance Society, the vanguard of Gorbachev's anti-alcohol army, employed six thousand five hundred state workers who were paid for by one-ruble-a-year contributions by fifteen million members. Unfortunately, over a third of Temperance Society members were heavy drinkers and dozens of their branch presidents were regularly retching their guts out night after night in the drunk tank. But the braces of Temperance Society bigwigs caught swilling bottles of confiscated moonshine only swelled their ranks. It was a state-sponsored binge to save the communist state, and the Tem-

perance Society had the *blat* to pull off the kind of cocktail party
Russians go to bed hoping to dream about.

Lenin's great pendulum kept swinging. All I had to do was
look out my window to be reminded of the absurdity.

The huge double-glazed window in my apartment at the Hotel
Peking overlooked Vladimir Mayakovsky Square, a large asphalt
and grass plaza encircled by cars missing stolen windshield wipers
and dominated by a fifteen-foot-high statue of the famed revolutionary poet, who committed suicide rather than prolong his slow,
syphilitic death. Mayakovsky Square was a favorite flashpoint for
Dr. Sergei Skripnikov and his Democratic Unionists. Every Thursday night, I'd gaze out the window to see Sergei and his white-
headband-wearing democratic shock troops being gimcracked,
water-cannoned, and hauled off for thirty-day hunger strikes behind KGB bars. Even the drunkest revelers in the Peking's imitation Chinese restaurant knew it was Thursday night when the
paddy wagon drivers and plainclothes KGB agents flashed their
red identity wallets for a few quick belts before the Democratic
Union's seven P.M. show.

"The state's current fashion is to devote itself to creating a free
market, when it should be more concerned with creating individuals who understand the democracy necessary to make a free market work," explained Sergei, a political anthropologist and leader
of the quasi-legal political party, which believed the entire communist system needed to be thrown aside before democratic markets could be established by cooperators. The Democratic Union,
formed in the autumn of 1988, called for the "form and essence of
a governmental establishment based on political, economic, and
spiritual pluralism, a multiparty system, a legal opposition press,
and trade unions independent of government control." This was
the party of the kids, disgruntled men and women in their twenties
and thirties with no connections to the Soviet Union's longtime
dissident community or the new cooperative crowd. "Free-market
democracy cannot exist alongside the current consciousness of the
Russian people," Sergei told me one night, a few hours before he
was to be arrested by the men gathering in the Peking's restaurant.
"The state has a monopoly on our lives—economically, socially,

politically, and spiritually. This is not an intrusion of the state into our lives. This *is* the state. This is our heart."

Right from the start of Gorbachev's plan to restructure the existing apparatus, Skripnikov and his radical followers had abandoned all hope of *perestroika*'s providing a Western political or economic solution to communist rule through the creation of cooperatives and the official exultation of democratic free-market values in the state sector. Although there were only a few thousand Democratic Unionists in the Soviet Union—most of whom had paid time in jail for membership dues—their effort to bust the Kremlin's ideological monopoly cut right to the marrow of the queer problem that all of the U.S.S.R. had with believing in Gorbachev's free-market flirtation. The DUs asserted that no one in the Soviet Union really believed that Gorbachev came to power to allow the cooperators a free hand in revamping the economy—not the soviets, not the diplomats in the Western embassies, not the *narod*, and not Gorbachev himself. Though no outsider could say exactly how Soviet policy was made and managed, it was apparent that the officials who were managing the transition to a new free market were the same clumsy bureaucrats who had administered the old, controlled market. And, depending on a Russian's personal politics, this dynamic was the result of willful misjudgment, grand conspiracy, or the ineptitude that resulted from decades of "revolutionary socialist" management techniques.

The Democratic Unionists—a goulash of communists, socialists, anarchists, monarchists, democrats, and a guy named Lev Schwartz, who always flashed a sign in front of Western television news cameras that said: MY NAME'S LEV SCHWARTZ AND THEY WANT TO KILL ME BECAUSE I'M JEWISH. I NEED A VISA TO AMERICA. PLEASE PHONE. 237-6087—were on the jazz all the time. The crowds that gathered to support them every Thursday night, screaming "Fashisti" at the white-helmeted riot troops and fireballing fistfuls of kopecks at the grim-faced KGB jailers in a symbolic gesture to buy them off, did not care that head-on confrontation invited more crushing reprisals in other places. The inventive dottiness of the DUs—noisy, loose, brilliantly unkempt—was too diffuse and twisted to have any impact on Russia's consciousness.

The only group of young people who stood a chance of up-rooting the system were the cooperators. But cooperators were hazardous material in Russia, and none more so than Volodya Ya-kovlev, of Cooperative Fact. The assertiveness of his character, despite his youth; the distinctiveness of his dry shoes in winter, a sure indication he had the perk of a personal driver; the cleverness he used to implement ideas, a clear signal they were somehow illegal and definitely profitable; and his vocal loathing of the Com-munist Party and its moribund attempt at restructuring were all qualities that made a young Russian being driven around Moscow with expensive shoes on his feet and clever ideas in his head either an undercover KGB agent or a damned fool asking to be ambushed.

There was another possibility, one that did not register on the faces of the people who greeted Yakovlev on Moscow's streets in 1987, the wild opening days of Russia's free-enterprise movement. If the public had known that he was a cooperator (as they would later hear all too frequently, until even Gorbachev became aware of Volodya Yakovlev), who controlled the only privately owned information business in the U.S.S.R., they would have over-whelmed him with questions. Soon they would have to pay for it. And Yakovlev, the only known salesman of accurate commercial information in a nation constantly in search of *istina*, was positioned to grow very rich in the process.

The rub was for whose benefit Volodya Yakovlev's wealth would function. He had taken controversial and revolutionary ad-vantage of *perestroika*. He would emerge as the main spokesperson for Russia's entrepreneurial system, creating pressure on an old generation of Stalinists and a new generation of Yummies (Young Upwardly Mobile Marxists) to disprove Dostoyevsky's notion that Russia was an unfortunate freak of nature. Even passively accepting the past was wrong, Yakovlev thought, and he was not going to tolerate the complicity of his generation in keeping the country's tormentors alive under a different name. The old way, the endemic corruption swaddled in patriotic emotion, was alive as ever. "Look at the misery on their faces," Yak said whenever we toured Moscow. "That's all the proof you need." It was an explanation I would hear often.

There were no genuine Soviet laws relating to cooperatives or the free-market system in 1987, although the freely elected two-thousand-two-hundred-fifty-member Congress of People's Deputies, of which the Supreme Soviet was the permanently sitting core, would awkwardly buck the odds to change the situation in 1990. What did exist was a merry-go-round of decrees issued by the Council of Ministers, an appointed body of Communist Party members who could, through authority and tradition, execute ersatz laws without any need for discussion or formal approval by elected officials. Formerly known as the Council of People's Commissars, the Council of Ministers was the bastard government of the Bolsheviks; and its often bizarre announcements were issued fast, furiously, and without prior warning to the population. Each Soviet republic had its own Council of Ministers and a great cobweb of corrupt professional bureaucrats loyal to the Party code of political morality. Intrigue ran every level of government to such an intense degree that it was impossible to discover where incompetence and stupidity ended and treachery and corruption began.

The cooperators, with whom I began to spend increasing amounts of time during the early months of 1988, were the only group who did not snicker at all the high-speed confusion dished out by the fringe radical groups, because they saw a lot of their own private fears reflected in the audacious and illegal adventures of youthful organizations such as the Democratic Union.* For example, the DUs prided themselves on getting arrested for anti-

*The Democratic Union, along with dozens of other unofficial political parties, achieved equality with the Communist Party under the law on October 9, 1990, giving the U.S.S.R. a legal basis for a multiparty system. The Supreme Soviet ruled that Communist Party organs, such as the KGB and the military, would no longer have any legally binding authority. Although the DU welcomed the Supreme Soviet's move, the group's leaders saw little practical change coming from the legislation, so long as the Party remained the largest landowner in the world and retained control over numerous newspapers, journals, and television stations, without providing any guarantees for mass-media access to the newly legalized parties.

Soviet slander by saying, often in pornographic terms, that Gorbachev was not irreplaceable, and unless any replacement emerged with his consent, the ensuing Russia without a Gorbachev spelled a social upheaval that would be gauged in body bags. It was a fear the cooperators voiced only in private. The DUs did not care who heard the message. "We are not telling the Russian people anything they don't already know," Sergei said whenever I questioned the rationality of his group's political agenda.

Men and women like Yakovlev also knew that the Soviet people were bloated and blackened from conflicting signals of past and present. The bureaucracy remained the dominant feature of daily life because written permission was still needed for virtually every human action, which reduced life to a scramble to get hold of a *propusk* (an official document that gave an individual the right to accomplish a task as mundane as buying sugar) or discover the *paroli* (knowledge of how to overcome the bureaucratic obstacles every Russian faces). Ivan Average, who saw bureaucracy as permanent and irreversible, tired of *perestroika* because all it showed was political confusion fostered by the new freedom and economic discord furthered by the cooperative movment. *Perestroika* might better have been defined for the general population as turbulence, a highly dissipative dynamic that drained energy and created an eroding drag on a Russian's daily life—a drag that kindled a nostalgia for the days when repressive authorities could maintain discipline simply by sending the unruly to count birch trees in Siberia.

The new generation of young elitist and careerist Russians— the aptly named "Golden Youth" children of the entrenched Party bureaucracy—harbored no deep desire to embrace the radical cooperators and change the system their parents had bred them to feed off of. The young and well-connected Soviets who had decided to stay in the country and participate in the system knew all too well that the bureaucracy never handed senior jobs to controversial men. The men who attained high status in the Soviet Union built a constituency within the system by spreading just enough graft around beneath them to ensure the loyalty of the *narod* they needed to implement their schemes. The few Russians who had embraced the danger of the challenge to restructure through cooperative ventures had become the object of punitive disfavor from those in authority and their street pawns, as well as from those preparing to assume official leadership roles. The survival of the old system was a matter of arithmetic and protein, supply and demand. The amenities of the bureaucracy—conveniences that every level of society would lose out on in one way or another if cooperative, free-market restructuring proved successful—were a suburban American shopping mall world of cigarettes, razors, radios, televisions, videos, tape recorders, blenders, toasters, food delicacies, sport shirts, airline tickets abroad, cement, shoelaces, medicine, linens, haircuts, batteries, books, cardboard, ballpoints, nails, watches, toothpaste, and cosmetics that fortunate wives and mistresses did not know how to apply. Anything and everything, whether a physical commodity or a service, yielding utility and commanding a price if bought or sold on a market, was chained to the *blat* system, which defined the Soviet economy and shaped the personality of the nation.

It was apparent to all of us involved in the cooperative revolution that the success or failure of the free-market movement, in purely economic terms, hinged on the ability of cooperators to disengage from the communist economy by breaking up the state monopolies. This was perhaps an impossible chore because of the extraordinary extent of Soviet monopolies and the pressure of the state to keep rigid control of its financial and industrial superstructure. The most basic goods necessary for cooperators to rebuild the Soviet economy—steel, plastic, concrete, plywood—were produced *entirely* by a single organization and a single factory.* The

*The extent of the Communist Party's monopolistic control of the economy through the state's bureaucratic maneuverings was both imposing and impressive, despite its inability to provide the public with anything but continually massive shortages. One hundred percent of Soviet sewing machines were manufactured by the state's Cheveinaya Association in Podolsk; 90 percent of the country's washing machines were built in the Elektrobytpribor Factory in Kirov; 87 percent of Soviet forklift trucks were assembled by the Autopogruzhchik Association in Kharkov, and 93 percent of its concrete mixers were built at the Tuva Works. Thousands of integral items were regulated by the state along every rung of the economic chain, from obtaining raw materials to the dispersal of any given product on a store shelf. The great fallacy of *perestroika* was that government moves to destroy this hydra created separate competing companies. Just the opposite

government ministries that controlled the system of manufacturing and service provision also exerted monopoly power over distribution through an infected network of territorial departments which made sure unhappy customers could not switch to an alternative supplier. The Kremlin crossed the taboo barring private property in late 1990 to help initiate economic reform through free-market enterprise. But this move to capture public enthusiasm for cooperatives and individually owned businesses remained tangled in the mechanism of the state monopoly, both practically and, more important, psychologically.

Day after day I heard stories that revealed the somber depth of the Soviet Union's incapacity to break through the past to the innovations advanced by the cooperative revolutionaries. Every one of these anecdotes began with the rush of new hopes and new fears that came with *perestroika,* like the sudden joy and pain of a new emotion making its way into the human heart. More than anything, the Soviet people were ill-prepared to handle the curiosities *perestroika* had awakened in them. One such anecdote concerned a young Russian woman who had made her way to West Germany for a job in a bakery, only to return to Moscow psychologically shattered. The woman was a good worker, but she grew more and more nervous with each passing day, until the owner was compelled to ask her why she was arriving at work in increasingly agitated mental states.

"I'm waiting for us to run out of flour," the Russian woman said in a reproachful tone.

"I've never heard of a bakery running out of flour," the perplexed owner said.

The woman stared at the baker in palpable disbelief. "This is too much to handle!" she screamed in complete distraction. "In

---

proved true: ministries claiming to move toward a market structure grouped each of their individual "enterprises" into one enormous state corporation. Workers wanting to break away to form a small-business market with their skills were forbidden from hiring the employees needed to ply trade effectively. Privately owned construction companies were allowed to hire up to two hundred people, and scientific companies, up to one hundred. Private industrial outfits could hire only twenty-five workers, and retail sales firms only fifteen. The suffocating tentacles of the hydra were being replaced with the crushing weight of a giant.

Russia we run out of flour every few weeks and the help is sent home. I can't work under these conditions!" And with that she walked out and returned to a life revolving around profiteers, black marketeers, and the wooden language of the Soviet bureaucracy.

The other side of the cooperative dynamic revealed itself in a well-worn but true anecdote that made the rounds of the American corporate grapevine in Moscow. It concerned what happened when a highly paid American petroleum consultant was offered a triple return on his investment, to be accomplished by paying off officials and factory managers to set artificially low valuations on enterprises possessing valuable Western machinery and developable real estate. A local official whispered that *perestroika* easily allowed him to sell off the assets and shut down the plants. The American explained the idea was called asset-stripping and that those caught doing it in America faced criminal prosecution.

"So what?" The official shrugged. "One third of the new government is too busy to know what's going on, another third is too idealistic to understand what's going on, and the other third is too greedy to care what goes on."

This was *perestroika*'s invisible sweep. People rose, only to slip back under the spell that still held them, bringing them back to the silent, obedient, and angry life under the bear.

"I have no idea what the free market is," explained one of many faceless Soviet shoppers, waiting on a Moscow grocery line a full five years into the *perestroika* process, her perplexed words echoing the national sentiment toward the new economic order advanced by the cooperators. "But I suspect this whole debate is really about how the same old apparatchiks are trying to control this new system and fill their pockets the same way they do now."

Volodya Yakovlev saw *perestroika* as a chance to end the nation's cynicism by involving the Soviet people in the free-market process. Unfortunately there were few people who believed in the sincerity of the government's various economic recovery plans or the cooperators' dream. The ring of the word *kooperativno*, like the leper's bell, announced a malignancy, possibly contagious, that prudent Russians thought better to shun in favor of the old methods of survival. Hobbled by their inexperience and impatience with

Western values and practices, too many Soviets found it easier and safer to work *perestroika* as an angle. In the bureaucrat's lexicon, *perestroika* was a code word for manipulating one's office to amass hard currency; *perestroika* on the street was often nothing more profound than an opportunity to score an exit visa or test a new angle on getting a beer. "We cannot have passengers endangered because of the whim of someone who wants to drink beer in Finland," said Valeri Kondratyev, the deputy chief of the Soviet Ministry of Aviation, commenting on the spate of Aeroflot hijackings by young Soviets toward the end of Gorbachev's first five years in office. Taking advantage of the new freedom to leave the country or hold a plane hostage for Heineken were *perestroika*'s most poignant metaphors.

"It really is an exciting time, so exciting that people are completely confused," Gorbachev said in a bizarre, self-deprecatory non sequitur on the never-ending reports of plots and coups against the government owing to his failure to realize the hopes for an economic miracle after six years of *perestroika*.

"Half the people who come to listen to me to speak on how to start a cooperative spit in my face," explained Artyom Tarasov, the chairman of the successful Moscow building cooperative Technica and, with Yakovlev, a leader in the cooperative movement. "The other half are visitors to a zoo; they come only to see what a 'millionaire cooperator' looks like."

On the streets, in the kitchens, and above the fray of the new and vibrant democratic discourse, the Soviet Union still ticked to the beat of Sharikov's dog-heart—an experiment of which both creator and subject wanted no part. The State Committee on Education and the Soviet emigration authorities predicted over seven million of the country's most qualified minds were planning to leave the U.S.S.R. by the year 2000.* "Only the professionals can bring the country out of its deep crisis," lamented Feliks Peregudov, the

*Analysts at Cooperative Fact believe that closer to 14 million Soviets will attempt to leave the country by the end of the century and that government statistics, although accurate, reflect the fear that many Soviets had of announcing their intentions to government pollsters, in the event their desire to leave should spark the reintroduction of harshly enforced emigration bans, quotas, and limits.

deputy chairman of the education committee and a vocal backer of using cooperative ventures to plug the brain drain. "We have extremely few of them. At any enterprise that demands a mind, everything depends on two or three dozen people—and they are the ones who are trying to leave."

The Soviet people were directing their energies toward exodus because there was absolutely no reason to stay. Russia was a bad day every day, and all its people were aching. Even the landscape was grieving: the houses were glorified slums and the fields were dead. There was no money and no food. There was no shortage of organizations to end the problems, but there were few organizers. There were clothes, but no zippers. There were potatoes, but no hands to pick them. There was timber, but no saws. There was no lack of logic, but there was logistic incompetence. There were cows, but no milk. There was the ability to read, but an inability to think. There were leaders, but leadership was forbidden. There were farms, but no farmers. There were cars, but no tires. Doors shut when they should open, and it was impossible for the government to offer anything to offset the allure of corruption and the seductions of leaving the country. Those who survived the Soviet banquet of horrors straggled off to contaminate the next generation.

By the close of 1988, the Soviet Union's future as a functioning member of the democratic world economy had been left by default in the hands of the cooperators. Although these democratic free-marketeers had received little Western attention outside the occasional story on their raw individuality and spirit, the cooperative movement, as such, was the essential element for the success of Gorbachev's political alchemy. Indeed, the more I traveled around the Soviet Union, where even now *perestroika* still causes more bitter regional and ethnic tension than it does economic and political harmony, the clearer it became that fledgling cooperators had the best chance to defuse the explosion. If I were going to gauge the validity of *perestroika* and the viability of Gorbachev's solemn vow to remove the trancelike political, psychological, and social blasphemies of the Lenin/Stalin inheritance that stood in the way of creating the Soviet Union's new democratic order, it was essential for me to relinquish my position as an American correspondent in Moscow in favor of observing the transition first hand as a Soviet cooperator. So I began reporting on and even advising Yakovlev's Cooperative Fact. There was a profound and compelling historical dimension to the job Volodya Yakovlev and I shared with the other members of Cooperative Fact. What we faced was bringing a democratic free market into a frontier of skeptics and chaos. Seventy-one years after the Bolshevik revolution that destroyed Russian capitalism and changed the world order, I found myself thrust into the undoing of that revolution, enthralled by what lay ahead. Yakovlev and I confronted, in 1988, a world much like the one encountered by those early Bolsheviks: harsh, unyielding, and with the capacity to erupt and lay waste to all that surrounded it.

2

> Where a vacuum exists, it will be filled by
> the nearest and strongest power. That has
> to be avoided at all costs.
>
> RICHARD M. NIXON

I T WAS DEFINITELY a zinc day. The air pollution levels
in Moscow are among the highest in the world. The industrial haze
that rolls in every day—a product of Stalin's construction of ele-
phantine factories throughout the capital—was a compote of zinc
and lead. Urban folklore said the lead made you tired and irritable;
the zinc fumes, on the other hand, energized your body and spirit
and made every plan and dream seem a distinct possibility. On
those rare zinc days the odds were stacked in your favor. Volodya
Yakovlev needed all the zinc he could get.

Vladimir Yegorevich Yakovlev was preparing to smoke on the
morning I first met him, standing atop a gray snowbank on a Gorky
Street corner and rolling a Russian cigarette between his yellowed
thumb and forefinger to loosen the cheap, tightly packed Soviet
tobacco inside. Volodya—the Yak—kept the flame of his ever-
present Bic lighter crushed against damp tobacco twigs dangling
from the cigarette's shredded tip, nervously waiting in the wind
for another day in Moscow to begin. Yak had already smoked too
many cigarettes for his twenty-eight years. Although he liked everything else about himself, the Yak hated the coal-black cough that
erupted from his lungs. But he had convinced himself that the

karate training he underwent three times a week would nullify the problem by his thirty-second birthday in 1992.

None of Russia's hazards fazed Yakovlev, not the food shortages, inadequate housing, shoddy medical care, wretched transportation, inoperative telephones, or clothes manufactured from flammable materials. Wearing a thin black leather aviator jacket, his brown hair flapping in the wind like frozen twine, the Yak gazed like a statue at the huddled masses on their way to meaningless work and empty shops. He had always been thin; the old photograph glued to his drab green Red Army registration booklet aped the grimace of Puck on the body of a scarecrow tightly stitched in fine Italian clothes. His face was starched-cotton white, and the fog that had formed on his round, wire-rimmed glasses hid the mischievous glint of his deep-brown eyes. Yak stood out among the human wreckage of Moscow. His energy was always at the highest speed, though, sometimes, admittedly, in reverse. The fact was that Yak was different to the point of danger. And he knew it.

Yak preferred thin-soled Western shoes, the kind that a Russian winter can destroy within thirty minutes of leaving your apartment on a really good day. The day we first met was a bad day. Bitter cold and cyclones of snow moved up the slight hill that marked the beginning of Gorky Street at the base of Manezhnaya Square.* The unclean chill swirled past the Executive Committee of the Soviet of Workers' Deputies of Moscow (Moscow's city hall), and out the broad stretch of Gorky that started at Pushkin Square and ended at the Byelorussian train station. Between the two points Yak surveyed an open-air shopping mall of doomed dreams. Thousands of people spilled out of the metro stations, shabbily clothed swarms moving in silence through a mixture of brown snow and syrupy mud, their brows furrowed nervously, their eyes scanning shop windows for a sly hint that something of value might be inside. Even Gorky Street was deceitful. The great thoroughfare had been called Tverskoi for centuries, until Stalin named it after Maxim

*On August 24, 1991, Russian President Boris Yeltsin changed the name to Square of Free Russia.

Gorky, his dearest literary apologist, in 1932.* The Manezh, into which Gorky Street's traffic was digested and belched out to the sound of rusty mufflers, was encircled by the façades of Soviet achievement. Gorky Street fanned out into the Manezh, at whose far side was the wide and steep stone path that ran between the history museum and the Kremlin's Arsenal Tower up the slope to the ice-slicked cobbles of Red Square. Beneath the Manezh, in the vast pedestrian tunnel that connected Gorky Street to Red Square, was another kind of action. Although the concrete cavity bustled with people during the day, at night it became a catacomb where Moscow's small-time street hustlers wandered like free agents in search of a team. The big-time hustlers, the politically powerful, had greased enough palms to be allowed entry into the hotels above, a forbidden zone for the rest of the country. But life was different underground. The small-time boys could not stand on the patio above Lenin's tomb on Revolution Day, nor taste the whiskey that flowed freely the night before in the hotel "dollar bars." These privileges, the entitlement of the *Kremlevsky Payok*, the Kremlin Ration, had to be earned. Those who worked Moscow's bowels, under the Manezh and in other subterranean velds and seedy apartments throughout the city, were in training for another kind of life above, as drones who would perish in identical fashion in the vicious cycle of the Kremlin Ration. Too many people lived below, entrepreneurs like Andrei Belopolsky, who had the bad fortune to meet a man in the dim cement hollow beneath the Manezh with a wad of labels taken from boxes of Russian mascara. Belopolsky went home and scraped the creosote off his chimney and packaged the soot with the labels and sold it as mascara. Demand for his product grew to such a pitch that he paid a Soviet mascara bureaucrat to cut factory production and turn the precious labels over to the enterprise. Belopolsky walked in the sun for one month in 1987, until it was discovered his creosote mascara was poisoning customers. Caught, tried, convicted, and shot, Belopolsky was buried for good in a sack.

---

*On July 27, 1990, the newly elected Moscow City Council voted to rename Gorky Street Tverskoi.

Volodya Yakovlev was an expert at fixing the free-market problems that hampered Moscow's would-be small businessmen. His
expertise at the maneuverings and countermaneuverings necessary
for surviving the Soviet system was not unique. His advantage,
according to several associates, was Yak's sense of who and what
he was in the proliferating organism of *perestroika*. Yak was a
cooperator and, although thousands of other Soviets had taken
advantage of restructuring to become entrepreneurs, he had
emerged, in effect, as the free-market movement's chief operating
officer by virtue of his position as its sole broker of the social,
economic, and political facts necessary to start a business. Yak's
product was information. His prowess in finding out anything from
the telephone number of a cooperative restaurant (not an easy task
in a city where phone books do not exist) to the address of a Moscow
carpenter who wanted to swap his lumber for an automobile had
turned Yak into a sort of casualty insurer. Solid information in the
Soviet Union saves time and cuts the risks Soviet people face whenever they transact "capitalistic" business beyond the orbit of state
supervision or, in Belopolsky's case, beneath the Manezh. The
answer was always the same whenever I asked Sabina or my other
Russian friends where to find information they were unable to
supply:

"Ask Yakovlev."

Yakovlev was a cooperator who had been elevated to the status
of living legend by Moscow's young crowd and by the state bureaucrats who approached him for information because government
reports were grossly inadequate and unreliable. But while many
people depended on Yakovlev for information, some of them re-
sented him and others hated him. The cooperative movement had
triggered a nationwide struggle for economic control between moribund communist bureaucrats who did nothing and eager cooperators who were convinced they could do anything. It took me
three days of phoning around the city to find this former journalist
whom Moscow called "the Fixer." We met one hour later and I
quickly discovered why Yakovlev, like any cooperator, evoked such
passionate reactions.

"Stalin would have had me executed for promoting the cooperative variant," Yakovlev said, a lump in his throat, remembering the death threats piling up in his office.

"I may still be shot."

The first thing Yak told me never to forget was that the closer the cooperatives came to moving in on the state's turf, the more panic they caused within the bureaucracy. It was an old war reignited. When the tsarist system of commerce and transportation fell apart during the Bolshevik Revolution, the consumers' cooperative societies, with twelve million members, fed Russia. Many of the Bolsheviks loathed cooperators because their activities mimicked the bandits who piled up private fortunes by taking advantage of the economic collapse that accompanied the revolution. The cooperators even had their own powerful political party during the lull between the February and October revolutions of 1917. Known as the Trudoviki, the party was headed by Alexander Kerensky, whose White Guard troops later battled Trotsky's Red Guard for control of the country.

After the Russian civil war, keeping the Soviet Union in the hands of the communists meant subduing the private sector and executing people like Yakovlev. The major economic debate after Lenin assumed power was whether or not cooperatives blocked the complete transfer of the means of production and distribution to the proletariat. Lenin's New Economic Policy, which was later obliterated in blood by Stalin, allowed limited private production, with the state maintaining control of heavy industry, transportation, and energy. The entrepreneurs, who functioned under the NEP, and who came to be called Nepmen, began to grow in power because they were the only ones able to feed and clothe the country with regularity. Although Stalin eliminated the Nepmen en masse in 1928, modern cooperators regard them as their martyred forefathers. Cooperators proudly referred to themselves as New Nepmen, and their commitment to risk arrest—or death—for their cause was a bonding passion the Soviet government never expected when the law permitting the new cooperatives was enacted in 1988.

The anger of everyday Russians toward the cooperators who dealt in manufacture and trade, as well as the misgivings of radical cooperators about moonlighting bureaucrats, was lubricated by history. Many Russians, in the privacy of street corners and park benches, complained that the cooperators were Gorbachev's Streltsy, the palace guard of soldier-tradesmen created by Ivan the Terrible in the sixteenth century. Described by historian Robert K. Massie as "a kind of collective dumb animal, never quite sure who was its proper master, but ready to rush and bite anyone who challenged its own privileged position," the Streltsy were Russia's first organized entrepreneurs by virtue of the shops and industries the tsar allowed them to establish. Because they were soldiers, the Streltsy paid no taxes, and their rank in society was passed down from father to son. So powerful were the Streltsy that they owned and controlled all the land that stretched south like the bell of a trumpet from the Kremlin wall to the gates of Moscow. Finally, in the late seventeenth century, Peter the Great hacked off Streltsy noses, ears, and cheeks and had their priests hanged by his court jester. He liquidated the group's ranks because they were hatching plots to keep Russia bound by traditional ways when Peter was trying to institute reforms and encourage foreign innovations.

The two forces in the Soviet economy in the late 1980s were the Party bureaucrats and the black market. It was a beautiful jungle balance, the apotheosis of a perfect and powerful criminal society. But on June 24, 1988, the cooperators became an official presence on the Soviet economic landscape, and they immediately vowed to change what Leningrad rock 'n' roll musician Boris Grebenshikov called "some kind of asylum in the middle of an empty field of danger . . . where everything that's mine will still go to somebody else."

Although a few dozen cooperators had been operating on the sly since 1987 in Moscow and Leningrad, paying protection money to local authorities for permission to conduct business without incident, it was not until a year later that the Council of Ministers of the U.S.S.R. declared legal those portions of the pervasive black market that filled the economic vacuum created by the accumulated greed and irresponsibility of the government. The shadow economy legitimized by the Council of Ministers in June 1988 had never been a clandestine affair. It was the natural order of things for Russians to accept the black market, which had become so powerful in political connection and preeminent in bounty that it would not bow, let alone relinquish its consolidated position, without a fight. Although, like most Council of Ministers decrees, the law on co-operatives was a confusing and contradictory proclamation, it did allow any three people over the age of sixteen to form a cooperative business by registering with the District Soviet of People's De-puties. The District Soviet, another layer of entrenched Party of-ficialdom who played both ends against the middle better than a Chicago alderman, had thirty days to approve the registration. If the cooperative proved to be too much of a threat to the existing order of things, its charter was denied, leaving the cooperator to appeal the decision in front of the Council of Ministers in his republic. Later that year, on December 29—a day that came to be known among cooperators as Red Wednesday—the decree was amended to preclude cooperators from activity in many aspects of medicine, environmental management, teaching, publishing, and telecommunications. A further series of loosely framed amend-ments, designed to force cooperators to be absorbed by state-owned companies, ordered that certain co-ops could exist only as subcon-tractors for state enterprises in the business of culture, travel, manufacturing, cassette-tape reproduction, and dozens more of the businesses that provide the foundation for a modern economy.

In ironic spite of the government's backhanded attempt to wipe out the private sector with a muddling series of ministerial decrees orchestrated to run cooperators out of business, the co-operative movement exploded into a full-scale industry that threat-ened the very essence of Marxist-Leninist thought and, more frightening to the Marxist mandarins, the legitimacy of the contin-ued existence of the Soviet state. Ownership equals political power in the Soviet Union and, as Igor Prostyakov, the vice-chairman of the Council of Ministers Bureau of Social Research, the govern-ment's cooperative hit-squad, loudly urged: "We must drive the co-ops under the roofs of state enterprises. This will ruin them and that's what we should do." Added the government representatives to the 1989 Naberezhniye Chelny Conference on Cooperatives: "The cooperator constitutes a threat to the public order, life, and limb of the Soviet people."

Yakovlev only laughed.

Those were the early days of the cooperative movement, and although I voiced serious concern about the government's portrayal of cooperators in light of *perestroika,* Yakovlev found extremely humorous the unwillingness of the Soviet leadership to support the alternative strategy it had adopted. Humor was his way of dealing with things, particularly the hollow pronouncements from the characters on the Central Committee of the Communist Party, the so-called *Banda Krasnaya*—the Red Gang. The Gang talked a very convincing game, but it had virtually no understanding, desire, or feeling for the realities of the free-market system. Cooperatives, taking advantage of the bribes, gimmicks, and intrigues of Russia's underground economy, had existed on the sly for years. To an outsider, formal sanction by the government looked like approval of the obvious, and certainly an inspirational endorsement of the free-enterprise system. But things were different on the inside of the cooperative movement. The December and June laws, although long overdue, smacked of what many cooperators perceived as the beginning of a counterguerrilla war against them, using law and decree to build a capability to crush their efforts. The cooperators may have agreed with the new legislation, but persuading them that a regime so professional in its manipulative abilities had enacted laws out of intelligence or good faith was something else entirely. A thousand years of Russian history told the cooperators differently, and the only thing of which they were certain was their fear.

Yet as I traveled the Soviet Union between 1987 and 1991, at first visiting cooperatives as a foreign correspondent and later as a member of Cooperative Fact, I never saw a cooperator display his fear in any way other than with humor. One afternoon Yak and I went to meet with Tofik, the big Armenian owner of the Saloon Cooperative Café twelve weeks before we were legally allowed to be sitting there drinking coffee that was not supposed to exist and eating a homemade sausage from a pig that had yet to be slaughtered. Yak surveyed Tofik's popular café and brushed off the crumbling concrete and flaking paint that had fallen on him as he entered the building, the legacy of a cheap system built on cheap materials.

The main question about any system of law-based government, Yak said, was the relationship between the legislature and the executive. The new parliament, which was still in the discussion stage, was hoping to be an effective legislature, but its committees would come to be dominated by the old-style Stalinist-Brezhnevite hacks. These omnipotent characters were the fatal dividing line between talk of and delivery on *perestroika*'s promise. Yakovlev and Tofik knew this gap was wide and dangerous. The Communist Party daily newspaper *Pravda* had already declared that multiparty systems had no place in the Soviet Union, going so far as to command there were to be "no other public forces in this country apart from the party of the communists." The cooperators preached another path of development and, as the two men scanned between the lines of the newspaper article, they agreed that the cooperative movement was the chief proponent of the multiparty system. Drowning a cigarette in a glass of water, Yak tilted his head to listen in to a conversation between a young Soviet army officer and his girlfriend. Moscow was in the throes of another toothpaste shortage. Rotting teeth had always been a particularly nasty Russian dilemma. (Yak's teeth were in such poor shape that they actually itched.) The only thing in shorter supply than dentists and toothpaste were the drugs, syringes, and other equipment required to repair oral disease. Root canals were performed without painkillers, decay was dug out with slow-moving drills, and teeth were bridged together with pieces of paper clips sterilized in boiling water.

"The reason there is no toothpaste, the reason there are no teeth," Yakovlev snickered, turning his yellow smile back to our table, "is there is toothpaste and there are teeth. Understand that and you will understand what this country is up against. The greatest problem is psychological. Russians have no experience in good work and do not understand there will be more money and more goods if they work harder. The government hates the cooperators for telling the people this and making money off of it. Take your basic forty-to-fifty-year-old Soviet man who has worked for years to make three hundred rubles a month, then say he wakes up to see a young cooperative dentist starting at five hundred rubles a month, over three times the average national salary. Imagine the conflict in his soul, imagine the hate in his heart."

"Imagine the pain in his mouth," Tofik said, tapping my front teeth with his index finger. "Then he will pay and gladly."

By April Fool's Day 1989 there were officially ninety-nine thousand three hundred cooperatives employing two million people in the U.S.S.R., and the conflict had turned to violence. Cooperators, the "hooligans" whom *Pravda* endlessly referred to as "wheeler-dealers and scoundrels," were shot and beaten, their businesses set ablaze by professional arsonists abetted by citizens pouring gasoline on the flames. Many cooperators would be stoned or clubbed with planks. So fierce would the hatred become that nineteen cooperatives were set afire in one day in the Turkmenian city of Nebit-Dag, with the six fire engines called to the scene destroyed by a mob of black marketeers, alleged plainclothes KGB agents, and disgruntled crowds screaming "*capitalisti.*" Other cooperatives would meet the same fate. Firebombings and black-market hand grenades were a favorite method of destruction, as were the burning and drowning of cooperative sheep and cattle, with no thought given to the country's abominably widespread hunger. After Vladimir Plotnikov's cooperative pig farm, built atop a garbage dump on the outskirts of Moscow, was burned down under suspicious circumstances, local residents openly rejoiced at the fate of Plotnikov and his "bourgeois pigs." Organized gangs descended upon cooperative farms in the Ukraine and Azerbaijan, ripping produce from the ground under cover of darkness, and then plowing tons of shattered and shredded glass into the fields to prevent further food production. Cooperative restaurants in Moscow, Leningrad, and Baku were attacked by chain-wielding bands of hooded thugs, scattering patrons and employees in fear. A gun battle erupted over ice cream in Glazur, an extremely elegant Moscow co-op restaurant that was a joint venture between Intourist and a Belgian beer company. The gunman, after pulling off two rounds and missing his intended target, fled down the Sadovaya Ring Road to hide out in the forty-kopeck-a-splash cooperative toilet on Smolenskaya Square, observers said. A few patrons told me the focus of the gunfight was a drug deal gone sour, the ferocity of the scene heightened by the alcoholic rage of the mysterious gunman. Two weeks and no arrests later, the street skinny on what went down and why became clear: Glazur's downstairs ice cream parlor and upstairs restaurant sold food for rubles, but Intourist wanted to transform the place into a more lucrative hard-currency-only restaurant that catered to deep-pocketed Western tourists. And the only way to do that was to scare away the Russians who found Glazur a charming and comfortable break from Moscow's ennui. Too many people, including Moscow's foreign community, who knew better than to use their credit cards, were paying tabs with worthless Soviet cash to avoid American Express and Visa conversion rates pegged at one dollar and sixty-eight cents per ruble. Intourist stocked Glazur with all of its provisions except beer. The greedy state travel authority, which ostensibly paid for the supplies in rubles, needed an excuse to turn the place into a *valuta* (hard currency) operation, thereby excluding rank-and-file Russians and increasing Intourist's hard cash stores. A staged gun battle was an ingenious solution, and it added a nice, chilly twist to the government's propaganda line on what could happen to good socialist Russians who frequented cooperatives. Glazur was shut down for three months. When the place reopened, the manager was crooked, the staff corrupt, and the beer watered down. Customers were immediately greeted outside by one of those hauntingly indefatigable Soviet doormen who shout: *"Tolka valuta! Nyetu? Davai otsyuda, zhopa!"* "Only valuta! Got none? Get out of here, asshole!"

The days I spent with Yakovlev turned into weeks as I gradually came to realize that there was a serious guerrilla war going on and nobody behind the battle lines seemed to notice. The hostility took the form of a dramatic three-way confrontation among the radical cooperators, the fanatical element in the Party who would not surrender their power and position to the capitalist system, and the iron-willed bureaucrat-adventurers who played cooperator when it suited their purses and politics. Flailing and thundering at each other like the clashing factions of a religion that had long ago abandoned its god, each group saw its goal as a purification of Russia in which they alone came out on top. The war was exacerbated by the need of each faction to exist outside the perversion of the laws and decrees because, as Andrei Faden, the political analyst at Yakovlev's cooperative, said: "The written rules of the Soviet game don't work, so you must work outside the law. Every one of us could be put in prison."

Guns in pockets and large kitchen knives under car seats became commonplace, especially among cooperators seeking a hedge against state-sponsored thugs and independent gangs of racketeers. Racketeering was a serious threat to cooperative development. Although there were laws to prevent extortion and destruction, the state did not enforce them. Cooperators were afraid to tell the police of their troubles because, with justification, they did not trust the militia. "The terror demands had to be met," explained Alex Finestein, a Moscow lawyer who defended cooperatives for violating their charters. "Families were being threatened with death. This is the reality." Valentin Kozakov, an ex-cop, brought together ninety men and women to start Cooperative Alex, the armed security firm that guarded us at Cooperative Fact. Kozakov, a discerning Leningrader wise to the system, understood there was big money to be made while *perestroika* tried to provide institutional solutions to personal defects. No one asked who Kozakov's guards were or where they came from. They shot back—that was good enough.

The state responded, too, unleashing against thousands of co-operators draconian tax laws and harsh regulations that suffocated their businesses with paperwork. High-level Soviet officials sensed an opportunity to use cooperatives as another method to extract hard currency from the planeloads of naive Americans who wanted in on the *perestroika* feeding frenzy. Institute of U.S.A. and Canada director Georgi Arbatov, who approached any visiting U.S. dignitary or network news anchor like a simpering pet just before mealtime, set up one of the first moonlight cooperatives to be established by a Party member. Arbatov, one of the many communist divas who cashed in their rank and license for dollars, privately rejected the cooperative movement; but his own cooperative—fully encouraged, serviced, and protected by the Party to which it kowtowed—made a bundle dispensing introductions and guidance to Westerners wanting to do business with the "new" Soviet Union. Russia's communist fat cats manipulated cooperatives as another procedure to *gladit firmacha,* literally, "to iron the

foreigner" out of money and items that would otherwise be unavailable in Russia. The directors of the big state-owned industrial
firms, who had done business with multibillion-dollar American
companies for decades, were never known for shrinking from such
shakedowns; the cooperative movement gave them, beyond a fresh
complement of nonindustrial bureaucrats from the arts and science
academies, a whole new wardrobe of Westerners to iron. Com-
mented Michael Mears, the former head of the U.S. Commercial
Office in Moscow: "There's a big crack between the poor fool who
is here trying to do business in this labyrinthine mess and the board
of directors and politicians back in the States who are reading
perestroika stories."

At the same time, government officials complained that the
cooperatives were draining new materials earmarked to produce
consumer goods to be sold in the eternally barren state stores.
Soviet banks were ordered to restrict preferential loans intended
for cooperatives that sold their products above state-controlled
prices; likewise, government suppliers were enjoined to curtail
deliveries of raw materials to noncomplying "enterprises," which
meant the cooperatives. District Soviets were granted emergency
powers to enforce price ceilings on restaurants, shops, and other
cooperative establishments as they saw fit. Cooperators were detained by the militia on trumped-up charges of hooliganism and
exploitation of the masses.

Anatoly Rutkovsky, the thirty-seven-year-old economist and
owner of the Come and Taste cooperative restaurant, whose dream
was to "re-create McDonald's . . . to feed the whole world with
sandwiches is genius," vowed to shoot himself if his cooperative
were forced to close. "If I can't find a pistol," he told me, "I'll
drown myself." A few days after Red Wednesday his place was
firebombed. The black-haired Greek-Russian restaurateur went on
the lam to Seattle, but came back alive to reopen his place, naming
the firebombed portion of the restaurant the "Mafia Room." After
the second wave of attacks on his cooperative, and the local government council's continued refusals to lend him police assistance
without large bribes, Rutkovsky emigrated to Greece.

"There is nothing left to say," Rutkovsky said a few weeks

before he departed Moscow in August 1990. "I will go and feed those who want to be fed."

In the early days of cooperatives, when the Western press dubbed the movement "the ride of the Cooperative Cowboys," cooperators had no coherent vision of themselves. This suited the government fine, because if you do not have some idea of who you are, then you are unlikely to form a coherent policy. Cooperators looked senseless, argumentative, hackneyed, and wrapped up in the personal melodramas that unfold when amateurs with good intentions try to illuminate the world. They had no way to agree or disagree, no way to debate and discuss, no means by which to communicate about political and economic matters. Cooperatives started from scratch and had no context in which to exist. The state-sponsored propaganda campaigns against the cooperative movement made would-be cooperators more cautious than curious about becoming part of the free-enterprise system. The state was making it quite clear that safety resided in drawing a small, socialist wage and moonlighting for extra money in the shadows. To come out of the shadows to establish a cooperative was an open invitation to all sorts of horrible catastrophes—particularly if you were successful.*

Mark Arnoldovich Portnoy paid Moscow's Armenian and Georgian crime lords two thousand rubles a month in protection

---

*So great was the public's fear of being tagged a *kooperativchik* that the free-market democrats in the Soviet legislature successfully passed a decree in August 1990 allowing individuals to set up limited private "joint-stock" companies outside cooperative codes. The decree was enacted in an effort to restimulate citizens opposed to becoming cooperators by permitting single individuals, distinct from groups, to own, invest in, and be responsible for a business. The decree in effect licensed what the Soviet Union's fifty thousand or so cooperative chairmen had been doing since 1988; it also did nothing to erase the apprehension about becoming a cooperator, because parliamentary decrees and laws could easily be ignored, rescinded, or overshadowed by other decrees and laws. The legal terms "joint-stock company" and "cooperative association" were interchangeable expressions everywhere except in the bureaucracy, although the semantics of the new legislation finally gave businesses a legitimate right to buy property and Soviet citizens a legal opportunity to enter into partnerships with foreign citizens. Nonetheless, bureaucrats and Communist Party officials, particularly outside the more politically liberal urban centers of Moscow and Leningrad, faced no great challenge in wrecking any sort of free-market venture, if its existence posed a threat to the local bureaucracy's capacity to dominate the area.

money. The short, stocky Moscow apartment building superintendent, director of Cooperative Moskvich and the founder of the Perestroika Association Cooperative and of Credit Moscow/The Perestroika People's Bank, said it was the price one had to pay to be a pioneer. On the evening of December 31, 1987, Portnoy opened his combination restaurant/nightclub/art gallery "44"— Moscow's first all-night club. Portnoy was graceful, in his own way, and he seemed to feel in his heart that at any moment he would change the face of Russia. The "44" filled up that first night. A long line of couples and young conscripts from the nearby army barracks snaked through the snowbank outside. Inside, people smiled. This was no small event. Portnoy went into the kitchen and wept. Business was very good—maybe even too good. Portnoy had swapped free food and drink and a couple of rubles under the table for peace with his bureaucratic *zashchitnik* (protector) and the guys at the militia outpost on the Leningrad Highway. In the early hours of January 1, 1988, local toughs from the murky Russian underworld arrived at "44" for their piece of Portnoy's pie. Nine months later the protection money had eaten up all the profits. Portnoy's revenue stream had dried up.

"From the very beginning," Portnoy told me on the grim October day he was forced to lock the big pinewood door of "44" for good, "the word *cooperative* has been bad."

Portnoy remained undaunted and announced he was going to open a bank. Although the Jewish handyman and entrepreneur did not have a kopeck to his name, Credit Moscow became the first privately owned bank to register in Moscow since December 27, 1917, when the Bolsheviks nationalized Russia's banks. A great many people questioned the wisdom of Portnoy's idea: the last batch of Moscow's private bankers had their vaults leveled by Red Guard artillery. "Whenever we didn't know just where the White Guards were," a Bolshevik gunner told American reporter John Reed during the battle for Moscow, "we bombarded their pocketbooks."

Credit Moscow was owned and operated by the directors of sixteen cooperatives that banded together to form the Perestroika Association. There were decorators, mechanics, traders, artists, restaurateurs, and jewelers. Included were Smirnov, a former ship's captain; Goldenberg, an auto worker; Kriolov, a cook; and Gorkin, a retired prizefighter with cannonball-sized fists ready to pummel any racketeer who strayed into his path. Their average age was fifty, and their goal was to lend money to cooperatives independently of the state-owned Gosbank, the biggest bank in the world. "The state hasn't given us a building yet," said Mikhail Goldman, one of Credit Moscow's largest investors, "so I figure we'll be loaded on boxcars and driven away to our headquarters."

Winter came early to Moscow in 1988, and every other Saturday morning I left Cooperative Fact and traveled out the Leningrad Highway, passing long lines of the huge snow-clearing machines the Russians called *Capitalisti* because, like capitalists, their gigantic metal talons scooped up every item in sight. Saturday was the day "44" opened its doors for the bimonthly Credit Moscow board meeting. Portnoy had pushed the dining tables together to create the atmosphere of a boardroom. Steaming glasses of pungent Georgian tea awaited the directors, who shook snow from their overcoats as they filed into the room to take their seats. There was never any talk, just the ritualistic clinking of sixteen spoons stirring Cuban sugar into tea. The managing director was Boris Nepomnyashchy, a twenty-five-year-old black-market itinerant who had found religion in the cooperative sector and whose last name meant "one who never remembers anything." Nepomnyashchy was always late, but as Arkady Osipov, a member of the bank's executive council, never failed to remind the board: "Bank chairmen are not late. They are detained."

The immediate issue that always faced Credit Moscow was finding money. If the Gosbank needed more money, it printed more rubles. If the government needed money, it printed more rubles. Depending on who cut the deal, the dollar-ruble ratio garnered anywhere from one dollar and sixty-eight cents to eight cents per ruble. The problem with the printing approach was that, because prices were fixed, an increase in the supply of rubles resulted in a shortage of goods and more bang for the buck on the black market. The ruble simply had no value and its fortunes were constantly taking immediate turns for the worse. Credit Moscow's idea was to give the ruble value by enabling cooperatives to produce high-quality goods and then letting the free market establish prices. But velocity-of-money theories were heady stuff for a group of bankers who did not even understand the concept of a checkbook. "What we are doing is an impossible task," Nepomnyashchy told the group on these occasions, "but every task is impossible until you begin it." Credit Moscow planned to offer its depositors 7 percent interest (Gosbank offered about 5 percent) and lend money at about 10 percent (roughly twice what Gosbank charged). The board never figured out how they could compete with the state bank if they had to sell more expensive money just to stay afloat. Said Vladimir Usachov, the director of a machine-building cooperative: "It doesn't matter. We are experiencing a greater risk just being at this table. There's no reason for us to pull back."

Nods all around.

The only deal Credit Moscow nearly pulled off came from a mysterious Zurich precious metals broker who offered to use the bank to invest fifty million Swiss francs in a state enterprise. Two of the directors went to the State Foreign Trade Bank and explained that the Swiss trader wanted Soviet platinum to be used as collateral on the loan to a state construction enterprise. The men were thrown out of the bank. "If the government cannot give a platinum guarantee to a five-year, fifty-million-franc loan," Portnoy told the board, "then it's not sure of *perestroika* and the cooperatives."

More nods all around.

Isaac Goldovsky, the director of Papyrus, a paper-recycling cooperative, and Yuri Rosenthal, the director of the Alice Bakery, invested fifty thousand rubles each in the bank. Mikhail Goldman, the fiery leader of the Acceleration design and construction cooperative, kicked in even more. Other directors seeded the bank with sums of from five thousand to twenty thousand rubles. Others gave nothing. Goldman was angry. "I'm against any liberalism," he screamed, denouncing his partners. "Those of you who haven't paid will be fired from the board if we don't have your money by Friday . . . and as for you, Osipov, when are you *really* going to join us?"

Maxim Osipov, a vice-minister at the Ministry of Finance, had failed on his promise to tell his state-sector bosses that he was a member of a cooperative. Goldman, sucking on one cigarette after another, gave a long and impassioned speech on Osipov's character flaws to a circle of frozen faces. "We must move to get insurance, we must make this bank work for the people and some of us are still working for the state!"

Osipov, nodding in distraught agreement with Goldman's tirade, responded delicately. "I agree I could be working harder. The ministry doesn't even know what I'm up to. I will work harder to make the banking association a success and to fulfill the plan."

"Then I'm done," Goldman said, grabbing Osipov's bald and oval head between his massive hands and kissing him twice on each cheek.

This same scene, with virtually the same dialogue, occurred every two weeks, until the bank and its directors went the way of most Russian dreams and disappeared without a trace. "I don't know what will come of all this," Igor Smirnov said to me in tears after Goldman and Osipov performed their final routine in front of the assembled board. "I don't think we need just insurance men and lawyers; we cooperators need an army to protect us from making mistakes." Smirnov had retired from the Soviet merchant marine with a captain's pension, but soon discovered that he could not stomach boredom. Seeing the world from the prows of tugs and tramp steamers had given him a vision of what the Russian people could achieve if given the chance. He started a trading cooperative that allowed him to travel around the country swapping commodities. He was a precise, practical man who attributed his common sense to the years he spent navigating ships around the icebergs of the White Sea. "Credit Moscow may very well fail. The state may change its mind tomorrow and tell us to go to hell, or we may not have the intelligence to make the bank work. But it doesn't matter. The struggle between the state institutions and the cooperatives is more than a clash. The state and the cooperatives, by decree, are supposed to be working together to rebuild the Soviet Union. This isn't happening. The state wants to control us, but it's hard for them to control hope. Please forgive us if we look amateurish. There's bitterness and pessimism in the blood of this country. If Credit Moscow, if the cooperative movement, can do anything to cleanse our blood, then we will have succeeded."

Portnoy's adventure cost the players nearly one million rubles and ended with very little satisfaction and a great deal of ruffled dignity. It was just Russia, they said. Civilization ended at the Soviet border. Beyond that, everybody entered the jungle, and not always right at the top of the food chain. The news of Portnoy's demise sent a rumble of bad vibes through the cooperative movement. The last thing they needed was to hear that one of their pioneers had fallen victim to a mix of mafia and mad ideas. Being Jewish did not help matters. If anything, it worsened and provoked more people to gang up on his failure.

Oddly, Volodya Yakovlev expressed no sympathy for Portnoy, who went back to his family and fixing apartment toilets. The co-op movement was very hard on those who indulged in being co-operators: it magnified a cooperator's sense of alienation from his own people, an estrangement that was, in a very ugly Russian way, made more acceptable by other cooperators' quietly equating Portnoy's failure with his being Jewish. Portnoy—tiny, ugly, loud—fit right into the venomous Russian habit of using Jews as the standard excuse for failure. Russian vanity is a repulsive creature, and it feeds on those who are different, people like Portnoy, who, despite his irresistible energy, never had the strength, connections, wits, or raw speed required to juggle the prejudice, the bureaucracy, and the black market over the long haul.

3

The most loyal are those who've been
found guilty.

SADDAM HUSSEIN

SABINA ORUDJEVA hated Volodya Yakovlev. She never
looked at him. A poised but mirthless smile passed quickly from
her lips, and then, after Yak's attention was drawn elsewhere, she
would roll her wide brown eyes and grumble something in Russian
that sounded like a fly beating itself senseless against a pane of
glass. Yak had never done anything specific to incur Sabina's wrath
and, for his part, did not find her dislike of him anything out of
the Russian ordinary. Sabina, who had considered working at Yakovlev's information cooperative after their first meeting over dinner, found him obsequious, ambitious, and full of the type of avarice
that eventually puts people behind bars or in the employ of the
KGB. Like all members of Moscow's Golden Youth, Sabina and
Yak had heard of each other over the years, but had not mingled
socially because of the differing political and personal circumstances
of their respective families within the Kremlin Ration. It was very
strange, she thought. Yakovlev, born with all the advantages of
favorably casted Party parents, had forfeited his birthright in order
to pursue crazy schemes among cooperators she dismissed as vaga-
bonds and peasants. Whenever Yakovlev voiced something Sabina
found particularly offensive (like his enthusiasm for the number of

57

Russians who were joining cooperatives without any attention paid to their backgrounds, or how difficult Yak said it was to find really talented and committed people among the idle and unskilled Golden Youth), she dropped her feigned disinterest and lashed into him with every fiber her petite body could muster. Yak just smiled at these outbursts. Better than anyone in Moscow, Yak knew that cooperatives brought together an unusually unsavory and flammable mix of charlatans, bums, ideologues, thieves, farmers, hustlers, priests, perverts, bureaucrats, gangsters, con men, and dead souls. Understanding that the movement needed to be completely reformed and overhauled to survive and to be accepted, Yak expected casualties, jealousies, and quarrelsome outbursts to riddle cooperative ranks until at least the turn of the century.

"The greatest problem in Russia is always the psychological problem," he would say breathlessly, after his attackers had calmed down. Lighting another cigarette, as he always did in moments of crisis, Yak would add quite matter-of-factly: "It's very difficult to train people to think."

"Well, we cannot think, Volodya, only you can think," Sabina would say, her voice shrill with mockery.

Yak would always turn his slitted eyelids from the smoking cigarette to Sabina. She was not all that different from himself, he knew. Yak and Sabina were both keenly aware of and troubled by the collapse of the country in which they lived. Sabina knew Yak was right, but she was suspicious of his motives and irritated with his commanding tone—the attitude of the Apparat. The electrical silence between their exchanges made Yak more confident of Sabina's talents. She was not willing to give up easily and he recognized the quality. He had only a few like her at Cooperative Fact and he understood the feelings. She was beautiful, intelligent, and possessed of the energy necessary to make things happen— but isolated, bereaved, solitary. His own experience confirmed that it was possible: emotions in riot and disorder, passions conspiring toward madness unless directed. By him.

"Why not come work for Fact?" Yakovlev asked. The question—which he asked Sabina frequently—opened a pathway into grief for Sabina. Sitting erect and gracefully flicking back her long and wavy blonde hair, Sabina wanted to say yes, but was unable to fend off the terrible strains of hope and fear. More than most of those around her, she led an imaginative existence, trying on two occasions to start her own art cooperative in Moscow. In contrast with the glaring inactivity of most Golden Youth, Sabina attempted to concentrate on tasks that might release her from being simply the on-again, off-again wife of the grandson of Leonid Brezhnev's Minister of Trade and, therefore, having access to a dacha with a driver, a maid in the country, and a spacious, two-room apartment to herself in the center of Moscow, as well as a European leather purse stuffed with rubles. Connections. Alliances. Correlations. Shades of significance. Communist bloodlines. That was the game. And everyone finessed it so well, except her. Failure did not suit Sabina and, more often than not, small tears welled up quietly in her eyes when something went wrong. "Zhal," she would say, murmuring the Russian expression for "It's a pity," until her body went limp, her bright face turning vacant and her mind set on finding a place to sleep off the disappointment of something that might have been, if only . . .

There were a great many "if onlys" in Sabina's life, as there were in all Russian lives, suspended overhead like clouds of bad weather. She had married Sasha Struyev, a childhood friend, when she was twenty. He was a short, kind man who reminded her pleasantly of the chipmunks her Afghan hound chased through the clumps of heavy birch and pine outside "grandfather's" dacha at Zhukovka, an exclusive estate run for the Party faithful but whose children had taken over. Lying atop a gentle bluff across a narrow stretch of the Moscow River from Gorbachev's countryside compound in the village of Quarrels, Zhukovka was guarded by aging veterans of the Soviet Union's Great Patriotic War against the German fascists. The old sentinels, sipping tea and the odd shot of vodka brought down to their plank hut by the babushkas who cleaned, cooked, and provisioned the dachas, were more babysitters than vigilant protectors of the Motherland. Zhukovka had become a country club for the Golden Youth, since their fathers and grandfathers—men with names like Sakharov, Shostakovich, and Brezhnev—had either decided it was better to live in Moscow or had died with the clout to prevent their real estate from passing on to the next Party factotum in line for a house in the country. "Why do we cultivate hatred toward the children and grandchildren of leaders who have left the historical stage?" asked Zhukovka's most controversial citizen, Andrei Brezhnev, the twenty-nine-year-old grandson of Leonid Brezhnev. "I must say that my grandfather didn't like it when people sought favors from him through members of his family and always told them to make official approaches." A refined and soft-spoken man, Andrei had been forced out of his job as a junior Foreign Ministry official to pursue a career as a music producer. But the perks remain pasted to his celebrity and, like the other inhabitants of Zhukovka, Andrei and his Western-dressed wife were not about to give up such exclusive rights as being bused to the fenced-off Council of Ministers' beach outside the village or having boats readied for them at the chic Party spa and beach two miles away at Petrovna Dalnee for the sake of restructuring the Soviet Union.

Zhukovka's guards, who earned a hearty three hundred rubles a month, cared little who lived there. The rows of medals—the siege of Leningrad, the battle of Stalingrad—pinned to their top-coats had tarnished with years, as had their faces, a result of a life revolving around the opening and shutting of a large green metal gate that protected their charges from the outside world. They were bored and laconic men, as was Sasha, whose own taciturnity was the result of his having nothing to say. Sasha could have done anything, but decided to do nothing well and everything badly while sinking deeper into depression with each failure. He was a painter, a writer, a designer, an art dealer, a filmmaker, a businessman, and a member of the innumerable other professions available to Russians who drive Western automobiles beyond heavily guarded gates. But he was patient and hospitable and, most important, impenetrable to the malice that beset Sabina in her youth. At first Sabina wondered how far she ought to go with this, but settled on an alliance of protection rather than a union of love. Russian women trust their instinct for survival in matters of marriage above all else, or they are dead. Safety and preservation are the most important Russian passions, although they never admit it, even to themselves. Shared dreams and orgasm and romance guided by the stars are the stuff of Western magazines and movies. Love is as passionless as a periodontal review; Soviet women are more concerned with finding food and shelter, and use their kisses as weapons to consummate survival.

"How I wish, how I wish that I could share in the confidence the West has in Russia," Sabina said, reflecting with a frown on the history that was taking place around her, almost apologetic for the shameless lack of expectation the Russians had in the system, lack of faith in themselves. "It's nice to have a rosy view of things, but I fear that is impossible here."

Sabina's birth certificate said she was born in 1960 to Irina Orudjeva (the daughter of Sabit Orudjev, Brezhnev's Minister of Natural Gas) and Simon Landsberg, a dim figure who trafficked in Soviet diamonds. Landsberg, who some suspected was a KGB agent drafted into doing personal work for Leonid Brezhnev's private mafia, made many trips to Western Europe during Sabina's youth, ostensibly as an agent for Soviet diamonds, which, after oil, were the country's chief generator of hard currency. Sometime during the mid-1960s Landsberg made a trip to Vienna from which he never returned. All Sabina knew was that something horrid had happened to her father. The only thing more powerful than the reluctance of her family to tell her what happened in Vienna was the speed with which her grandfather went about altering the documentation of her birth. Sabina's new papers stated she was born in 1958 and that her guardian was Sabit Orudjev, who had gained great fame for keeping Azerbaijani oil flowing to Soviet troops during World War II and who later came to be known as the father of the Soviet air conditioning industry, having turned idle Baku factories into assembly lines for the ubiquitous BK-1500. Landsberg, wiped out entirely, became the man who never was. Despite her new papers and, if discovered, risking serious documentation problems with the state martinets, Sabina launched her own investigation into what had become of her real father after her grandfather's death. While obtaining a degree in advertising at Moscow State University, she discovered that Landsberg had died in a mysterious automobile accident in Vienna in 1974, but that other people were claiming to have seen him walking about Moscow as late as 1980. Her chief source of information was a Georgian black marketeer named Atari, who claimed to be a friend of Landsberg and who would meet with Sabina only at the restaurant in the Sovetskaya Hotel. Atari recounted a bizarre tale of tangles and deceits: Landsberg was still alive. The fatal car crash was an elaborate ruse, designed to allow Landsberg to continue his illicit diamond deals for powerful Soviet officials (all unmentioned) from the safety of nonexistence. The burned and mangled body recovered from the flaming wreck was not complete enough for a true identification. Claiming the time was not right to say any more about Landsberg, the cryptic Georgian told Sabina to stay in touch with him through a uniformed Sovetskaya waiter. Soon after, Atari, too, disappeared into the underworld.

The astonishing news threw Sabina into personal turmoil. Sabit, who raised and sheltered Sabina as a child of the Kremlin Ration, was dead, having left her cherished memories, a medal that proclaimed him "King of the Bear Hunters," and a gigantic, narwhal-tusk-handled Siberian knife inscribed "Good fortune against the bears"—of the Politburo, according to the family story. Her mother had moved to Helsinki, where she married a Finnish businessman and started a new family. Sabina was alone, an only child with forged documents provided by the state to give her entrance into a world both she and her grandfather detested. Her strange and uneasy mood was compounded by the fact that no one in the Kremlin Ration knew quite how to receive her: the traditional "Party discipline" under which leaders, apparatchiks, and their families were forced to follow strict rules of hierarchical behavior had made her an orphan of sorts. Sabina returned from Sabit's funeral to discover she no longer had a powerful *zashchitnik* (protector) to watch over her life. Her cheery personality grew listless and her days and nights more scornful. Enough of her childhood had been spent in church to give her a belief in God. Although she would not tolerate blasphemy of any sort, life, she judged, was a cruel caricature, a masquerade of lies, distortions, and perversions. It was then that she met Sasha, who shook his head over the painful gyrations of her history and thought no less of her for it.

Sabina's greatest talent was a flair for tart and wry humor. She savaged both the Party hypocrites and the democratic reformers who were growing sleek and pompous at the expense of *perestroika*. No one was spared. Gavril Popov, the reform-minded mayor of Moscow and Sabina's former economics professor at MGU, was "Hans Christian Popov" because his boisterous support of a free market was a "fairy tale" that contradicted the information she was receiving from the Party members who inhabited Zhukovka. Yegor Ligachev, the orthodox communist member of the Politburo, whom Gorbachev had put in charge of agriculture after a drawn-out and bitter political struggle over the country's new capitalist tendencies, was the "patriarch of food who is doing his utmost to keep Russia's belly empty." Her intelligence was nourished on the sights and sounds around her, not on the skilled presentation of state reality. "The West thinks the KGB is gone," Sabina said with a chuckle as we drove past the drab yellow and gray secret-police complex on Dzerzhinsky Square to visit a cooperative in July 1989. "They are no longer concerned with investigating *people*, but they are very involved in destabilizing *perestroika*. Last week the KGB created a new division of forty agents to do nothing but start joint ventures with Western firms. This is their experimental sociological work. If the crowds rush in tomorrow to kill Gorbachev, the KGB will do nothing because they are concentrating on their scientific experiments."

"How do you know this?" I asked, captivated with the news that the two-hundred-ninety-thousand-member KGB had formed a special cadre of agents to infiltrate U.S.–Soviet joint ventures and cooperative partnerships with small American firms. The new unit was a variation on a 1970's espionage technique in which KGB agents posing as Soviet businessmen hopped freely between Western trade fairs to pay cash under the table for items they were forbidden to purchase legally because of trade sanctions.

"How does one know anything is real in the Soviet Union!" she exclaimed, exasperated with the question I would ask her over and over, whenever she related some amazing bulletin. "There is evil here and you correspondents never want to write it because you want *corroboration!* The communists are experts at hiding their intentions and you help them because you cannot get some official to tell you the obvious. We Russians wait and watch and see things you can never hope to see. We in this country know little, but we do know enough to keep indoors when it rains and to what lengths the communists will go to keep their power."

Sabina had a way of putting people wise to what was going on around them very quickly. It was a difference between big-dog and little-dog politics, she said. "Look at the faces in the street," she would say whenever I pointed out some bit of government news claiming another grand step toward democracy. "Do you see any democracy among the little dogs?" At heart Sabina was a democrat, but survival dictated it unwise to relinquish the perks she received from her marriage by openly supporting the destruction of the existing system. Life was safe, particularly for a cynic, which Sabina had matured into with amazing strength. Cynicism, laced with animosity toward the big-dog politicians whose factional schemings had very little to do with day-to-day life, was bred, as the old Russian grandmothers said, in the milk of the mother.

Sabina said that Soviet politicians excelled at vague definitions and, for all their romantic talk of restructure, played the game to suit only themselves. Even the *perestroika* puppies, the Soviet Union's freely elected liberal politicians, were growing fat off the Party's agenda for liberty and justice, and democratic rebelliousness was not part of their diet. Yevgeny Beyshenaly, a writer at *Sovetskaya Kultura*, described the new group of parliamentarians elected in 1989 as no better than a clique of schoolboy pilferers. "Many of them in the election campaign assailed the existence of VIP Rooms for deputies at airports and train stations," he mocked, "but now they do not say a word. Now they go to the head of the line everywhere."

Publicly, Soviet leaders spent a lot of time talking about getting away from communism, but privately they are still mired in the system's boiling asphalt. Any talk of change in the system has all the television pull of the Reverend Pat Robertson denouncing sodomy inside a gay bathhouse; making the mechanics of change actually work involves political maneuverings so massively complicated that it flummoxed even Niccolò Machiavelli. "A small section of the populace desires to be free in order to obtain authority over others," the great Florentine political tactician observed of corrupt societies in *The Discourses*, "but the vast bulk of those who demand freedom desire but to live in security. But when the only security is through corruption, in the course of three generations the corruption inherent in the leaders would have begun to spread to the members, and, when the members had become corrupt, it would no longer have been possible to reform them. Whether it is possible for change to be made in a noncorrupt society I do not know."

Democracy was no easy feat in a nation where almost nobody laughed and everybody told you only what you wanted to hear—and then there was the question that my Politburo and Central Committee friend Trusishka kept pondering whenever we got together for a drink. It had to do with borders and boundaries, and the point at which any peaceful pursuit of democracy becomes violent through the sheer velocity of the collision between the incompetence of a ruler and the dissatisfaction of those he rules.

Trusishka was in a state of fear. "People are afraid," he jabbered over coffee at the Margarita cooperative café on the corner of Moscow's beautiful Patriarch's Pond. "The whole Party seems to be closing down and growing more powerful at the same time. No one knows where it will lead." Trusishka was one of Gorbachev's men, a *perestroichik* who had cruised high on the *bronya* since his birth into a noble Party family in 1951. Enough of his teenage years had been spent abroad to give him an interest in democracy, and the foresight to understand that the Party's predatory habits only increased its alienation from the country. The desperation of the public—"Lenin's children"—was a vicious cycle that *perestroika* had aggravated as it had improved for the better, he believed. "Let me tell you something," Trusishka said in his British-accented English. "Let me tell you what the majority of the educated Soviet people who can make *perestroika* work actually want. They want to be in on the good life that the Party controls *now*. If not, they want to leave the country. Among themselves they talk of democratic pluralism, but it's too late in mankind's history for the Soviet people to go through further pain and sacrifice to have the kind of life you have in America. They all want to arrive at their destination today. We don't have another seventy years to complete the journey." It was a harsh travel report: *perestroika* was a rattletrap held together with words, not deeds, and it was lurching forward over bumpy ground. Only one outcome was possible.

Trusishka went into his office at Central Committee headquarters every morning at nine A.M. looking bad and departed at seven P.M. looking worse. I had first met him while taking a weekend walk alone in the Zhukovka woods; so startled was Trusishka to see an American wearing a Pittsburgh Pirates baseball cap inside the exclusive dacha compound that we immediately struck up a conversation. Trusishka's fascination with America proved to be a boon, particularly his interest in the power of the black talk-show hostess Oprah Winfrey to influence white, middle-class American women. "Oprah is an amazing example of how race relations have improved in your country," he said. "If only something similar could happen here." Whenever I needed a special favor, like the backstage pass to the decisive Twenty-eighth Party Congress (which I slipped back to him at Margarita's), he would come through "out of curiosity to see what you think about what is going on." *Perestroika* had happened so fast, he said, that most people in the West thought it had always been part of the Russian stew. Democracy in the Soviet Union was boiling down to a choice between conservative communists and liberal communists, with nobody humanly appealing in either pot. The Twenty-eighth Party Congress, and its failure to engender *perestroika,* exposed the Party in all its calculating ugliness, betraying *perestroika* to be nothing more than a well-orchestrated sham.

Gorbachev's men, who had traveled tirelessly in the West to spread *perestroika's* gospel, were not about to risk further trouble by explaining and defending *perestroika* in the provinces let alone mobilize the critical Twenty-eighth Party Congress in July 1990 as a proselyte to export restructure to the countryside. Despite further abdications from the Party by Moscow Mayor Gavril Popov and Leningrad Mayor Anatoli Sobchak (more would follow), the independent Soviet weekly newspaper *Commersant* headlined the street-take on the congress with: PARTY CONGRESS: NOTHING NEW and, commenting in a later English-language edition on Sobchak's long-range personal blueprint for vitalizing the Party-controlled economy, "How much wood could a Sobchak chuck if a Sobchak could chuck wood?" Yet is was Gorbachev who drew the Party's line on the whole treacherous mess. "Those who leave now and seek refuge elsewhere I view with contempt," he said.

In the West, Soviet reform—the hemorrhaging of the Communist Party—was interpreted as evidence of weakness in the system and not understood for the strength it actually reflected, even in the minds of the new *Narodny Deputaty* (People's Deputies), who complained the loudest against the process. Gorbachev's game plan had been to rise above the system through, among other maneuvers, an acceleration of his willingness to endorse the reduction of Kremlin power, blaming the slowness of the change on the conservative, anti-*perestroika* factions.* His divisive move concocted a stalemate. Dramatic reduction in central power led to immediate anoesia among the Bolshevik dinosaurs and the tens of thousands of local Party factotums who feared, as Yegor Ligachev said of their lot at the Twenty-eighth Congress: "Our Party and our state are facing a great threat, and our federation is being taken to pieces. If we continue to make one concession after another we may lose everything." Added conservative, Leningrad Party boss Boris Gidaspov: "Radical political change is helping plunge the country into an orgy of chaos." Gorbachev, who had slapped down bureaucrats such as Ligachev and Gidaspov for bogging down restructuring and democracy during the first four years of his administration, entered the fifth year in 1990 saying the Russian people were at fault. Gidaspov, for example, had been humiliated publicly at a rally of twenty thousand people in November 1989. "Boris, you're an ass," shouted the crowd. "Boris, retire!" Although Gidaspov was light-years removed from *perestroika* and utterly out of sync with the aspirations of the Russian

---

*This political dynamic only strengthened the power of Russia's ultraconservative factions such as *Pamyat* and other nationalist groups. "It is very dangerous politically and economically because the conservatives can unite faster than us," explained liberal People's Deputy Alexander Trofkin, a construction worker. "The conservatives speculate on our lives, going from bad to worse like moneychangers. Our confusion and indecision are their power and profit."

people, Gorbachev promoted him to full membership in the Politburo seven days after the people of Leningrad were ready to stretch his neck from the nearest oak.

Conversationally, philosophically, and never pausing to weigh the consequences, Soviet leaders had shaped the Russians' anxieties about life into a national, institutional melancholy obliging the people to keep faithful to the Communist Party, which was always hard at work, sorting out the "complexes" with the heroism and transcendence of Lenin. Practically and intellectually, the Soviet Union was shamelessly and recklessly managed like a medieval religious inquisition from which there could be no deviation from scripture, lest the gargoyles come down off the cathedral to devour the unfaithful.

The three-hundred-and-five-member Central Committee of the Communist Party, a Soviet parody of a tenth-century college of cardinals sitting on tall-backed chairs, relinquished through imperial edict its historical monopoly on power in early 1990. But the teachers and their new communist students at the Higher Party School, the training ground for budding apparatchiks, were having none of it at the Twenty-eighth Congress. With the obfuscational skill and sedate concentration of Jesuits redefining dogma to prevent their pope's power from being wounded in schism, the Party loyalists constructed a deliberately hazy communist missal for the twenty-first century. Entitled "Toward a Humane Democratic Socialism," the encyclical paid absolutely no testimony to the needs of the Soviet people in the modern world, while shedding tired light on the country's mass misery under the system. There were evil archangels, of course, like the "confused establishment of cooperative ventures."

When the Twenty-eighth Communist Party Conference voted in July 1990 to redecorate the Politburo to include representatives of all fifteen Soviet republics, the move was heralded by Gorbachev and his reformers as a devolution of political clout from Moscow to local authorities and a change in power from the Party to newly elected legislatures. Economic power was now positioned to trickle down into the hands of the people. Although the outgoing Politburo, made up of twelve full members and seven candidate (non-voting) members, was grossly tilted toward Moscow politicians, the real power to affect people's day-to-day lives had always been in the hands of local Party officials in the smaller cities and provinces. The new and improved Politburo would have. twenty-four members, including representatives selected from the two-hundred-and-fifty-member Central Committee, with each one responsible for a specific policy area. Gorbachev, using all the right buzz words, called this "ideological renovation" and an "ecology of the soul"— but the mood on the street was a reluctance to rely on this faddish body because republic-level Party organizations and the Central Committee were with rare exception contaminated with corruption and for nearly six years under Gorbachev's rule had shown a loathing for using *perestroika* as a tool with which to sever the tug of mass social and economic misery. Indeed, at the level of the republic, the district, and the local council, communism had achieved a degree of truly exceptional vulgarity; a further deputation of authority from Moscow for this crowd to use at home was foreordained to become but a further delegation of cruelty. The spin on Gorbachev's maneuver to transform the Soviet Union into a confederation of sovereign states, each controlling its own resources and "acting independently and really influencing the Central Committee and Politburo," was an echo of what John Reed had observed of Kerensky's panic-stricken Mensheviks on the eve of the 1917 October Revolution: "In the relations of a weak Government and a rebellious people there comes a time when every act of the authorities exasperates the masses, and every refusal to act excites their contempt."

While I stood watching Gorbachev's prearranged homespun political chat with CBS News anchorman Dan Rather on Red Square during a break in the Twenty-eighth Party Congress, or while reading *Time*'s adulation of the Soviet leader as "Man of the Decade" with Sabina and my other Soviet friends, it was clear Gorbachev had the gusto of a reform-minded American politician and the ability to command a television screen, boost *Time*'s circulation figures, and influence the Dow Jones Index in the process. And the American people, who were more afraid of suburban crack peddlers and Japanese bankers than hastily launched Soviet missiles and Marxist dogma, liked the Gorb because he was friendly, optimistic, and answered the same kinds of questions American network news readers asked of their president. But Gorbachev's cannily deft American style was surface flash in the U.S.S.R.; he was a Soviet politician running a country whose reformers approached the ideas of political pluralism and private property with the same anger with which the Pope once challenged Copernicus's notion that the sun was the center of the solar system. *Perestroika* Politburo bad guy Yegor Ligachev inadvertently described the naked corporeality of restructure when he told an applauding Twenty-eighth Party Congress session that he was not a conservative opposed to *perestroika*, as his opponents were claiming, but a "realist" who understood how the system operated. Or, as *Perestroika* Politburo good guy Alexander Yakovlev fearlessly informed students in a boggling speech he gave at the Higher Party School in early 1990 on the Communist Party's struggle for survival in the modern world: "The Party has acknowledged family farms. Isn't that a step forward?" It was like debating whether or not to invent the wheel while airplanes buzzed overhead.

"Only the naive believe that the attempts to create independent, democratic political structures in Moscow and Leningrad will affect the entire nation in any benign pattern," Trusishka explained of the spiritual struggle in the communist convent. "Moscow and Leningrad are not the Soviet Union. What happens in those cities peacefully may be exported to the rest of the country violently. This is a variant." Trusishka was one of Sabina's "big dogs" and we argued long and often about what was going on in the kennel. The outcome was always the same. Trusishka was not terrified of change, but as *perestroika* continued on its lurchy voyage into a cloudy future he grew continually fearful that Lenin's "*Homo Sovieticus*" was destined for a "blood spasm": his none-too-subtle euphemism for a civil uprising against the system.

But the huddled masses—*Homo Sovieticus*—were in too dark and sluggish a mood to care what the big dogs were barking about—at least not yet. Historically, Russian populism was the stuff of fairy tales, much like the flare that momentarily lights up a dark sky with a cascade of brilliance, only to fall scorched and spent to earth.

And the "giant" of the Russian night, as Vladimir Nabokov alluded to in *Transparent Things,* was "especially terrible." Nothing ever *really* changed, certainly not the genuinely frightening woe one felt when walking among the Russians on Moscow's dingy shop-lined streets, or Azerbaijanis as they coughed their way through Baku's petrochemical atmosphere, or Armenians stumbling over Yeravan's earthquake rubble in search of Party-controlled relief supplies that never arrived, or Georgian sheep herders forced to graze their flocks on the dust-coated weeds that grew inside rusted and abandoned factories, or Uzbeki surgeons performing delicate operations in medical theaters with the sanitary standards of a Tashkent stable. Pain meant nothing to these people, pressed together like lemmings on their way to a cliff, and *perestroika* . . . well, that was just a temporary assignation the Party was having with the West—a *blat* scam on a global scale that was bringing the Big Dogs all kinds of financial and high-tech treats in return for a promise to marry Miss Liberty. Only vaguely familiar with the problems and passions of Ivan Average, the Party's number-crunchers at the All-Union Center of Public Opinion, a group that portrayed itself as the Russian Gallup Poll but was cracked more in the mold of the research department at "Family Feud," decided to survey 2,696 Soviet citizens to see how they felt about life as Gorbachev entered his fifth season in 1990. Four percent expressed confidence in the Communist Party; 6 percent believed Leninism provided an answer to the Soviet Union's malaise, and 63 percent said they were not willing to work harder if it meant making more money. There was no shortage of spleen directed against the state or against cooperators, of whom 40 percent said "they cannot make any money honestly." Fifty percent of the respondents revealed that they went to the black market to have their shoes repaired. Only 25 percent favored the passing of big state factories into private, cooperative hands. Dwarfed by the strangeness of the query, some 64 percent did not know how to answer the question: "Are you happy?"

I found happiness to be an unaccustomed condition in the Soviet Union's moral wilderness, even to Gorbachev, whose eyes had begun to take on the cold gleam of anxiety as *perestroika* spun further out of control, the consequences of the endless struggle between economic truth and political expediency entirely of his making. He tried to look good in public—on his own turf—but reality's hard lump was beginning to show. Nearly six years of restructuring and openness had made him look old, rather tired, and increasingly in need of benzedrine. "You know people are saying 'chaos, chaos, collapse, collapse,' " Gorbachev hectored in exasperation, stroking his white knuckles, preparing to drop the big shoe on the reporters who milled around him inside the echoing hallways of the Belyi Dom on the final afternoon of the 1990 Congress of the Russian Republic.

Gorbachev grew momentarily solemn before delivering the kicker, the crimson People's Deputy badge pinned to his lapel shining like satin beneath the pale light that reflected off the palace's slabbed marble and glass walls. Maybe Gorbachev had slugged down one too many cans of the free Stella Artois beer that millionaire cooperator Artyom Tarasov had been handing out to eager delegates ("For a democratic Russia!" shouted Tarasov, the director of Cooperative Technica) from the trunk of his Mercedes-Benz, because, instantly, the renowned Gorby smile of relaxation and health returned. "When Lenin watched a similar revolutionary process, he said, 'You know, this chaos will crystallize a new form of life,' " Gorbachev reminded the crowd, tempting them to smile with his last reserve of charisma. His words, although obediently felt by the Party, were desperate, and despite their Marxist eloquence, as functional and empty to the Soviet people as the line of refrigerators that Central planners had named after a squirrel.

"And we all know what *that* form of life did to us," Sabina grumbled in a mix of nausea and guilt as we headed across the Belyi Dom's vast concrete plaza, up to the Sadovaya Ring and into Moscow's busy late-afternoon streets. "What is radical in their scarecrow brains is normal everywhere else in the world," including the parliament of the Russian Republic, which took keen pride in defying the pronouncements of the Twenty-eighth Communist Party Congress to enhance its populist image in the minds of the electorate. Russian Republic president Boris Yeltsin understood that economic torpidity was the most effective weapon to use against Gorbachev and the ideology-driven Party faithful, who would lose their status once the planned and centralized system was junked in favor of a democratic free market.*

Yeltsin wanted "privatization now" to soak up hundreds of billions of excess rubles through the sale of state assets. The idea looked flawless on a blackboard because it would create a balance between supply and demand, allowing the government to free prices without the risk of science-fiction inflation. The only problem was that Soviet assets had extremely limited value. Why? Because factories and buildings from the Dnieper to the Amur ranged from decrepit to nonfunctional; geriatric equipment could not be used competitively in a modern economy, and threatened workers' health and even survival. Unless an enormously expensive Western cash-and-technology aid package went along with privatization, the transfer of ownership from the state to the individual would accomplish nothing but gloom under a different aegis. Kremlin bureaucrats demanded yet more vain and worthless Party conferences, Supreme Soviet committee meetings, and "sociological studies" produced by official Soviet institutes, conservatories, academies, societies, ministries, and collegiums to "further study" the impact of the free market on Lenin's socialism. But it was too late, no matter the plan. The Soviet economy was no longer a contradiction in terms. It had reached such a critical mass of lunacy that

---

*Russian nationalists, pushing for the republic to secede from the U.S.S.R., demanded their free market to be underwritten by the Kremlin's turning over half of its hard-currency revenues from oil extracted on Russian land to the republic. The Russian Republic was the source for over 85 percent of the U.S.S.R.'s oil-producing wells. The state purchased oil from its "enterprises" at twenty-three rubles a ton, less than one dollar at the black-market exchange rate. Even at the "official" exchange rate of forty dollars, equaling twenty-three rubles, the state sold its own oil to Soviet industry at less than one-third the international price. The popular panacea of using the hard currency generated from the export of Russian oil to fund an exclusively Russian free market was another of *perestroika*'s magnificent fallacies. Obsolete pipelines, major accidents, parts shortages, antiquated drilling equipment, poor transportation, ethnic unrest in the petroleum areas, and an annual loss of millions of tons of oil and tens of millions of cubic feet of natural gas from fire, leakage, and negligence added up to an economic and social turmoil that did more to endow total economic collapse than it did the dreams of Russian nationalists.

by the end of the Twenty-eighth Congress *perestroika* looked to have been scripted with all the logic of "Monty Python's Flying Circus"—not the winner of the Nobel Peace Prize.*

Creating a condition of normality in a nation of absurdity meant an end to useless bureaucratic discussion, and the rapid privatization of the system through the enactment of radical economic measures. The Communist Party would launch a long political insurgency against Yeltsin's "500 Days"† to a free market because the idea possessed the inertia first to frustrate and then topple Party control in the Soviet Union's fourteen other republics. But "500 Days" also held the promise of throwing millions of *myzhiki* (Ivan Averages), already angry with *perestroika*, out of work, as well as putting their collective acrimony to use as ammunition by the powerful old guard against the loose coalitions of free-market democrats whose policies had created soaring food prices, plunging fuel reserves, and emotionally draining unemployment.

Although Gorbachev claimed commitment to creating a basis

---

*The burlesque of the Nobel Committee's awarding Gorbachev the Peace Prize while his country decayed was not lost on the Soviet public. "The awarding of the Nobel Peace Prize to Gorbachev is a standard Western gesture designed to shore up the authority of the leader of a crumbling empire," said exiled Russian poet Irina Ratushinskaya, who spent four years in a Soviet prison camp and was stripped of her citizenship after traveling to the West for medical treatment. Added exiled Russian dissident Vladimir Bukovsky, recalling the twenty demonstrators killed in the republic of Georgia in April 1989: "I really don't understand how someone could have given the Nobel Peace Prize to a man who condoned the intervention of soldiers' using poison gas and the shovels with which they dug toilets to disperse a nationalist rally." Or, as one man who was standing on a Moscow shoelace line asked me: "What does the Peace Prize have to do with me when I can't find any milk?"

†"500 Days" was the strategy to slam-dunk the Russian Republic into capitalism between the autumn of 1990 and the spring of 1992 through republic-wide privatization of industries controlled by the Party and the Soviet government. It was also known as the Shatalin Plan, so named for its author, Stanislav Shatalin, an economist and member of Gorbachev's Presidential Council. Gorbachev's alternate strategy, written by Soviet Prime Minister Nikolai Ryzhkov and amended by economist Abel Aganbeygan, was in complete opposition to the "500 Days" revitalization package. Despite economic policy differences between the two plans in the areas of taxation, profit, and ownership, the real dogfight was over law: Gorbachev insisted that Soviet law prevail over the respective laws of the country's fifteen republics; Yeltsin was determined to shatter the U.S.S.R. as a centrally controlled economic entity legally administered by the Kremlin.

of a market economy by October 1992, he was consciously vague about a timetable for selling state property to the private sector— the first step of any plan to wrestle economic control from the corrupt central planners and into the hands of the cooperators. Communist Party publications, such as *Pravda* and *Sovetskya Rossiya*, the windows into the critical concerns on Gorbachev's mind, spent their decreasing supplies of newsprint-ink on investigative reports into the "barbarity, vandalism, and sacrilege" of people illegally dismantling monuments to Lenin. Nurtured by the hostility of the Twenty-eighth Congress and the ditherings of Russia's "economic experts," the guerrilla war waged by the cooperators against the communist economic order since 1987 had been thrown onto an open battlefield by the conclusion of 1990.

On one side of the battle line stood Yeltsin's free marketeering Russian Republic legislators, an obstreperous lot of new-age Soviet democrats who thought Gorbachev and his policies might best be poleaxed like Saint Paul on the road to Damascus. On the other were Gorbachev's docile, obedient, and freely elected Supreme Soviet parliamentarians, exhorting the central government to retain control over the export of oil, gas, gold, diamonds, and other raw materials for a cruel mix of realpolitik reasons. Somewhere in the middle was Volodya Yakovlev, who knew that the only trait shared among all the Soviet Union's new democracy-lovers was an acute need for getting their hands on a dwindling supply of hard currency. Soviet democracy and the cooperative revolution were both starting to echo what the great jazz musician Paul Desmond said about dating fashionable glossy-magazine models: "They'll go out for a while with a cat who's scuffling, but they always seem to end up marrying some manufacturer from the Bronx. This is the way the world ends, not with a whim but a banker."

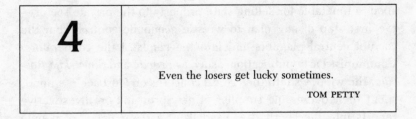

4

Even the losers get lucky sometimes.

TOM PETTY

T HERE'S SOMETHING WRONG in the transmission," Volodya Yakovlev complained, sitting in his modernized office on the ground floor of a drooping Moscow tenement, opening a sealed envelope with one of the razor-sharp Japanese shuriken flying stars he often flung at unwary employees. This time Yak hurled the eight-pointed ninja claw into a newly painted sill and gazed with steady incomprehension at the pallor on the other side of his heavily barred window. "Look at those two," Yak said, twisting the assassin's star out of the sill, drumming one of its tips on the glass pane toward a young mother in white go-go boots. She was trying to excavate the stroller that held her screaming child from Moscow's thick and oily mud. "Do you think they have found *perestroika?* Do you think they trust *perestroika?* Somehow I don't think those are variants."

Variants. Modifications. Mutations. These were the things Yak sought out in his new Russia. *Perestroika* was the symbol for it all—like a toy that has a disturbing realism about it but in the end is just an unreal plaything. Yak admitted that he never *really* knew the difference between Soviet truth and fiction. "Too many ideas and powers at work out there," he said. "Too many variants. Tracking them all down is my great adventure."

Yak's quest began on November 5, 1987, when, against the wishes of his family, friends, and colleagues, he sacrificed a guaranteed good life as a feature reporter at the magazine *Ogonyok* to start Cooperative Fact. The day Yakovlev walked out on the best job in Soviet journalism to become *perestroika*'s most unlikely and reluctant revolutionary was the day Gorbachev's so-called second revolution took to the streets, many of Moscow's cooperators would later say. Three months before Yakovlev opened the Soviet Union's first news and information cooperative in a one-time accordion store on the outskirts of the capital, *Ogonyok* editor Vitali Korotich had directed him to write a story about *khozrashiot* (the new economic accountability that Gorbachev was demanding of state-owned firms) and the few dozen struggling cooperatives that had been established and allowed by the government to quietly operate in expectation of the Kremlin's relaxing restrictions on private enterprise in 1988. Korotich wanted an insider's account to be published in his popular and boldly controversial Communist Party–owned weekly, so he gave Yakovlev the demanding assignment of physically starting a cooperative and chronicling the results.

"It all began as a journalistic adventure," Yakovlev said. "Then we discovered that people who wanted to be cooperators had no idea how to make their dreams happen. They didn't know how to ask questions because they were never allowed to ask questions. I knew how to ask questions because I was a journalist. It became very clear very fast that many people wanted to start their own businesses but were frightened of going to the state bureaucracy for information and help."

In the best tradition of storefront journalism, Yakovlev enlisted Viktor Zolatarov, an engineer; Gleb Pavlovsky, a dissident writer; and Kseniya Makahnenko, a journalism student at Moscow State University, to launch a cooperative that manufactured and sold stylish, high-quality clothing out of a converted apartment on the road to Leningrad. Overnight, Yak's band of investigative reporters began to make money; moreover, they discovered that the people who supplied them with raw materials kept asking questions on how to deal with *mudestika*, literally the state's "bureaucratic bullshit" one encountered while trying to get a business off the ground. Yak and his colleagues had stumbled on a niche in the market: people wanted to turn a profit from *perestroika* but had no idea how to do it, so why not charge money and do it for them?

The group's most interesting member was thirty-eight-year-old Gleb Pavlovsky, the formerly exiled publisher of the underground magazine *Searches*. Brezhnev had sent Pavlovsky off to paint propaganda murals on the sides of Siberian buildings for his efforts. He returned from exile in 1986 loaded for bear, joining the Club for Social Initiatives, a small, unofficial Moscow political group where he first met Yakovlev. Pavlovsky wore Bulgarian sneakers and looked to be a renegade from the pointed-star and leather-jacket set—a man of the street with the kind of enormous, brooding Russian presence that makes patrician Party members uncomfortable. Yak and Pavlovsky were the cultural odd couple: the suave Volodya was interested in the economic possibilities of *perestroika;* Gleb was drawn toward the political freedoms it offered. At first Pavlovsky thought that Yak talked revolution only because it was fashionable. Pavlovsky had suffered for fashion. The two men argued for weeks: dogma, ideology, dialectic—the kind of talk that comes as naturally to Russians as talk about batting averages and sports cars comes to Americans. "What we discovered together," Pavlovsky said, "is that this country had a total vacuum of information. Yakovlev and I realized that *perestroika* was wonderful for providing people with information, but not for making the information work."

Viktor Zolatarov was unemployed, so there was no problem convincing him to become a full-time member of Fact's ranks. Kseniya Makahnenko, however, was a problem. Yak, then twenty-seven years old, had designs on making Makahnenko his fifth ("and absolutely last") wife, and the knotty difficulty of convincing Yassen Zazorsky, the dean of the Moscow State University School of Journalism, not to send her out to a provincial newspaper—after Soviet students graduate they are generally assigned jobs by the state. Those with connections secure good positions in Moscow or Leningrad; those without them are rerouted into the wasteland. Yak, who never married Kseniya, hustled every connection he had at the journalism school and in the government apparatus to get Makahnenko on his staff. The urgency of his task had more to do with than just love: at the time, Fact had no computers with which to track the cooperatives, and Makahnenko, whose nickname in Fact's early days was "the Computer," was the only person who knew the details of every cooperative in Moscow by heart. The Makahnenko data store was vast and varied. Cooperative Chance provided medicine and private health care, Navator designed and repaired doors, Exhibition fixed electrical equipment and plumbing, Mantelpiece made jewelry, Mushroom Rain catered parties, People of the Same Thinking bartered commodities, and Today washed windows and built nuclear reactors. Today, which survived for only a few weeks, reflected the all-too-frequent and disheartening downside of trying to open a business in a country that does not understand business and still uses abacuses to calculate profits and losses. Most individuals who want to form a cooperative have no idea how to go about it, and common desire often replaces common sense. That at least was the case with Today, an ill-fated but glorious partnership between an atomic engineer and a friend who washed windows. Although absurd to the Western eye, the venture seemed quite logical to two people with absolutely no feel for a free-market system. Fact was going to sell Russia the feel.

With twenty-five rubles in startup capital and using Yak's coveted *Ogonyok* press passes as shovels, *Kooperativ Fakt* began to dig up information on everything from opening a bank account to obtaining plumbing supplies. "We placed our first advertisement offering to help people find work in the cooperative sector and assist them in opening their own cooperatives in late November 1987," said Yakovlev. "The next day we had two hundred thirty-five responses. I was amazed. We sat down that morning, looked at each other in panic, and asked, 'Well, now, how the hell are we going to help these people get work?' We had no idea. Everyone thought we were crazy to open Fact, but at the same time the bureaucrats were scared of what we might accomplish."

Ogonyok editor Vitali Korotich was the first to express annoyance, and in no small part because his assignment to Yakovlev had spiraled into his reporters' forming a cooperative that made *Ogonyok*'s bureaucratic bosses at the Central Committee very uneasy. The former medical doctor from the Ukrainian city of Kharkov was the big power in Moscow journalism, and his state-sponsored magazine, which in Russian meant "little flame," had transformed the pediatrician turned poet turned Communist Party editor into *perestroika*'s most potent public voice. *Ogonyok*, which began publishing during the rule of Nicholas II, had become a code word for dull Party-journalism during Brezhnev's Era of Stagnation, following the trail Stalin had laid out for the magazine after Lenin relaunched it in 1923. Popular mainly for its crossword puzzles and its use as kindling in dacha stoves, the Little Flame began to set major political fires from the moment the Politburo put the former editor of the Ukrainian weekly *Vsesvit* in charge of *Ogonyok* in 1986. One of Korotich's first moves was to eliminate the Order of Lenin medal that had adorned *Ogonyok*'s cover for nearly fifty years.

"It takes up too much space," Korotich said.

"The Party went apeshit over that," *Ogonyok* writer Artyom Borovik recalled. "I thought they were going to take Vitali out and shoot him."

Korotich survived, and within a year the magazine's weekly circulation had doubled to a million, and in three years sales had increased to over three million. Readers' letters skyrocketed from under twenty to over eight hundred a day. Sixty percent of the Soviet public voted *Ogonyok* as their favorite publication in 1989; its mix of investigative journalism, letters, poetry, culture, art, photojournalism, and historical research into Stalin's terror gave the magazine an exciting edge over the other Party publications and its staff the ability to get into formerly forbidden areas by simply flashing their red *Ogonyok* press cards. Korotich's office had an open door, and his directive to the writers who clogged the passage was simple: "I don't want you bringing in articles on anything that you don't talk about at home. If the subject doesn't interest you, it doesn't interest me." With the face of a happy Humphrey Bogart and the quick and agile frame of a welterweight boxer, Korotich encouraged a type of journalism unknown in Soviet history. He dispatched Moscow teenagers into the streets in search of *lyubers*, young gangsters from a southeast suburb intent on roughing up

Moscow hippies and punk rockers; published a frightening tale of a criminal suspect tortured by cops in Petrozavodsk, and pushed out older "stagnation" staff members in favor of writers in their twenties, who were assigned stories on prostitutes, pimps, war, and corruption. "Now we have to talk about what is painful, and publish it," Korotich explained. "We used to divide everything into periods—prewar, postwar, pre-Khrushchev, post-Khrushchev, pre-Brezhnev, post-Brezhnev. We must have one life. We must make it all one strand with one internal logic."

Vitali Korotich was a terrific editor, who, while giving reporters like Yakovlev and Borovik virtual carte blanche, never let them forget that he was Gorbachev's favorite editor-in-chief, using his dry sense of humor and endless supply of patience to guide and protect his eager reporters from the Communist Party censors and Central Committee power brokers whom he battled with hourly, either in person or over specially built and constantly rasping Party phone lines.* Although he sent Borovik into Afghanistan, so that "we can write about how the soul of a seventeen-year-old is shaped when he falls into that situation," there were boundaries that the feisty editor would not cross. Publication of army cases was taboo, and he dubbed the exiled Nobel Laureate Alexandr Solzhenitsyn a "fool" who was "not a writer, but a political opponent." Until July 1990, *Ogonyok* was a Party publication that cultivated much dissent publicly but tolerated very little privately. Like all great editors, Korotich was dictator, priest, and guide; and, much like American magazine editors, who often shape or spike stories to keep advertisers happy and revenues flowing, he had to accommodate Party interests that held little concern for the young staff he had assembled. For example, when the magazine planned to publish a critical article written by the disgraced and retired KGB

---

*I worked at *Ogonyok* as a guest editor for four months in 1988 and had the opportunity to watch Korotich in action on an almost daily basis. Professionally, Korotich was a brilliant editor who personally disliked being continually used as an on-camera sounding board for *perestroika* by Moscow's Western press corps. He always dealt with the press with a smile on his face, but felt his professional credentials as a journalist were cheapened when foreign reporters hit him up for the latest inside information in the Kremlin.

spymaster Oleg Kalugin in June 1990, Politburo members huddled
with Korotich and made him kill the piece over worries that hard-
line Party members might exploit Kalugin's charges that the KGB
was as heavy-handed as ever to discredit its now-ascendant liberal
faction. Korotich buckled. It was an echo of what he had said
through a shattered speaker system to the embittered whistles of
the crowd gathered for Moscow's first major pro-democracy demonstration in February 1990:* "The system of fear is over, but today
we do understand that the Party is the driving force of *perestroika*."
Of course, for Soviet readers unaccustomed to Korotich's new
brand of journalism, *Ogonyok*'s pages had moxie, but it stretched
only to the point the Party drew for its journalistic subsidiary. The
magazine published stories only *after* Korotich decided (usually by
consultation with his allies on the Central Committee) whether or
not the political fallout could be contained by the Party and the
government. The process was a time-consuming and methodical

---

*The demonstrations in support of democracy that took place on Karl Marx Square
on Sunday, February 25, 1990, and later on Sunday, March 25, were early ex-
amples of the disunity within the democratic forces and the lengths to which the
government would go to prevent public manifestations. *Pravda* warned that civil
disturbances were inevitable and would happen on the street under the cover of
democratic slogans. The government, which had ordered all state employees to
their jobs for those Sundays, had failed to issue the proper permits until the very
last minute, and anxious Muscovites remained glued to their television screens
at home the nights before in hope of hearing an update. One channel broadcast
nothing but gruesome clips from American horror movies cut into film of marching
Soviet soldiers on the evening of February 24. Another station showed an hour
of artists sitting in pain on tree stumps that had been embedded with nails. Moscow
awoke on February 25 to find columns of horse-mounted troops shielding Lenin's
tomb and scores of buses and dump trucks pushed together to barricade Red
Square and other central points within the city along with heavily armed military
troops and riot police blocking off motor and pedestrian traffic. The demo went
down as scheduled, but it was never made clear who was in charge, how many
people were there, or how many of them appeared out of curiosity. Soon-to-be-
elected Moscow Mayor Gavril Popov said there were 500,000 people at the
February 25 demo; the militia counted 300,000, the English-language broadcast
of Radio Moscow reported 250,000, the Russian language broadcast of Radio
Moscow said 100,000, and Associated Press reported 80,000. Popov boasted that
1,250,000 people had amassed for the March 25 demonstration. There were fewer
than 75,000. "No change will come of this," Sabina said, pointing to the solidly
armed units and the fragile and frightened looks on the marchers who trudged
past them during both manifestations. "The government accomplished everything
they wanted from these demonstrations."

nuisance that forced Korotich and his staff to spend more hours covering their backs than covering events. But to publish without seeking such advice and consent could have ended in tragedy for those involved.

Ironically, one member of Yakovlev's *Ogonyok* cooperative investigation team, Kseniya Makahnenko, was the daughter of Yuri Makahnenko, the late editor of the Ukrainian-language magazine *Banner*. It was Makahnenko who had given Korotich his start in journalism by first publishing his poems in the early 1960s. "My father told me they were good and brave poems," said Kseniya, "but Father was a hard person and constantly in trouble with the authorities. He always wanted to take more and more chances. Korotich and Father split apart soon after the poems were published."

Yet Korotich was no paper tiger. Artyom Borovik's artillery-like coverage of the war in Afghanistan shocked the country into the realities of war and Borovik into having to defend himself from charges that he was an agent for both the KGB and the CIA. Volodya Yakovlev's savage, blow-by-blow accounts of the Soviet mafia and black market caused a scandal that prompted the Party and the public to question the veracity of the reporting, but it was all true—too true. Rabidly communist publications such as *Young Guard, Our Contemporary,* and *Moscow* regularly pummeled Korotich for being everything from a Jew ("I am not a Jew, but anyone who wants to change the Soviet Union is a Jew to *Pamyat,** so

---

Pamyat (Memory) was the name given to a loose confederation of five right-wing Russian ultranationalist groups believed to have cultivated great power and influence with conservative elements in the Communist Party and the Soviet military. Their influence was rooted in the Russian idea of *rodina* (the motherland), and the group's manifesto was extremely popular with many Russian intellectuals and peasants because it fostered the notion of traditional Russian values and the ultimate power of Russia over the Soviet Union at their rallies. *Pamyat* never actually urged Russians to institute pogroms against Jewish citizens or the new democratic organizations, but they did often tack leaflets on the lobbies of Moscow and Leningrad apartment blocks that harshly criticized Soviet Jews as Russia's "Zionist enemies" and the cause of the nation's economic ills. Whatever the group's tactics, its very existence stirred great fear in the minds of most Soviet citizens, many of whom believed that Pamyat was the work of the KGB and the military to continue the officially instigated anti-Semitism of the past. The group's most remembered outburst was led by fifty-four-year-old Konstantin Smirnov-

then I am a Jew—We are all Jews") to having been a Brezhnev toady in his youth. One screed published in the pages of *Pravda* called *Ogonyok* "the scum bubbling on the crust of the mighty stream of renewal." Korotich retaliated in print, causing an internecine war that forced Gorbachev to call for a meeting of all Moscow's editors to plead for "unilateral disarmament." But the brawls to discredit Korotich and the others who supported a speeding-up of the restructuring process continued. The older the *perestroika* revolutionary, the more of his past he has to hide, or at least not talk about with any frequency, lest he spark a crude and thuglike public skeleton hunt that makes American supermarket tabloids seem tame in comparison. Korotich's blight was the pro-Brezhnev article he had once written in the journal *Kommunist;* this indiscretion, which followed his every move like a bad rash, was capitalized upon by both left-wing and right-wing Party factions. The yoke around People's Deputy Yuri Afanasyev, nicknamed "Big Glimmer in the East" by Western political pundits, was his former stewardship of the Young Pioneers, the Communist Party Boy Scout and Girl Scout troop. Gavril Popov, Moscow's popular new mayor, owned a sixty-thousand-ruble dacha in Zhukovka, a home that was hard to afford on an economics professor's salary of less than two hundred rubles a month. Slamming and shaming reformers with their often unsavory activities during the Era of Stagnation was a popular political blood sport and, as Borovik sadly pointed out, "denials meant nothing. The attack is all that counts because it will always be successful, making the public question the credentials and intentions of the reformers."

"It's time for people to read the papers calmly and accept them as a possible version of the truth," Korotich said of the continuing

---

Ostashvili in January 1990, when he used a bullhorn to direct a black-uniformed gang into a Soviet Writers Union forum, screaming, "Kikes—go home to Israel!" Smirnov-Ostashvili, who insisted the charge was a lie, was found guilty by a Moscow court in October 1990 of fanning interethnic enmity and sentenced to two years at hard labor. Although the decision of the Moscow court was geared to send a message to *Pamyat,* dozens of the group's defenders, waving fists in clenched fascist-style salutes in behalf of Russian nationalism and contending Smirnov-Ostashvili had done nothing but exercise the right of free speech, poured out of the raucous courtroom shouting, "Shame! Shame!"

melee. Yet Korotich's initiatives, vital as they were for the public to get behind *perestroika,* did not go to the heart of the immediate problem facing young Russians like Yakovlev and Borovik. Although Korotich assiduously supported his reporters once they were in print, the cardinal distinction was that *Ogonyok's* driving editor was a fifty-two-year-old reformed apparatchik who rocked boats, while Borovik and Yakovlev were twenty-six-year-old Young Turks who sank them. As the magazine's young contributors saw it, calcification was taking place: a hardening of attitude toward the risk-taking that gave *Ogonyok* its credentials simultaneous with the enshrinement of the Communist Party as the *perestroika* team leader.

To work at *Ogonyok* during *perestroika's* early years was to look through a political and moral kaleidoscope that offered the eye far-reaching endeavors and limitless possibilities. But to make the entire farrago real would have diluted *Ogonyok's* stake in *perestroika.* Korotich was intensely aware that both he and the magazine could be used as scapegoats for the failure of restructure. To go beyond the official bounds of criticism would only further provoke the Party's powerful conservatives, the bureaucracy, and the right-wing power cliques. In the West Korotich was a hero, but in Moscow, particularly among the young intelligentsia and new-age cooperators, Korotich had been assigned the role of *perestroika* quisling, despite the fact that he incubated many of their radical ideas and gave Volodya Yakovlev the idea to open a cooperative.

"When I told him that I was leaving to start a cooperative," Yakovlev recalled with a taste of bitterness in his mouth, "Vitali just turned away from me. We haven't spoken since." Korotich was never really all that comfortable with cooperatives because his editor's eye saw the possibilities for old-style Soviet corruption in their basic functioning. The differences between Yakovlev and Borovik ran deep, too. The professional respect each man had for the other was punctuated by an antipathy for the tactics each used to make the framework of *glasnost* wider, so that the word would no longer be necessary in the language. For Borovik, Yakovlev was a "hustler who still owes me ten rubles from university." For Yakovlev, Borovik was "too much of an apparatchik for my taste."

Despite the sourness, both men appeared at first very much the same. There was no easy way out of Russia's problems, and neither Yakovlev nor Borovik was willing to back down from changing society by using their positions to score the coveted documents necessary to leave Russia's mess for the West. Borovik lived with his wife and her child in a series of small apartments loaned to them by friends; his own salary of a little under three hundred rubles a month was hardly enough to make ends meet.

Vladimir Yakovlev was named after his paternal grandfather, the boss of the Cheka (a forerunner of the KGB) in Odessa during the Russian civil war. Like his son, Yegor Yakovlev, a former special correspondent for the government daily newspaper *Izvestia* who became the editor of the weekly *Moscow News*, the utopian revolutionary who fought alongside Lenin believed in the dreams and aspirations of the Bolsheviks. "There were Russian families and Soviet families in our country," explained Irena Yakovleva, Volodya's mother. "The Soviet families were the communist romantics, but the Russian families were the real revolutionaries. Many of the Russian families, as such, didn't follow a clear Party path at home, and they paid the price, even though they were Party members. The Soviet families ran their households strictly according to Party directives. The first big problem the children encountered was in school, where the teachers were under orders to break students of any un-Party-like habits they had learned at home. Well, Volodya stuck out because Yegor and I ran a home that was open to all ideas and people. This irritated the teachers. The things we spoke of at home were not accepted at school, by the Party. Our family and friends became very excited when the American astronauts first landed on the moon, and we discussed the marvelous achievement at great length with the children, but when Volodya went to school with this excitement the teachers yelled at him and said that he should be thinking about what the Soviets could have done to abort the American moon mission. The state tried to crush our children's spirit and curiosity, and my husband and I wouldn't stand for it. When Volodya entered journalism school, a teacher asked his class about the pawnbroker character from Gogol's *Dead Souls*. Since the class was made up predominantly of the children from

Soviet families who wouldn't be found dead in a pawnbroker's shop, only Volodya was able to describe how a pawnshop operated, because our family needed to use pawnbrokers. The other students looked down on him for this knowledge. True communists didn't need pawnshops.

"We did have some political problems with Volodya," added his mother, who was also a professional journalist. "But we didn't have the right to hinder his path. Yegor and I are proud of what he has accomplished, but we are still afraid of the cooperative movement because Volodya's career is based on opposition to the system and its regulations. The unknown fear is whether or not he will be able to sustain himself if the old ways come back. Yet Volodya is from a hopeful generation; my husband and I are from a frightened generation."

If Irena Yakovleva's "frightened generation" had an ogre, then it was undoubtedly Genrikh Borovik, the father of Artyom Borovik, a man who believed in the communist system with a biblical totality. Indeed, whoever it was who once said that having an infamous man for a father was like living in the shadow of a statue that casts nothing but cold light knew the Boroviks. Genrikh Borovik was, according to one's point of view, the Communist Party's clinically ruthless chief apologist, the KGB's most diabolical colonel, the insouciant chairman of the Soviet Peace Committee, or the Russian Count Dracula. Nobody admitted to liking the man. Nobody. The elder Borovik, well known to the Soviet public from his frequent television and newspaper stories on the horrors of America during the 1960s and later as the hit man the Kremlin dispatched to denounce its political and cultural opponents on national television, was apparatchik-terror incarnate. Every word Genrikh spoke on television was full of tension and contempt for any idea that even approached democratic pluralism. After leaving the state press agency *Novosti* to take the helm of the Soviet Peace Committee, a clearing house of Marxist rhetoric whose mission was to waste paper on the publication of insipid English-language booklets filled with grammatically incorrect communist gibberish, the name Borovik became a national synonym for the human manifestation of Brezhnev Russia. "It's true, everyone dislikes my father," said

Artyom, laughing from the sheer enormity of the loathing the Soviet public had for the man. "People see him on the street and walk to the other side just to avoid him . . . my dad *really* believed in the Soviet system and he cannot truly accept or understand what's going on now and is suffering for it."

Whereas the Yakovlev family sent Volodya to the more plebeian Moscow State University, the Boroviks sent Artyom to *MIMO*, the International Relations Institute, a training ground for diplomatic office that caters exclusively to the children of high Party officials. For a public accustomed to the *blat* system, there was no way of getting around the idea that, whatever Artyom accomplished in journalism or Yak accomplished in business, it was their fathers who made it happen. The symmetry of such arrangements in the Party system was not without its appeal for many Golden Youth, even in the age of *perestroika*. Yet Artyom's rapid rise from obscure reporter on the daily newspaper *Sovetskaya Rossyia* to foreign editorship of the country's most popular and influential magazine by the age of twenty-seven was entirely his own doing. An uneasy peace existed between the two Boroviks, as well as the irony, lost on the Soviet public, that the son of Brezhnev's foremost hired character-assassin was a guerrilla fighter in the war to usurp the power of the *Banda Krasnaya*—the Red Band. Artyom, in fact, used his vast network of contacts to expose the moral and political debaucheries of the very people with whom the public believed him to be in cahoots because of his family name.

Yegor Yakovlev had been a liberal communist all his life, but there was something sad and poignant about Genrikh Borovik and the conservative scene that whirred around him. The people I knew in Moscow said that Genrikh operated entirely on the cruel impulse of a man whose dreams had taken an unfortunate turn, and was to be avoided at all costs. Whereas Yegor Yakovlev had written radical columns on the pages of *Izvestia* that represented the future, Genrikh Borovik's writings and television appearances never overstepped the cleanly cut communist boundaries of the past. Meaningful conversations with men like Genrikh Borovik were impossible because every friendly gesture was tainted with the possibility of provocation. Genrikh was a Soviet of the ancient regime who saw life in terms of neatly colored sequences of plots and counterplots; it was an existence in which every human action needed to be expressed carefully and in utterly unsentimental terms to ensure that the message could not be misinterpreted or become malformed in transmission. There were many like him in the Soviet Union: powerful old and middle-aged men blinded against *perestroika* by outmoded political grammars and bitter and doubting attitudes; powerless young men fearful of embracing Gorbachev's new order with the sacrificial zeal necessary to keep it alive through the years of crisis to come. One never really knew what they were thinking, except that life under Gorbachev was becoming a set of fast-moving and contradictory events with no meaning or relationship to one another. The distinctions between Russians and Soviets, state bureaucrats and private cooperators, and democratic pluralists and Marxist ideologues were real enough, but down in the rueful trenches of daily Soviet life, every man and woman, no matter his or her politics or position, agonized from a private grief that tracked back to the system of Lenin and Stalin. Some struggled through fantasies of making it to the West, others were affected by the weariness and pollution that helped account for a 6 percent annual increase in birth defects, many withered from being isolated from light and color, and yet others suffered from acute strains of cynicism that appeared as tangibly as measle spots. All their faces dripped with the brooding and boiling sentiment the Russians called *bweet zayela*, "everyday life has eaten me." It was an eerie countenance of blankness, animation, and frustration. The look of the bear.

I HAD JOINED Fact as an adviser to Volodya Yakovlev in 1988 with a keen understanding of the cultural and bureaucratic problems we all faced in marshaling a national and international consensus in favor of the cooperative movement displacing the so-called free-market order officially pushed by the "new look" Communist Party. For me, Fact was the bricklayer of a foundation for a fresh political and economic system, and my mandate in its architecture was to develop American and Western European markets for Fact's economic news and business-advisory services, and to assist in training Postfactom reporters and editors in the American journalistic standards and practices necessary if Yakovlev were to successfully sell the information abroad. Things were supposed to be different at Fact: we were the phoenix from the ashes. But, as the co-op grew from a few enthusiastic dreamers in an accordion emporium into one of the Soviet Union's most influential cooperative institutions, Yakovlev seemed determined to prove that, for all the grand talk about a new political and economic order based on pluralism, integration, and morality, in the end the powerful still make their own rules.

There was no heat in Volodya Yakovlev's cluttered back office at Cooperative Fact, but the place cost him only ten dollars a year at the unofficial exchange rate, so there was no need to provoke the local Soviet into replacing the cracked window he had covered with a torn sheet of orange plastic. There were cooperators who could have done the job, but the ministry of windows, Yak joked, had run out of panes. A cold wind was blasting through all the lopsided apartment blocks up and down Khoroshovskaya Shosse, the sinkholed four-lane blacktop that meant "Good Highway" to the bilingual reader and broken axles to the actual traveler. This included carloads of Russian citizens and foreign businessmen and journalists who drove down the street in hope of finding their own window repairman from the man Moscow's Western community had come to call the "Fixer."

For Yak, the chilly autumn of 1988 had turned into an extremely profitable winter, forcing Fact's employees to use all their electrical outlets to power ten computers and an illegal photocopying machine. Instead of electric space heaters, Fact's staff wore gloves and huddled for warmth around the bare-wired teakettle in Yak's frowzy communal office. Fact's single phone rang incessantly atop a battered table, and people hurdled briefcases, coats, and boxes of shoddy stationery to dig the coffee-and-nicotine-stained receiver out from under a pink piggy bank, scattered cigarette stubs, leaky pens, and a heap of muskrat hats. There was plenty of money, but there was no big easy at Forty-one Good Highway— the flashpoint of the cooperative movement.

Yak first opened Fact's brightly varnished wooden door to the public at noon on November 5, 1987, and what greeted him was a line of dour faces that sometimes stretched for two hundred yards through a small park and into Good Highway. Yak had transformed the ramshackle storefront (which had belonged to a state appliance repair company with the tongue-twisting name of *Mosgorremelektorbytpribor*) into one of the first twenty cooperatives to exist in Moscow by giving it a clean, Western feel that customers could sense from the moment they cleared the doorway. Once inside the outer office, Fact's Russian patrons invariably dropped their mannequin expressions and stared, enthralled by their country's only free-market information exchange, which was, in effect, a virtual-reality Yellow Pages. The sensation was warming, like drink. Hypnotically high-tech globe lighting fixtures hung from the ceiling, bathing the shiny green exotic plants decorating the large rectangular room in a glow alien to the Russian epidermis. Behind a long counter were seven well-dressed and cheerful women who responded to requests for information with such speed and courtesy that Fact's Good Highway branch was raking in fifty thousand rubles (eighty-three thousand official-exchange-rate dollars) a month. One of Fact's thirty-five Moscow-based employees always roamed the tight column like a carnival barker, telling those who did not want to wait in the cold weather to phone a special number at Moscow's Central Telephone Exchange, where one of Fact's eight operators provided an oral directory of information and mailed bills for the service the following day. But this was the Soviet Union. So many of the people on line did not want to believe what they were being told: Fact's cooperative colossus stretched from Leningrad in the west to Vladivostok in the east, with small branches in Central Asia, the Caucasus, and many points in between. But they came by the thousands anyway, begrudgingly at first, either paying ten rubles to fill out a questionnaire that offered their talents to other cooperatives or individuals seeking employees, or paying between fifty kopecks and a ruble to locate a Fact-registered restaurant, a ton of cement, or a clown.

"Most of our first-time customers get upset because they think a woman can't help them with their problems," explained Yakovlev, who instructed his receptionists to tell clients seeking clowns for birthday parties to call the Council of Ministers. "Russians are used to receiving information from highly connected people. They can't believe that what they're receiving here is real."

The Council of Ministers, however, knew Fact was frighteningly real, and had spent the first quarter of 1988 trying to shut Yakovlev down. The Soviet bureaucracy was a beast made up of layer upon layer of federal ministries, ministries of republics, regional committees, city councils, area authorities, and local Soviets. The pronouncements of these bodies on civil matters such as "who gets an apartment" and "how many toilets are delivered to a new office" were in theory a result of the sound application of Marxist theory as defined by the Central Committee of the Communist Party and the Politburo. More often, however, the official permission needed to initiate a task first went to those with enough *blat* to favorably influence the decision. Corrupting a local official to find a vacant space or have a window repaired was a relatively simple procedure in comparison to affecting a ministerial decision. Influencing decrees made higher up the bureaucratic ladder were exceptionally difficult and costly, as well as requiring dangerous applications of *khitry* (cunning) that could backfire if not exercised with extreme political caution.

One of my chores while working at Fact in 1988 was to help unpack and set up new office equipment. When I started to uncrate a small photocopier that had been collecting dust in a corner, I was stopped by Roman Kudriavstev, Fact's twenty-three-year-old computer technician. "No!" he screamed. "We haven't yet taken care of the bureaucrat in charge!" Kudriavstev said we would all go to jail if the machine were unpacked prematurely, and his explanation, delivered in a nonstop staccato, was an anthem to the Soviet bureaucracy: "For us to use that machine we need to build a room with a special metal door that has a specifically sized window that only opens on an approved set of hinges." Brief pause. "The state must sanction the door and the window and the person who will run the machine with special state documents that allow him and him alone to operate the machine, but only when the door is locked and the copy person is sitting in the room alone." Another pause. "The door must always be locked and what we want copied must be handed to him through the window and an official record of what's being copied must be made to prevent the machine from distributing subversive material."

Yakovlev had no problem in making a deal with the manager of *Mosgorremelektorbytpribor* in late 1987 for the shop's idle two hundred square meters. He had a much bigger predicament. Shortly after the Council of Ministers decreed cooperative ventures legal in 1988, they realized that information co-ops were potentially too profitable and dangerous to be left in the control of individuals from the private sector. "The state wanted to create the official cooperative information service," Yak explained. "The same stupid bureaucracy that started the economic nightmare that made co-operatives necessary now wanted to create and manage the private sector."

"The government provided us with much of the information we used at the time," said Gleb Pavlovsky, one of the founders of Fact. "More often than not, the information was incorrect. We were continually told that we would receive better information if we cooperated with the state. I said no! They wanted us to become part of the same bureaucracy that we wanted to destroy. No honest cooperator was behind this provocation. The government wanted us to become part of their machine, to eat us up and spit us out. I said no!"

Since it was practically and politically impossible for Yak to influence judgments taken on a ministerial level, his only defense against a hostile takeover by the state was to go loophole-hunting in the new law. He discovered a big one. While the decree prevented new information cooperatives from registering with the state, it did not prevent already licensed cooperatives from branching out into the information business. So Yak cut his first deal. He approached Igor Gorbashov, the director of the Rainbow clothing cooperative, and offered him 20 percent of Fact's first-quarter profits in exchange for the right to run his information co-op as a subsidiary of Rainbow. Yak had beaten the bureaucracy with *khitry*. This time. When Rainbow later went out of business, Fact became the only registered information cooperative in the Soviet Union and Gorbashov went home with about ninety thousand rubles when his clothing operation went under.

"Cooperatives allow people to show their talents in many ways, and this is unique for us," explained Kseniya Makahnenko, the Moscow State University journalism student who was a founding member of Fact and "the fifth Mrs. Yakovlev"—a feat of marital juggling that had left Yak with angry ex-wives and cartons of clothing scattered all over Moscow. "It was a big risk for Gorbashov to leave a state job, where he could get paid for not working, to start a cooperative, where he must work against impossible odds to survive. To become a cooperator, fail, and then be forced back into the old system can destroy your life. It's sad when they fail for lack of knowledge. Their initiative dies with them, and the fear of the system comes back to haunt them.

"Mikhail Gorbachev did so much for us, such great things," Makahnenko said with an odd sadness in her petite voice, and then, nearly growling with anger, "but the ideological ones control us. Those fools who must approve this and authorize that will never understand. Everything is organized in the Soviet Union—even the madness."

"At first all our customers were furious, wondering why they needed to pay money for information," added Yak, who began Fact paying his employees six hundred rubles a month, almost four times the national average. "Many of them told me that I sold them air . . . I told them that for the first time in their lives they were able to breathe. There was a successive and predictable strangeness to the process over the first five months. First we got the crazies tempted by the opening of their individuality. Then came the enthusiasts, who were encouraged by the first successes. Then we got the losers, all the people who couldn't make money from state work. Now we have a lot of very successful people, even ministry officials, who see cooperatives as an interesting alternative and are leaving state work to join in. Their wonder over paying money turned into a wonder for making money."

The wonder apparent on the faces of Fact's Russian and American clients, who left the co-op firmly gripping Hewlett-Packard LaserJet printouts of the names and numbers of Soviet freemarketeers, was one of the rare, legitimate results of the *perestroika* phenomenon. To deliver Fact's payroll, cash flow, and the *blat* and *vzyatka* (payoff) necessary to keep the various layers of Soviet bureaucracy at bay, Yak did some scheming. The object of his scheme was Lorrie Grimes. Her name did not matter as much as her U.S. passport and the valuable computer hardware she brought to Moscow from Seattle in breach of American State, Commerce, and Defense Department policy directives, federal statutes, congressional legislation, and—as both Lorrie Grimes and I would discover—the street smarts one uses when cutting a deal in an economy that draws no distinction between entrepreneur and hustler.

Veteran American businessmen in Moscow understood this characteristic particularly well. One of the earliest moves made by Western businessmen during the opening hours of *perestroika* in 1985 was to offer smart and well-connected Soviet managers 50 to 100 percent more money for working with the newly legitimized joint business ventures between Soviet and American companies; others provided treats to their "moles," those officials who gave the inside story on what was going down in ministries that had contracts with American firms. Western businessmen in Moscow had greased Soviet palms for years, but *perestroika* had opened an untouched range of hustles that gave businessmen more latitude in playing the game. The big American companies, as well as their European counterparts, quietly enticed entrenched bureaucrats with large clothing allowances, access to shops reserved for Westerners, Concorde tickets to New York City, and gifts of stereos, video recorders, washing machines, television sets, porn movies, and envelopes thickened with dollars.

Vladimir Sushkov, the Soviet Union's powerful deputy foreign trade minister until Gorbachev sent him to prison in 1988 for corruption, was so good at *gladit firmacha* (the popular Russian expression used to describe the ease of "ironing foreign businessmen" for money and other unavailable items) that he rose to cochair the influential U.S.–U.S.S.R. Trade and Economic Council in a long line of men including Pepsi's Don Kendall, ADM's Dwayne Andreas, Dresser's Jack Murphy, and former U.S. Secretary of Commerce C. William Verity, Jr. According to Soviet and American diplomatic and business sources uniquely familiar with Trade Council operations during the 1970s and 1980s, the organization that began with a mandate to build a business bridge between communism and capitalism degenerated into a "combination country club, home-improvement contractor, tailor, frequent-flier program, and electronic department store" for Soviet foreign trade ministers and Trade Council executives. Although the Trade Council's money was managed on a daily basis over the years by executives James Giffen, Dmitri Solyukh, Vladimir Cheklin, and William Forrester in New York and Richard Spooner, Vladislav Malkevich, Boris Alekseyev, and Edward Perper in Moscow, the association was funded almost entirely by Fortune 500 corporations, who had millions of dollars tied up in exceedingly risky trade deals. As many of these "Council-backed" deals began to shatter or spiral into huge cost overruns after Sushkov's conviction on charges of smuggling Japanese video recorders, American members of the Trade Council, who paid between four thousand and fourteen thousand dollars a year in membership fees, began to compare notes and discovered that the Trade Council's endeavors and expertise in the Soviet market were long on form but short on substance. So secretive was the Trade Council that it refused publicly to disclose the names of its approximately 315 American members and 150 Soviet enterprises and ministries; until 1989 it maintained an unlisted phone number in New York City. As one angry senior executive from an American automotive company explained: "The Council cost us over two hundred fifty thousand dollars and all we ever got out of it was a fucking table near Gorbachev at a Kremlin dinner."

In theory, Russians holding dollars could be charged with a crime, as Soviet citizens were prohibited from having large amounts of hard currency without an officially acceptable explanation of how they got it.* But dollars were in high demand everywhere, including in the pockets of the ambitious young bureaucrats charged with policing the hazardous no-man's land that separates the black market from the Party-managed market.

But it was computers—specifically those incorporating the Intel 286, 386, or 486 microprocessing chips—that were in unique demand between 1985 and 1990 because of Western export restrictions accompanied by stiff jail time for those Americans convicted of illegal technology transfers to the U.S.S.R. Although it was unthinkable for major American corporations to freight sophisticated computer equipment to Moscow because of U.S. Customs probes and the qualms of corporate legal departments, there was absolutely no problem for a commercial airline passenger to

---

*Fact did business with some twenty-five American firms in 1987 and 1988, charging them one thousand dollars for an initial consultation, two hundred fifty dollars an hour after that, and one thousand dollars more for a detailed analysis of a specific Soviet market.

haul as many outlawed personal, portable, mainframe, or laptop computers as he or she wanted into the Soviet Union as checked luggage. Indeed, nobody ever checked, and in what must rank as the most magnificent irony in the history of IBM, so much banned computer equipment flowed into the Soviet Union during the second half of the 1980s that IBM's Moscow office manager, James Donnick, left his post in disgust in 1989 because the selection and availability of illegal one-hundred-megabyte, 386 hard-disk computers, and thirteen-inch VGA color monitors on Moscow's black market far outstripped his ability to offer customers anything more radical than a Big Blue service contract for hard currency. The black market provided a wider inventory of cheaper, more easily obtainable, and more advanced computers than the outmoded models stored in IBM's West German warehouse; moreover, Moscow's computer hustlers furnished their customers with service contracts costed in rubles.

"The computers came and came," Artyom Borovik said, describing one of the ways in which the state put its computer hardware to work. "We have people who know how to use them better than the Americans, but we have a country that doesn't know how to take advantage of them. Too often, the computers gave the criminals a data base. Take the food situation. A family that runs a large collective farm in the southern Soviet Union keeps one of its sons on the farm and sends the other to the Foreign Studies Institute in Moscow. He graduates and is given a good job with the authority to commandeer a plane from Aeroflot. He sends the plane south once a year and has his brother fill it with apples or tomatoes. The plane goes to Siberia or the Arctic Circle and the apples and tomatoes are sold for twenty rubles each. A fortune is made yearly. How else can these bureaucrats afford their dachas, cars, and girlfriends? This is the system and it is now computerized."

Computers conferred the pull and power of a multinational wheeler-dealer on every visitor to Moscow. All anyone with about two thousand dollars in his pocket and a dream of cracking the chic *perestroika* market in his head needed was to dial the 800 number of a computer discounter and order an Intel 386 machine to be

Federal Expressed to him for collection at the Pan American Airline's Clipper Club at Kennedy Airport for the nonstop trip to Moscow, where it would fetch one hundred fifty thousand rubles (around two hundred fifty thousand dollars at the official exchange rate), possibly twice that in the provinces. The American entrepreneurs rushed Moscow like airborne Oklahoma Sooners, so many that the Soviet Consulate in Washington, D.C., had to conscript extra embassy staff to process the thousands of business visas that arrived at its door weekly by Federal Express. There were California entrepreneurs wanting to sell the Soviets swimming pool tarpaulins, Texas entrepreneurs pushing bull semen, Florida entrepreneurs extolling the virtues of prefabricated houses, and North Carolina entrepreneurs peddling sod. There were New York entrepreneurs hustling collegiate football games, Georgia entrepreneurs trying to sell cosmetics and hair pomades manufactured for black people, even though there are no blacks in the Soviet Union, Virginia entrepreneurs vending lawn furniture (there are no lawns), and Arizona entrepreneurs flogging imitation hawk-feather dusters. Others tried selling Arkansas catfish farms, others New England lobster tanks, and still others women's lingerie à la Frederick's of Hollywood. Jane Fonda jogged around the Kremlin peddling her exercise videotapes; Ronald McDonald pranced down Gorky Street marketing Big Macs, and Vermont ice-cream magnates Ben and Jerry wandered through rusted Soviet ice cream plants with dreams of Raisa Raspberry and Mickey-Mocha Gorbachev.

"Virtually all of them had no idea what they were doing," explained Michael Mears, the U.S. Commercial Office counselor in Moscow during the late 1980s, who estimated that each entrepreneur who visited Moscow spent at least twenty-five thousand dollars per trip. "It was an entrepreneurial nightmare. Every one of them had a guaranteed scheme to make a million dollars out of an economy that had no money, no equipment, no convertible currency, and absolutely no idea what to do with or how to make the products people were trying to sell or manufacture in the Soviet Union. But they came anyway. Nothing would stop them."

"It was a totally wild and out-of-control scene, joint-venture madness," said Sidney Reiner, the late veteran Soviet business specialist and the president of Cosmos Travel in Manhattan, who arranged the visa support, airline flights, and hotel rooms for many of America's would-be Soviet-market millionaires. "I had one client tell me that he was going to sell the Russians frozen sperm for Soviet racehorses. Moscow was like Dodge City without Wyatt Earp." But even Wyatt Earp had come to Moscow, at least in the form of Hugh O'Brian, the American actor who played the famed U.S. marshal on television. "I'm here with some students from my foundation who want to learn about the Soviet Union," explained the man who cleaned up Dodge. "Maybe Russian television might be interested in buying some of the old shows. What do you think?"

No matter the deal, what Soviet cooperators and state-employed businessmen were initially interested in was computers, and every American entrepreneur arrived either with one in his luggage or with the promise of one. The computer, whether sold for rubles to provide a millionaire's cash flow in local currency or exchanged for normally impossible services and favors, was a magic wand; and any foreigner with one in hand had the wizardry to accomplish miracles.* Or so Lorrie Grimes believed when she first entered Forty-one Good Highway in the summer of 1988, hoping

---

*Although a few hundred thousand rubles amounted to a great deal of money for a Russian, it was totally worthless for the visiting Americans, who were forced to pay for all their services in hard currency usually exchanged at the inflated official exchange rate of approximately one dollar sixty-eight cents per ruble before they arrived in the Soviet Union. Americans could use cash-rubles for cab rides and restaurants, but not much else. It was at this point where the cooperators and the state officials with whom the Americans had come to do business entered the picture. The Soviet Apparat was simply too big and chaotic for an American to double-deal for services without local help. Hotels, airline and train tickets, theater and circus seats, guided tours, rental cars, works of art, fur coats, caviar, and most high-quality souvenirs had to be paid for in dollars converted at the official exchange rate—unless an American businessman had contact with a Russian who knew how to prevent his colleague from being financially flogged and humiliated by the Apparat through the judicious application of a cash-ruble stash. With such assistance, a round-trip Aeroflot ticket between Moscow and Tbilisi in Soviet Georgia that cost around five hundred dollars in hard currency ended up costing less than twenty dollars in black-market converted rubles. Two kilograms of caviar that sold for over three thousand dollars in a state hard-currency-only store sold at less than twenty dollars on the black market. Sable fur coats, which went for upward of fifteen thousand dollars, could be had with the right contacts at less than one thousand dollars. In some circles, this exercise in financial management came to be known as the *Perestroika* Gambit.

to turn a profit from sating the American appetite for Soviet chic with a diet of Moscow rock 'n' roll bands, Leningrad folk singers, and cultural exchanges that placed Russian chefs in American restaurant kitchens and Hawaiian hula dancers in Siberian dance halls. Lorrie Grimes and her husband, Doug, headed up the MIR Corporation, a classic American entrepreneurial venture run on a grubstake of guts, a spare bedroom, and subscription to *INC* magazine. Grimes was no innocent to the Soviet scene. MIR had specialized in operating unusual Soviet–American exchange tours for cooks and musicians since 1985, so it was natural for Grimes to explore the growing cooperative restaurant sector for potential clients and fresh opportunities. But Moscow had changed. Lorrie Grimes never realized just how much. "Yes, I was the first to trust Yakovlev," the twenty-nine-year-old Washington native recalled with a cheerless laugh. "So let this be my testament," Grimes began in her fast-paced voice.

"Yakovlev was known everywhere in Moscow as an authority on the cooperative sector. I called to meet with him and spoke to his translator and assistant, Svet Raikov. I met with him at the offices of Fact, with Svet translating because I spoke very little Russian at the time. Yakovlev agreed to assist with the chef-exchange project and asked me to give him more concrete information about my needs in our next meeting. He didn't introduce me to anyone, even though people were walking in and out of his office all the time. The phone never stopped ringing and no one ever answered it. He smoked one cigarette after another, not stopping to drink tea with me. But then he never drank tea, only coffee, four or five cups in one sitting. At the time I thought this was the sign of a real serious Soviet entrepreneur. The first meeting was a test for me. If Yakovlev liked me there would be a second meeting and he would seriously listen to me then. I walked away from that first meeting feeling like I had done well on my Scholastic Aptitude Test.

"In our second meeting at Forty-one, Yakovlev actually listened to me and I was surprised to learn that he spoke English very well, better than his translator, Svet. I told him what I needed and he added his own vision and ideas to it, giving me the feeling that he really understood the project. He said that he really didn't like my client and preferred to work directly with me. This, of course, flattered me. I didn't understand the game at the time and started to become consumed by his game of politics. I promised to act as the middle person with my American client at all times so that he wouldn't have to come into contact with her.

"The deal was for him to provide five Soviet cooks from five cooperative restaurants and I would, through my client, provide five American cooks from five restaurants. They would work in each other's restaurants for a period of three weeks and he would provide the hotel and visa support in the Soviet Union while I provided everything in America. This part of the meeting took a total of seven minutes. At the close of the agreement portion of our meeting, he started to talk about the cooperative movement and how he saw Americans fitting in. Since the Soviets had introduced the cooperative system to the public, I had been interested in being part of the action. There was great potential for Americans to come in and exploit the Soviets if the cooperators were not careful. I also understood that if nothing was done to help the young, entrepreneurial Americans understand how the Russians did business, the Americans interested in creating a healthy relationship would become disenchanted and discouraged almost immediately and quit.

"I had an idea running around in my head to set up a seminar for Soviets and Americans to learn about each other in business. I wasn't sure how to go about it or how to find the people interested. So Yakovlev starts telling me of his ideas concerning the same subject. I was stunned at the way in which he put my ideas into words. It was as if he had listened to my thoughts. In 1988 there were very few Americans willing to get involved with the cooperative sector because of the risk of not knowing if they would survive. The Soviet system had just started to change and the first summit between our two countries had just taken place the year before. Everyone was waiting to see what would happen, if Gorbachev was really serious. I had some experience in doing business with the Soviets and understood how to do business with them on their terms. And Yakovlev was the king of the cooperatives and I wanted to get in on the beginning of something new and exciting. His flattery helped dispel my doubts about my lack of confidence in feeling qualified to work with someone of his obvious genius. I was to learn a whole new way of doing Soviet business from Yakovlev, a way of doing business that I have run into since then and now know to run in the other direction when I recognize it. I only remember bits and pieces of what happened next, I guess because I have tried to forget.

"We created a whole new world for ourselves every time we met. It was like beginning some sort of a new revolution every time we got together. Our revolution needed computers and money to get started. The idea was to put together a catalog of businesses. We would start by printing a catalog of the Soviet businesses interested in American contacts. Then we would print a catalog of American businesses interested in Soviet contacts. The businesses would pay to advertise themselves and the Soviets and the Americans would pay to buy the books. Yakovlev had about twenty computers of mysterious origin on hand, but told me that he needed six more computers to get started. These six computers were to be sold for rubles. The rubles would be used to pay for the publishing of the catalog in the Soviet Union. The deal was that I would come up with clients interested in marketing their businesses and he would pay for the publishing and production of the catalog. He put together a contract, saying that it was for the state authorities and that it didn't mean anything.

"Yakovlev had a deadline for me to come up with the clients and businesses interested in being in the catalog. The deadline was one month after signing the contract. I told him this was impossible, that we could not possibly market, sell, and collect the payments before that deadline. He assured me that he would not adhere to the date, that he of course understood that it was not possible. He went on to explain that he could not proceed further without a contract from me, that the state would not grant him the permission to set up a business with me without it, and that in a sense it was to protect me. If I didn't come up with the clients in time, and research showed there was no market, the deal was off. No pressure. I wanted to trust him. I trusted him.

"Yakovlev told me that he could not consider me his partner until I gave him the six computers. It was understood that we had an unwritten agreement that I would not work with other cooperatives without his consent and he would not work with other Americans without my consent. I gave him almost twenty thousand dollars' worth of computers, and he introduced me to everyone as his partner. Then, in December of 1988, Yakovlev came to America on an invitation from Harvard University. MIR paid for his trip to Seattle from Boston. We picked him up in a limousine, introduced him to all our friends and family, wined and dined him, took him for a flight in a private plane, and talked business. He met with the cooks group and assured them that he had everything set up and ready to go for their February arrival in Moscow. Again, he assured us that he was not going to adhere to the deadline date for the catalog and that the contract was only a piece of paper he needed to show the bureaucracy that we were serious about the project. I thought I was being naive, that he never intended to use the money from the computers to finance the catalogs. But I wanted to trust him. I trusted him.

"One of my employees accompanied Yakovlev back to New York. During their last conversation at the airport, he told my employee that he should take over the catalog project without letting me know because I was incapable of conducting any form of business, being a 'bubblehead and a woman.' My employee informed me of this immediately. I returned to the Soviet Union on New Year's Eve and met with Yakovlev that night. We celebrated the new year and then I didn't see him for a week. At our next meeting I confronted him with the information from my employee and he explained that he had sensed some tension between my employee and me concerning the catalog project and thought that by making an alliance with him as such, that he would back the project. I wanted to trust him. I trusted him.

"Then he started asking for more computers. I refused. So he asked for a fax machine. I consented because we were having problems with our communications. I returned home to tell the cooks everything was ready. They arrived in the Soviet Union with the notion that they would be staying in the homes of Russian cooks and cooking at the cooks' restaurants. These cooks, a confusion of cooks, were the cooks that they were expecting to come to America. Well, the American cooks did cook in the Russian cooks' restaurants. They did not stay in their homes as planned, however. They stayed at the Ukraine Hotel and the whole thing was a disaster and no one could turn it around. Yakovlev wouldn't meet with the leader of the American cooks' delegation, and Fact had set nothing up for the group, not even meals. The Soviet cooks who were coming to America didn't even know the American cooks were in town until the group tracked them down. The American cooks called me in a panic and I rushed to Moscow to find out what went wrong and create a better system so that these mistakes would not repeat themselves. I had no intention of cutting my relationship with Yakovlev, but he avoided me for one week. Finally, when he met with me, he blamed me for everything and then treated me as if nothing had happened. It was then that I knew I couldn't work with him any longer and that I'd lost a lot of money.

"I realized Yakovlev was incapable of taking responsibility for his mistakes and was only interested in getting press and computers for himself. He wasn't interested in doing business at all. His only motivation was computers and social profile. Businesswise, he never thought anything through to the end. If it created a press interview or a computer, that was enough. He needed money and equipment to run his business and saw me as a way to do that. He was always playing catch-up and cover with the Americans he dealt with. He never had the time to think of what to do to clean things up and start everything in the right way again. Our working relationship ended with a Telex from me telling him that he owed me the money for six computers and one fax machine. The whole thing for me has been one big learning experience. I wanted to trust him. I trusted him."

It was easy for the Americans to put their faith in Yakovlev and the co-op movement because the cooperatives were made up of young Russian men and women who exuded the same fire that drove the American entrepreneurs on to recast the U.S. business scene in the 1980s. Uniquely aware of the American entrepreneurial dynamic through his readings of American business publications, Yak targeted small U.S. companies to become his partners in selling the Soviet Union as a market. "We can easily manage to develop contacts with large Soviet industries," he explained. "But we want to deal on a more personal basis with American firms that gross around one million dollars a year and are interested in working with cooperatives to rebuild the Soviet economy. Too many of the American businessmen who come here think big and fail. Small succeeds with fewer problems."

Think Small was the Big Amen of the American entrepreneurial gospel, and men and women like Lorrie Grimes listened and responded to Yak's cooperative sermon with all the enthusiasm of a Chautauqua congregation. But, unknown to the idealistic young Apple-computer-fed MBAs who filled the cooperative tent, Americans with cash and computers were rare delicacies in the Russian co-op crowd, a dish heretofore eaten only by ranking ministry officials. In the hands of Yak and many other cooperators, the Great American Dream became the Great Russian Scheme. Yet the new action in the cooperative sector fused with the paralysis of the Soviet trade ministries and the high-cost/low-return membership frustrations experienced by members of the U.S.–U.S.S.R. Trade and Economic Council to create an entirely new vehicle for dealing on a big-time basis with the Soviet market. American companies with long histories in the Soviet Union began to explore the cooperative sector as a cheaper and more effective pipeline into *perestroika*. Cooperators certainly had the *blat* to accomplish tasks that the Trade Council and the government ministries had said were impossible and forbidden. More important, the cooperators were the only Soviets in the country's economic stream who grasped and acted upon the concept of a free market with any initiative.*

---

*The economists and ministers whom Gorbachev had put in charge of erecting a free market shortly after he came to power in 1985 still had no idea of what a free market was over five years after they had been given their mandate. The inability—or loathing—of Soviet officials to master free markets was cannily captured by John Phelan, Jr., the chairman of the New York Stock Exchange, during a trip to Moscow to discuss the creation of a Soviet stock exchange. "Despite all

"We knew most of the cooperatives were no different psychologically from the state ministries we had been dealing with for twenty years," explained the Moscow director of a large American construction firm that used cooperative help in exchange for computers. "But they possessed an energy the state didn't have. We wanted to give them a shot, and if they failed or disappeared or the laws were changed, well, the cost to us wasn't near to what we were losing from kowtowing to the ministries and the Trade Council to stay in good graces with the bureaucracy."

The biggest problem facing companies such as Combustion Engineering, General Electric, Dresser Industries, Dow Chemical, and the Ford Motor Company was how to tap the cooperative sector for the specific services they required. Cooperators were notorious for telling potential American clients that they could do *anything*. And—quite often and usually illegally—they could.

The explosion of black-market crime that engulfed the entire country was as overwhelmingly massive as it was hard to pinpoint statistically. The government never released any reliable figures on the scope of economic crime, but KGB Chief Vladimir Kryuchkov admitted that he "never expected this scale of organized crime. There are rather stable gangs, having access to the black market and even their own investment funds. They have the opportunity to accumulate power." Added Soviet Justice Minister Venyamin Yakovlev: "Our American colleagues ask us why we fight speculation, a normal phenomenon in a normal economy. But our criminal code stipulates as illegal things that are normal in a market economy."

But the guerrilla management techniques employed by the cooperators did not play well in corporate suites, where Soviet deals were crafted as much for political profit in the Kremlin as for financial gain in the bank. "This was the catch-22 in dealing with the cooperative sector," explained John Minneman, vice-president of the Chase Manhattan Bank in Moscow, the only American bank with a Soviet office. "A cooperator's definition of jeopardy and my

_____

the talk of free markets, the Soviet officials kept asking when does the state come in to set the price," said Phelan, who visited Moscow in October 1990. "They still have only a vague notion of what a market is."

definition of jeopardy were not the same." The people who ran America's corporate outposts in Moscow perceived the critical necessity of acquiring contacts with Soviet cooperators, but they also recognized the dire need to have the route swept for mines by an American go-between who understood the cooperators and the danger in dealing with them.

This man was Charles Bausman, a twenty-six-year-old graduate of Exeter and Wesleyan who was as fluent in Russian as he was expert at what brand of industrial-strength winter boot was needed to outlast Moscow's winter. Bausman had learned how to deal among the Soviets while growing up in Moscow as the son of the local Associated Press bureau chief. He had married a Russian woman in 1987 and brought her to America. After separating from her in 1988, Bausman returned to Russia to begin 1989 as the "owner" and principal resident of his ex-wife's courtyard apartment in central Moscow that became the clearing house for deals between cooperators and American companies. "Charlie," as everybody, from the U.S. Ambassador to Yakovlev, called the blue-eyed, clean-shaven prepster from Greenwich, Connecticut, was calm, honest, reliable, efficient, and ambitious; he was also savvy enough to con the shoes off any Russian who even thought about filching his gold wire spectacles.

Bausman had designs on becoming a journalist when he arrived at NBC's Moscow bureau in early 1988 for a job as a summer intern, but departed the daily grind of covering *perestroika* to become a participant in the Second Revolution. For a profit. Charlie had the Moscow jazz, and he liked the place. He liked its characters, its smells and sounds, the look of its crumbling history, its *beau-parleurs*, and even the brutal bluffs of its inhabitants. His two-room apartment, excluding a kitchen that resembled a Pittsburgh beer distributor's, and the spacious underground American bathroom that a cooperative construction company had dug five feet beneath the old water closet, was an electronic wonderland of computers, telephones, faxes, answering machines, and dot matrix printers that, as he often said, "make the Russians weep." But Bausman was no black marketeer. Instead, he invested time, energy, and equipment in Russian cooperatives with the understanding that he could use their contacts and facilities to work his own deals with American businessmen.

The scope of Bausman's knowledge was impressive, and there seemed to be no limit to the information he could uncover for his American clients. "Every new American businessman coming to set up shop in Moscow made three mistakes within his first forty-eight hours in town," Bausman explained. "They bought Finnish office furniture, ordered a German car, and believed that the government agency in charge of taking care of foreign businessmen actually took care of foreign businessmen. All three moves were ridiculously expensive and unnecessary if you knew where to go instead." And Charlie knew where to go. Using a network of cooperators, state bureaucrats, street people, and artful dodgers, Bausman's free-market bandits provided furniture, apartments, cars, translators, drivers, information, and ruble-priced gasoline to a vast and varied list of American clients at a fraction of the cost and headache of dealing with the state. All they asked for in return was complete secrecy.

"Charlie was like Robin Hood," said a Western attorney who used Bausman's services. "He was gifted and intuitive. His best attribute was a willingness to be the first one to stand up and say some scheme was a sham before it turned out to be no more than a sham and got everybody in trouble with the authorities. He knew how far to go, and he damn sure knew how to deal with the Soviet con men."

W. Douglass Lee, Jr., the director of the large London countertrade company Intertech Resources, called Charlie the moment he heard rumors that a cooperative known as Biocor had received permission from the Council of Ministers to buy and transport Soviet supplies of strategic and nonferrous metals out of Odessa and Vladivostok and, more interesting for Lee, outside the tightly controlled confines of the trade ministries. Lee, a twenty-year veteran of doing business in the Soviet Union and Eastern Europe, had met Bausman a few weeks earlier in a Moscow cooperative restaurant and decided to put Charlie to the test. The rumor mill said Biocor's chairman, Alexander Kuzen, was claiming eighty-two offices worldwide, fifteen hundred employees, and immediate ac-

cess to Gorbachev. Lee's ministry sources had never heard of
Kuzen, but balked at dismissing the rumors that were sweeping
the international metal-trading fraternity. Charlie called Lee a few
days later and said: "You gotta meet this guy."

"Yeah, but is he for real?" Lee asked skeptically.

"Just come and meet him with me," Bausman urged. "Kuzen
is too good to miss."

It was early and Moscow's nine million inhabitants were en-
joying clear blue skies. Zinc-day skies. The possibilities were
endless as Bausman, Lee, and I pulled an illegal turn off Kropotkinskaya and into the Zubovsky Boulevard stretch of the Sadovaya
Ring Road. From Zubovsky, there was a view of Progress Publishing, the biggest publishing house in the world, and the steady
stream of Moscow businessmen filing out on the circular road from
their power breakfasts of German beer and scrambled eggs at the
cooperative restaurant Kropotkinskaya Thirty-six. The sun and icy
morning breeze were making the old stucco fixtures on all the
stained and peeling buildings shine like hammered platinum. Even
Bausman's green and crippled Volvo station wagon seemed to be
working well as it lurched to a halt in front of Biocor's "world
headquarters."

The three of us were greeted at Biocor's third-floor front door
by a lone worker cursing to himself in Russian and smashing away
at walls with a broken sledgehammer. The two Americans, dodging
chunks of flying plaster and live electrical wires that scattered
sparks throughout the seven-room apartment, inched their way
unguided into Biocor's presidential office. "Here!" a Russian voice
shouted over the din of loose concrete and metal fragments splash-
ing around the floor. Fanning the dust away from his eyes and
snorting a cloud of plaster out of his sinuses, Lee barely had enough
air to shout "Where?" before a large figure appeared, wraithlike,
out of the fog. "I am Kuzen," proclaimed the president of Biocor,
slumping into a chair and picking dandruff out of his hair while his
younger brother was trying to crush a pair of pink woman's bedroom
slippers on two of the largest and most aromatic feet in the hemi-
sphere. It was no longer a zinc day.

"I'm very impressed," Lee whispered to me. "Although Kuzen

really does need to do something about his personal hygiene, his slippers do match his shirt. Charlie was right. Kuzen is just too good a show to miss."

Our trio spent the next hour listening to the story of Kuzen and Biocor—and what a story we heard. "Yes," Kuzen said, "I have more metal than you can ever afford to buy. I am also one of only twenty-five people in the world with special top-secret clearance to all of the Soviet Union's top-secret inventions. Gorbachev is my friend and my patient. You see, I also am the inventor of a cure for diabetes. It's not available on the market yet because the West German pharmaceutical house I'm dealing with wants to make money from it and I want to give it away for free. They have put two million dollars in my Liechtenstein account to tempt me. Gorbachev is a diabetic, you know. I visit him weekly and give him injections of my drug.

"We can do business, good business. Americans are my best customers," said the thirty-two-year-old cooperator, paying no attention to the sledgehammer that crashed unannounced through the office wall. "Just tell me what you want and where you want it. We can attend to the letters of credit later. I could use a computer right now, though. I'm working on a cure for cancer with my new heat-pack invention. Let me give you a copy of the study on both the diabetes cure and the cancer cure. I need help with the West Germans. People are dying because of their greed. So about those computers . . ."

That was the game, and if the amount of American goods stacked alongside the piles of Russian rubble in Kuzen's flat were any indication of the number of people playing, American businessmen were buying into Kuzen's scam in a big way. Yet within the concentrated weirdness of characters such as Kuzen was a grain of illuminating reality that Bausman had the capacity to isolate. Hustlers of Kuzen's ilk did not appear out of nowhere with stories of mainlining Gorbachev with mystery drugs, and the state did not just give them seven-room apartments on Zubovsky Boulevard without getting something in return—or thinking that they were getting something in return. Kuzen built the Biocor con, as Bausman discovered, on a videotape he had made of thirty seconds of news footage that had been a lead story broadcast on the Soviet news program *Vremya*. The nightly news program had sent a camera crew to follow Gorbachev during his visit to an important trade exhibition in the Ukraine in the winter of 1989. Kuzen had somehow managed to spend the entire thirty seconds walking next to Gorbachev and was filmed chatting with the Soviet leader like an old friend. The soundless news item, broadcast to the entire nation as *Vremya*'s important kickoff story, gave Kuzen the opportunity to fill in the dialogue as circumstance required. Bausman speculated, and probably correctly, that Kuzen flashed his *Vremya* tape in front of the bureaucratic authorities who were needed to authorize, credential, and provision Biocor. The "My Friend Gorby" tape was Kuzen's *paroli* (a password or secret sign) to getting whatever he wanted from the state, so long as he did not run the con too high up the bureaucratic ladder. No Soviet dared to question Kuzen's credentials; to do so *might* incur the wrath of his good friend Gorbachev. The Kuzen con, although preposterous, worked in the Soviet Union for the simple reason that it *might* be true.

Bausman realized that all cooperatives operated on a variation of the Kuzen con because villainy was the only available method for beating the Apparat. Nobody was ever really sure what was criminal anyway. Not even the Soviet and American lawyers—whose job it was to understand all the decrees, laws, ordinances, constitutions, codes, and edicts that flowed out of the ministries, congresses, Soviets, committees, and trade unions—understood completely what was legal and what was illegal. "The entire Soviet Union is in confusion," said Barbara Dillon Hillas, an attorney and Soviet legal specialist for the Washington, D.C., law firm of Steptoe & Johnson. "The laws reflect that confusion." Added Soviet attorney Alexander Finestein: "I don't know the difference between right and wrong because the government has yet to discover the difference."

"The cooperatives fed off the crisis of morality," Bausman explained. "Some cooperators had staff attorneys to advise them, but more often than not they just went out and grabbed everything in sight, paying people off along the way. The judgment businessmen had to make was whether or not a cooperative's activity went too far beyond what a cooperator had the ability to get away with. It was a tough call for American businessmen to make, but when the state authorities screwed up—which was all the time—and people needed to have something done quickly, there was no place else to go."

And no one knew how to ease the fears of American businessmen better than Yakovlev, who had built Fact on the principle that malfeasance was endemic to Soviet society and that criminals could be judged guilty only if they failed to realize and act upon the sheer corruptness of the system. Yak realized that foreign businessmen, no matter how long they had been in Moscow, were continually hampered by their superficial acquaintance with how the system operated. Dishonesty, in the Western sense, was common business sense in the Soviet Union. The Russians calculated the morality or immorality of a deal based entirely on what was in it for them. An immoral cooperative was one that charged an unaffordable fifty rubles for a pair of shoes made from leather *blat*ed away from the state bureaucrats, who were supposed to be selling the same shoes for five rubles. A moral cooperative was one that knew how to bribe the shoe leather off a bureaucrat, pay its workers five times the national wage, and keep subsidized five-ruble shoes out of the state stores to embellish the free-market system. It was hard to see any moral difference in the degree of crime necessary to get shoes—unless you were a Russian without a pair of shoes.

"Yakovlev was very smart in knowing how to handle the bureaucracy," Bausman said, "but he was incapable of following through on the promises he made to Westerners. He didn't need to lie to us. It didn't serve him well at all, because people like Lorrie Grimes accepted his hustling the system for Fact to survive. It took each of us who dealt with Yakovlev a long time to realize that we were being hustled in the same way. Yak was that good at it. A pro."

Bausman's soft manner and attention to precise dealmaking for profit were incompatible with Yakovlev's velvety voice and predilection for vague but resourceful schemes to make hard currency. Yak was discomforting, but his focus on the system's elemental fury was sharper than anyone Bausman had ever met. Such a vision was profit . . . and there was always something new to learn about the temperament of the system. It had always been like this: Yak giving the orders and those around him being carried along by what appeared to be free-market energy and determination. It had been like that the first day Bausman met Yakovlev.

"Volodya's office stank to high heaven," Bausman remembered. "There was no ventilation, and he sequestered himself in the back chain-smoking and drinking coffee. He wanted to start a translation service, which was a great idea, so I agreed to contribute two personal computers as a start to our business venture. Then he never showed up at the meetings we had scheduled with potential customers. He was always too busy or sitting in the computer room playing Space Invaders on the color monitor. It took me weeks to nail him down on the specifics of this translation venture.

"Finally I cornered him to discuss getting furniture for the new office. All of a sudden he jumped up from Space Invaders and was full of enthusiasm. We got in his car and drove off. For the next three hours we drove from one furniture store to the next, of course not finding anything we needed, and I was getting more and more annoyed. There were the obligatory stops for Turkish coffee at all sorts of strange haunts around the city that he had memorized. We stopped at a local police station, where he just happened to have a meeting to find furniture arranged. It was completely ridiculous. We eventually found fourteen chairs which I announced were suitable, at which point it turned out he had no cash on him, so I paid.

"Until the furniture hunt, I actually thought Volodya did something important for Fact because there was such a constant flurry of activity around him. I told Volodya that this was a ridiculous way for someone like him to spend his time, and he just laughed at me and said that doing things like looking for chairs was what made his job fun, just do whatever comes into your head—Space Invaders, furniture searches, saunas at the Council of Ministers baths—whatever. 'Do what strikes your fancy,' he said. Everyone and everything was expendable—employees, contacts, meetings, and contracts. It was at that moment that I realized I was dealing with a person who played by a whole different set of rules, was completely unreliable, and probably dangerous."

Nonetheless the remarkable achievements of *perestroika* had gotten American business interested in cooperators, and it was Bausman's responsibility to tell them that cooperatives were not places for those interested in making any quick money. The Soviet free market was for cool heads who could afford to adventurously experiment with their money. There was a whole new mood in the Soviet business community, too, the same feeling of adventure that the monster had when it walked out of Dr. Frankenstein's door. Things were looking up for the boys in the state business machine because *perestroika* had given formerly abandoned managers the opportunity to spend the hard currency held by their factory in any manner that helped to release the centrally planned system to laissez-faire economics. Yak was the first to realize that the hard-currency reservoirs the state had put under the control of down-and-out local and district officials were untapped sources of wealth that could be opened to those outsiders who provided provincial factory managers with unavailable consumer goodies and trips to warmer climates under the sponsorship of Fact-arranged business conferences.

Yak's first foray into this lucrative arena was a fashion seminar he sponsored in Moscow with his Cypriot partner Markos Shiapanis. Arriving from around the country at the Sporthotel with two thousand four hundred American dollars in their pockets, some one hundred thirty engineers and factory managers with designs on doing business abroad spent five days learning "How to set up business lunches, dinners and comradely meetings," "Basic principles of behavior at a reception," and "The contents of the briefcase of the businessman." One lecture centered on the sensitivity of foreigners to smell and the importance a Soviet businessman should attach to changing his shirt after every shower.

"The fashion conference was another Fact fiasco that made money," explained Bausman, who was conscripted into delivering a lecture on the importance of proper dress when conducting business with a Western client. "The results can only be described as freakish. Shiapanis brought the worst wardrobe of third-world clothing imaginable, really *bad* stuff: rubber-soled Greek shoes, ugly ties, horrible socks, and polyester shirts that he probably acquired through a deal with the Salvation Army. Volodya is passing out these really awful coffee-colored shirts stuffed in Samsonite briefcases while I'm telling these guys the importance of white cotton shirts and never to wear blue boots. Soviet factory managers are built like boilers, so it was obvious that none of the clothes would fit. I didn't have it in me to stick around for the fittings after the lecture, but I know that some of them stayed there trying to figure out the clothing until four in the morning.

"I'm sure every one of them went home happy because the black-market value of the tape recorders, cassettes, watches, and pens Yakovlev gave them was worth a fortune out in Siberia," Bausman added. "It was vintage Volodya. Nobody knew the Soviet free-market system better than he did, but it sure as hell wasn't *perestroika*."

Perestroika had made power a relative term: the passage of the cooperative laws, coupled with the power to deliver computers, hard currency, and simple Western-made gadgets did more to ameliorate Fact's authority than it did to encourage progress toward genuine democracy. Bausman never had a difficult time calling Fact a corrupt institution that grew mighty by feeding off the cracks in *perestroika*'s shell. Soviet opinion polls had consistently indicated that a majority of Soviets opposed the entire cooperative movement for that very reason. A slight plurality of those polled, however, still favored some sort of free-market structure. But the problem remained that no Soviet knew exactly what a free-market system was nor how to make it function. Why, most Russians asked, should they restrain their appetites when both the Kremlin regime and the cooperators connived ever more imposing economic perks? Yakovlev duly seized upon this rationale to build his own vision of a free market—one based on a new level of caprice and craftiness and hypocritical enough to frequently employ the standards of the Kremlin Ration. Based on my own experiences at Fact and other Soviet co-ops, the growing corruption at Forty-one Good Highway was by no means an aberration of what was taking place in the cooperative movement nationwide. Corruption was reality; hypocrisy was elevated to philosophy, and, as Sabina had scolded when I proudly displayed my blue leather Fact membership card, "Yakovlev creates and manipulates the same conditions that allow the communists to thrive."

6

Don't look now, but someone is stealing
your potatoes.

RUSSIAN PROVERB

VOLODYA YAKOVLEV was a child of the Soviet bourgeoisie, but nearly all the people who worked at Fact had been plucked out of Russia's vast pool of *narod* and thus lacked the long and sophisticated experience of their boss in fingering Westerners or maneuvering the Soviet bureaucracy. Fact's senior employees were well paid, of course, but Yak's superior attitude toward many of the rookie Factoids began to sow the seeds of disenchantment and schism by the middle of 1989. This was no small phenomenon. Some thought Yak was taking too many chances playing the corrupt cracks in the bureaucracy, others felt that he was not spreading around enough of the hard currency garnered from the sale of information to Western clients, while still others—like Svet Raikov and Roman Kudriavtsev—believed the time was right to try beating Yak at his own game.

Raikov and Kudriavtsev made no secret of their desire to use the cooperative movement as a means of making it to America. Raikov, twenty-eight, had learned his English working as a houseboy in the stylish home of American expatriate journalist Edmund Stevens, the former Moscow correspondent for *Newsday*. Before moving into Stevens' trendy Arbat home, Raikov had swept Moscow's streets and built cars at the Moskvich factory. "Edmund Stevens taught me the psychology of Americans," said Raikov, whose mother was the director of Moscow's Institute of Hypnosis. "Yakovlev taught me how to be clever. He was very, very clever."

Kudriavtsev, who lived in a communal apartment with his wife, two old ladies whom he did not know, and a battered guitar on which he butchered the Beatles for every American he met, learned his English hustling American tourists on the streets. Raikov was one of Fact's ubiquitous "organizers," a job best described by Yak's often-heard line: "Svet, do this." Kudriavtsev, however, was Fact's resident computer wizard, a title the thin and wiry twenty-two-year-old acquired by virtue of his former job of sitting in front of a state computer terminal, dispatching trucks and snowplows around the capital after leaving the Department of Applied Mathematics of the Moscow Oil and Gas Institute.

While Svet drove around the Moscow doing "this" in his white Saab, Roman sat in Fact's large computer room wrapped against the cold in scarves and sweaters, cranking out lists of cooperatives and creating the government forms that needed to be filled out (the state authorities never seemed to have any of the forms available) if a client wanted to start a cooperative. When not operating his bank of LaserJet printers, the bearded Armenian updated Fact's cooperative data and crunched his hard disks to tender marketable statistics such as the fact that 52 percent of Moscow's cooperatives in 1988 were owned by individuals with Jewish surnames and that this could provide the government with the basis for a pogrom against the cooperative movement. Roman and Svet were bored. They also wanted to grow rich and leave Yak in their dust.

"I want to do two things with my life," Roman explained to every American who crossed his path. "Make a lot of dollars and go to America to fuck as many girls as possible."

"Yes," Svet agreed, "this would be good."

Although Yak was the consummate cooperative con man, always ready with glib promises and the unconvincing excuses that inevitably followed them, he was capable of flamboyant generosity and kindness toward his most essential workers. When Fact's net profits topped one million rubles a month from the sale of data and business intelligence bulletins to an information starved public,

Yak told his section heads to set their own salaries. "Whatever you want," he said. "Your wallets are not big enough to hold all the money." Fact operated on eighteen-hour days, and should one of his cooperators tire to the point of clinical exhaustion from the pace, Yak was there to provide the staff member with an airline ticket to the Cypriot beach house he had arranged with his Greek partners as part of their deal to sell polyester suits and vacations disguised as fact-finding business trips abroad to rural state-factory managers with hard currency who wanted to visit the West. Yak, like the bureaucracy he was fighting and making money off, took care of his own. And the only thing he did not like was not knowing what was going on with the cooperative movement.

At first Yak was very angry when Svet and Roman, two of the earliest Factoids, took off with help of Charles Bausman to start the Moscow Business Center, a cooperative designed to provide Moscow's Western business community with clerical, secretarial, and translation facilities outside the state sector. MBC was a great idea, Bausman thought, but only if he could convince Roman to stop spending all MBC's hard currency on German beer he and Svet drank while interviewing young girls for secretarial positions atop the MBC bed. MBC's six-room apartment cost three thousand rubles a month and was located on the top floor of a nineteenth-century building off Patriarch's Ponds, one of central Moscow's most beautiful sections. MBC's rickety wooden elevator smelled like cat urine, however. And the building's other residents eyed the comings and goings of MBC staff, customers, and secretarial candidates with fear and loathing. Despite the drawbacks, MBC was exactly the kind of operation visiting and permanently residing American executives needed in Moscow. Yakovlev, strapped for space, realized foreign businessmen lacked a place to work, and once he got over his anger toward the two Fact "turncoats," provided MBC with computers, software, and an impenetrable metal door that looked to have been screwed off a Mosler vault. Protecting the other side of the gateway was Tolya—a bare-knuckled professional boxer, who, being on the lam from the police, voiced the sincere conviction that becoming a cooperator was the safest way of avoiding arrest.

MBC blossomed quickly and with all the flourish of a splendid flower fated for a short life. The first order of business was to make the place look like a business center, so Roman snatched the annual stockholders' reports of Xerox and Exxon from the U.S. Commercial Office library and scattered them around the MBC waiting room for his American clients to scan while they lolled beneath a five-foot-wide blow-up of Lenin wearing an MBC earring. Lorrie Grimes provided a fax machine, Bausman brought clients and computer software, and everybody tried to keep Roman hidden in the back room. By the spring of 1989, MBC's client list boasted a Japanese television executive in Moscow who provided equipment and hard currency in return for translations of Soviet news programs and a hard-currency kickback to supplement his salary. Peter Schonwald, the visiting area manager for Polaroid, used MBC for secretaries, phones, and drivers, while selling medical camera equipment to the government. Bronislaw Dvorsky, the director of international relations for Budget, tried to set up a rental car network out of MBC. The U.S. Embassy purchased MBC T-shirts and cooperative restaurant directories, and advised visiting American businessmen to check out MBC's facilities. Combustion Engineering, the first American corporation to enter into a joint venture with the Soviets, contacted MBC to see if Roman had the means to ship spare parts that their partner, the Ministry of Petroleum, was unable to move the several hundred miles from Moscow's airport to the Tatar Republic. Even the Central Intelligence Agency showed up, in the guise of a Commerce Department Soviet economic analyst who had been sent to Moscow for a few months to replace a vacationing embassy employee. "Why did you take me to see this place!" she shrieked at me, bolting past Tolya and down the stairs, muttering a litany of unintelligible U.S. governmental acronyms. "Those people are not supposed to have all that computer equipment! It's illegal. I can get my ass pee-en-gee'd [State Departmentese for *persona non grata*] out of here for seeing that stuff and meeting those people. They're breaking the law! Where did they get it?! Someone is breaking the technology transfer laws!"

But there were no laws to break, only laws to buy and sell as American business went along trying to squeeze a buck out of *perestroika*. Even MBC's cooperative charter was of shady origin, as were its salaries, its equipment, its employees, its automobiles, even the illegally sublet offices it filled with American, German, Austrian, Japanese, Australian, British, and French clients. The bonanza Roman and Svet had counted on proved to be illusionary, however. Western businessmen were happy to pay a few hundred dollars under the table for the use of MBC's translation and secretarial facilities, but Svet and Roman did not have the allure that Yak used to pull off the big deals that made him a millionaire. Roman, in particular, thought brokering Moscow–New York round-trip Aeroflot tickets for Americans could become an enormous hard-currency moneymaker. Aeroflot tickets were sold to Westerners for hard currency only, and the cost of a round-trip flight floated anywhere from nine hundred to two thousand dollars, depending on when the seat was booked. Aeroflot, of course, had to sell a certain number of tickets for rubles because the ruble was still officially considered to be Soviet currency. A more adventurous Westerner in Moscow might discover the popular scam of bribing an Aeroflot official into selling a ruble-priced ticket; a few hundred dollars or a fistful of cheaply purchased rubles passed under the counter worked wonders.

Roman claimed to have high-level connections at Aeroflot. He told MBC's clients it would be no problem for him to arrange ruble-based round-trip passage to any point on the airline's international and domestic network, as long as MBC was paid between fifty and five hundred dollars for the service. There were a lot of takers at first, until word spread that MBC's "international travel bureau," as Roman called it, had a tendency either to ground its clients or send them off in the wrong direction. One of MBC's Kennedy Airport-bound passengers, a young American businesswoman who had paid Roman for her ticket eight weeks in advance, arrived at Patriarch's Ponds after Roman had failed to pick her up on the morning of the scheduled departure. Roman, who was in bed interviewing a secretary, had absolutely no recollection of the reservation. Grabbing two large bundles of hundred-ruble notes and hijacking Bausman's Volvo for the airport dash, Roman blasted off for Sheremetyevo Two with less than ninety minutes to spare before his client's flight was scheduled to take off.

"Roman insisted the ticket was waiting at Sheremetyevo," the perplexed passenger recalled, "but when we arrived he tried to bribe—right out in the open, mind you—a woman in an Aeroflot outfit who turned out to be a flight attendant who had just arrived from Bucharest. Roman kept telling me 'no problem, no problem' and started to wave his rubles like a Kabuki dancer in front of *anyone* who vaguely looked to be from Aeroflot. Needless to say I never made it to New York or got my four hundred dollars back, but I was thankful, because, as it turned out, Roman did have some successes. One man he sent to London ended up on a flight to Newfoundland. This man had fallen asleep on the flight out of Sheremetyevo, and woke up as the plane was leaving Gander for Havana."

"We had problems," Roman explained with a sly laugh. "This is Moscow. What can I tell you? This is why I'm going to leave. Right now I have an offer from a Catholic university in Vermont. It has a very serious curriculum on business for kids aged eighteen and nineteen, fresh from high school, who are offered a short course of orientation in the business environment plus a number of more detailed programs covering finance. These young students would like to start business relations with the Soviet Union and are interested in talking to a Soviet businessman like myself."

"Don't underestimate Roman," Bausman warned upon first hearing of Roman's new career as a university lecturer. "He may look like a slob, but under that gross and unattractive exterior there is the future of the Soviet Union. Everything here is Roman. He is the new biological creature that took seventy years of Soviet history to produce."

If Gorbachev's goal of achieving a Western-style mixed economy was to be successful, it would require a unified and Herculean effort on the part of honest cooperators, who would replace ambitious *perestroika*-Party functionaries as the vanguard of the free-market movement. There was a catch, however. Although Gorbachev was reluctantly burying the muddled, utopian economics of Marxism-Leninism, the jobbery of communism as a civil process of government was perpetual. "To create a real market, deep changes will be needed in the structure of our psychology," explained deputy Soviet Prime Minister Leonid Abalkin in a none-too-subtle reference to the undertow of Yaks and Romans exerted by the old system. "All this will require at least ten years, perhaps an entire generation."

Exploitation was both the irresistible force and the immovable object in the Soviet Union and remained so during *perestroika* because individual survival depended upon harnessing the energy of the dynamic. Ersatz free-market power, which was primarily evident in the democratic political strongholds of Moscow and Leningrad, flourished not because the cooperators had changed the game, but because they had learned how to use *perestroika* to tap the inertia of the old system's devious tricks and complex lies, half-truths, and betrayals; the few young democratic politicians and cooperators who had been successful in wresting power from provincial Communist Party officials were discovering just how defenseless the free-market system was against the country's overall economic and political rot.*

"Moscow business has changed," described Ivan Russov, the

---

*In autumn 1990, many of the disaffected democrats united into the largest political bloc opposing the Communist Party. Calling themselves the Democratic Russian Movement, the group joined up the Soviet Union's new-age democrats with labor unions, scholars with peasants, and Red Army officers with disabled veterans. The group united around a broad platform that called for Russian sovereignty and the immediate resignation of Gorbachev, the Politburo, and other Kremlin leaders. The chances of the DRM becoming a unified political force were slim because each member had sharply divergent views on what to do after Gorbachev's government *ushol po sostoyaniya zdorova* (retired for reasons of health). Gorbachev pulled a political trick out of his hat during this time that Soviet liberals said symbolized both democratic decline and the growing power of the conservative cliques. The Soviet parliament passed a bill that gave Gorbachev the right to dismiss "heads of state enterprises and social organizations" and employees down to the last worker if they failed to comply with central legislation. It also gave him the power to "limit the powers" of local councils and their executive and administrative bodies for the same reason. These so-called vertical structuring actions were in direct contradiction to the promises Gorbachev had made to local authorities earlier in the year at the Twenty-eighth Communist Party Congress. In practice, vertical structuring would mean if any republic proceeded with plans for an independent bank and the removal of industry from Kremlin control, the directors, managers, and all their staff would be threatened with unemployment. Even more important to the freemarketeers were provisions in the bill that sapped the power of the pro free-market councils in Moscow, Leningrad, and other cities.

former chairman of the board of Raznoimport, one of the richest of the Soviet Union's sixty-two state-owned corporations to be decentralized and reorganized by *perestroika*. He appeared to have grown shorter over the years, his mustachioed, gray-featured countenance less relaxed than when we first met in 1984. Russov was the original Comrade in the Gray Flannel Suit; and, before Gorbachev, the sixty-five-year-old broker of Russia's natural resources had been a bureaucratic kingmaker and his company an "official sponsor" of the ill-fated 1980 Summer Olympiad in Moscow. Razno had made big money selling strategic metals during the years of stagnation between Brezhnev and Gorbachev. Golden years that had given the Georgian businessman time for golf outings to the West and an American Express card with which to pay green fees. Then, as Russov referred to those years, Soviet debt was serviced on time, Western bills were paid within sixty days, and Russov had socked away enough hard currency under his own name in the West that Soviet authorities arrested and subsequently released him on charges of corruption during Gorbachev's heralded 1987 ministerial cleanup. Over two years later, tightening his fingers around the grip of his putter, cocking his head to better study the lie, and then stroking a golf ball gently across the floor of his corner office, Russov whispered: "I still practice my putting as much as I can, but I don't get to play as much as I like to. Things are different here now.

"Today there is confusion," he added. Russov had left government service under a provocative cloud to become a freelance consultant to Western trading firms. "Each new generation wants more and more. Business used to be conducted under a family setting. Now all these new young businessmen are different when dealing with the West. My generation never outright lied to our Western partners."

Russov had been one of Moscow's precious touchstones for Americans waiting to do business in the Soviet Union. Until *perestroika*, Americans with no track record of doing business in the Soviet Union had to be invited there by the Russian corporation he wished to deal with. Once the invitation was secured, often with the assistance of the U.S.–U.S.S.R. Trade and Economic

Council, the American businessman's road to Moscow was through London and British Airways' Sunday-morning 711 flight. Seven-eleven was the dice roll into the Soviet market, and the American businessmen who chanced the trip seldom stayed more than one week, usually at the International, a bunkered, Hyatt Regency–like structure built with the pomp and circumstance of Armand Hammer and the convenience of a health club and two floors of hard-currency French perfumeries, Russian furriers, Japanese electronic stores, Austrian delicatessens, British pubs, Hollywood cinemas, Italian ice cream parlors, and Japanese, Russian, and German restaurants. Armed guards and foulmouthed doormen double-checked the documents of everyone who entered the International, making sure that average Russians could never get inside to see what they were missing.

It was within the International's cocoon that visiting American executives operated and from which they seldom strayed; their only contact with the system was through men such as Russov, chauffeured black Volga saloons and larger Chaika limousines ferrying the executives to and from meetings. Copying machines were frowned upon by the authorities, and police regularly visited Western offices to check a machine's copy counter to see if the number matched that kept in the office ledger. Formal meetings with Russian executives did not resemble the American way of doing business. There was no business lunch and American executives were rarely invited to a Soviet businessman's home. Virtually all of Russia's corporations were housed in the two wings of the Ministry of Foreign Affairs in Smolenskaya Square, one of six buildings constructed by Stalin that resemble multitiered wedding cakes. The American executive entered a huge marble and granite reception area, where two armed military policemen urged him to take a seat on one of the ripped blue vinyl chairs and wait to be collected by a factotum from the appropriate corporation. Nobody called the individual the executive was scheduled to meet to say that he had arrived. If the executive requested that such a call be made, he was most likely informed that the phone was out of order. Schedules meant nothing to the Russians, and executives were often left waiting for hours. Finally a woman would appear and usher the executive up to an office where tea, coffee, and cookies were always served. Invariably, a man who was never identified sat quietly in the corner taking notes.

"It was essential to bring gifts," explained Intertech Resources director W. Douglass Lee, Jr., a frequent visitor to Smolenskaya Square during the 1970s and 1980s. "Calendars with naked women were very much in demand. So was scotch whiskey. We always brought them scotch. Christ, I sometimes thought you could have bought half of Moscow for a case of scotch.

"They were happy to deal," Lee added, "and they always paid on time. They were extremely loyal to their customers. Once you did a successful deal with a Russian, he would do everything possible to continue doing business with you. They were tough negotiators. You needed an iron lung to smoke as many cigarettes as they did and an iron stomach to keep up with their drinking, but the hustle factor was not as intense as it is under Gorbachev and they never expected anything more from you than what you could pick up at the duty-free store at Heathrow Airport. If you were signing a deal worth a few hundred million, then maybe a stereo or an air conditioner. That was the way the Russian did business until Gorbachev. The bottom line was that Russov actually knew what was going on and Razno paid. Gorbachev's crowd doesn't seem to have a clue about what's going on and their hard-currency reserves are so low that they never pay on time."

Yakovlev knew that *perestroika*, for all its ballyhoo in the West, blundered in providing American businessmen such as Lee with the necessary information that was once supplied by men like Russov. Soviet ministries, roiling in a reorganization that could take decades, were losing clients and capital for reasons as senseless as failing to publish their new telephone and Telex numbers. Moreover, business visas were extremely difficult to secure because those Russians who had authorized them in the past had vanished into the bureaucracy with the coming of *perestroika*. Arriving in Moscow with easily obtainable tourist visas, American buyers and sellers called on Smolenskaya to discover doors locked, offices changed, and police guards shaking their heads when asked if they knew where everyone had gone. "There was a virtual stampede on our office for such information," explained Michael Mears, the U.S. Commerce Department chief in Moscow. "Our staff would phone around and ask the Russians questions, but nobody ever knew anything. Representatives of companies that had done business in the Soviet Union for years faced, for the most part, the same problems of first-time entrepreneurs fresh off the plane. The best unofficial advice we could give them was to go home."

"Things are worse despite the gains," complained Vladimir Karyagan, the director of a Minsk hotel and construction cooperative, describing the results of the industrial and commercial breakdown caused by *perestroika*. "The state stores are empty, the black market is too expensive, and democracy isn't repairing the problem," said Karyagan with a pained smile that reflected the smoldering national sentiment toward the total economic collapse of the Soviet Union. It was a catastrophe, said Gorbachev, based on the "clear reason that we have lost control over the financial situation in the country."

The cooperators had hoped to repair the damage, but too many of them, like the Bolshevik revolutionaries of 1917, argued that their ends (complicity with the bureaucrats who controlled the political and technical apparatus necessary to revitalize the economy) justified their means (the creation of a free-market democracy void of the Apparat). Yakovlev's rationale was quite simple: "Fact deals with the bureaucracy or Fact doesn't exist. The Soviet Union deals with the bureaucracy or the Soviet Union doesn't exist. The only other possible option would be civil war." Another serious problem affecting the cooperative mind-set was the types of Russian the movement attracted. The fear and desperation on the streets had fostered a growing class of young Russians motivated by nothing more than a desire to amass as much money and as many American contacts as possible. Yak had started Fact to give young Soviets an opportunity to recover something of themselves, going so far as to hire a staff psychologist to help his workers make the difficult transition from idleness to activity. Yet no amount of counseling could change Soviet reality. "Many of my friends work with Yakovlev and none of them are crazy about the place," explained Olga Kapetonova, a twenty-five-year-old graduate student who turned down positions at Fact and MBC that would have made unique use of her English-language skills. "It's better than being a waitress in a cooperative restaurant, and you have a chance to meet foreigners. Yakovlev thinks he knows everything, but he is no different from the bureaucrats he fights," the Soviet diplomat's daughter added. "My friends who are there stay only because Fact is a good environment to find a way out of the country. But I cannot work at Fact. I don't have the strength to put on a stately democratic front for him like many of the others do. It's a very difficult thing to be noble and to struggle for food and a way out of the Soviet Union at the same time. I will leave the Soviet Union, but I will leave honestly.

"Honesty is the great lie of the cooperative movement," said Kapetonova, who traces her bloodlines back to a family of St. Petersburg nobles and priests. "They are morally dishonest in everything they do, just like the communists."

The cooperators who felt a suffocating pressure because of limits placed on registering and licensing their ventures were those who refused to play the game, those who did not have the *blat* to play the game, or a combination of both. According to People's Deputy Vladimir Tikhonov, the rebel economics academician and founding father of the cooperative movement through his articles and tutorials, Soviet freemarketeers were destined to face a dishonest system of "bans" instead of an honest system of "permissions" for decades. "We haven't developed the concept of a transfer to a market economy," said Tikhonov, who earned his radical spurs with Boris Yeltsin at the politically liberal Sverdlovsk School of Science in the Ural Mountains, a haven for disaffected Party members who wanted to chart a new course for the country. "The word *market* scares off the people who work in the state Apparat. It scares them in part for ideological reasons, but only insofar as it would destroy the ministries' monopoly on production and all the benefits that go along with it. The state monopolists will continue to use all the powers at their disposal, including the creation of new cooperatives and corruption of existing cooperatives, to prevent anyone else from getting to an outside market before they do."

Yakovlev used graft to keep the state from infringing on his market and to keep Fact operational; codes of morality and democratic principles were unimportant because the cooperative's survival was at stake. Truckloads of wine went to the bureaucrats in charge of dispensing the newsprint necessary for Fact's weekly information bulletins; briefcases of women's hosiery went to Bela Petravitus, the Council of Ministers' chief bureaucrat in charge of overseeing cooperative laws and taxes; a co-op known as "A Bunch of Guys Who Do Things" was underwritten to pilfer Western construction supplies from embassy sites around Moscow; state-owned publications and radio stations were given cash incentives and Western computer software to broadcast flattering stories on Fact; local Soviet bureaucrats were bribed to provide apartments; state telephone officials were given thousands of rubles to install direct phone lines to the West; and some of Fact's men traded jobs for sex with prospective female employees. There was nothing out of the ordinary in this, and that was the problem that many ordinary Soviets saw in the cooperative movement. The cooperators were supposed to be the springboard to changing the system. One of the methods available to them was to financially support political candidates running for district, republic, and national office. On the surface these candidates were to reflect the public's desire for the honest, free-market system the cooperative movement claimed to represent. But nothing works in the Soviet Union unless it is somehow rigged, even an election.

The slate of candidates vying for seats on the local Krasnopresnensky Soviet that administered the Good Highway district was long, impressive, and included the name of Alexei Novogelov, a quick and clear-eyed member of the Fact board of directors. Novogelov, a husky man in his mid-twenties with a thick crop of blond hair and a muscular stride, was Fact's in-house fixer and a virtual one-man shopping mall. Rugs? Stove? Apartment? Automobile? Soviet Navy admiral's uniform? A toilet seat? It did not matter what it was, because Novogelov knew where it was. Fast. Novogelov delivered—an exemplary talent, said Yak, for a local Soviet councilman to have at his disposal. Young men and women of Novogelov's resourcefulness were particularly needed within

Moscow's reforming administration, which continued accusing members of the old administration and the state Apparat of frustrating their reform efforts and deliberately engineering shortages of food and consumer goods. "Cooperators can help in this task," said Yak. Yet it was never very clear how Novogelov won his Fact-financed race against the other candidates. By his own admission he never campaigned. No posters went up. No leaflets were handed out to voters and he never showed up at the debates. When asked, Novogelov said that he did not even know whom he was running against nor the duties of an elected official. "I have no idea what's going on," Novogelov said, running out the door to score a case of Brazilian instant coffee for Fact's kitchen on the morning after his victory.

"The local council dispenses apartments and we needed someone on it," Yak said wryly. "Our campaign logic was our requirement for more office space."

This was cooperative reality, and not all cooperators were pleased with the circumstance. Vladimir Tikhonov, the father of the cooperative movement, was vocally opposed to accepting material advantages for himself. But while he defended the rights of cooperators to become millionaires, Tikhonov also understood that the underlying corruption that supported the system bred dissent, confusion, and an ill-will that pitted cooperator against cooperator. He was nervous about the public's growing irritation over cooperative prices and tactics, frustrated as everyone was by the unwillingness of civil authorities to curtail the bombings, killings, and extortions conducted against the country's new capitalists. Western capitalism was never a perfect embroidery, but it had become possible to get eggs, butter, or airline tickets without first unfolding some magnificent con. The cooperators, like the Soviet Union itself, needed new reputations from which to weave democratic cloth. Politically, the nation needed Lincolns, Churchills, and Bolívars. Economically, it needed Morgans, DuPonts, and Paleys. What it got was more Volodya Yakovlevs.

Yakovlev did not want to know that each of his duplicitous acts bred further public suspicion as to his motives. Honest cooperators—there were few—were reluctant to condemn or criticize Yakovlev too openly for fear of an outcry against them that might disrupt the little public support that existed, and on which they depended. The companies of special state security police, rumored to be trained and backed by the KGB and right-wing military cells to harass cooperators, were believed to have been placed on various cooperative payrolls to afford protection. Although I had never physically viewed the racket in operation, the willingness of cooperators to fuel such stories only added to my own growing suspicions that Fact was becoming part of the state bureaucracy it had vowed to supplant. Many Russians believed the cooperatives were another creation of the KGB that the state had turned to their private purpose. I placed little faith in this theory, but at the same time I remembered Sabina's warning that all wild rumors in the Soviet Union contained kernels of illuminating truth. Clearly, however, there was no way for any cooperator to cleanse the corrupt old system internally without being tainted by its filth. I did not dare to approach this issue too directly with Yakovlev at first because of his courage to buck the system and, later, because of the near hysterical anger he used to tell me that, as an American, I would never understand how the Soviet system operated.

What I did understand all too well was that the foundation Yakovlev had helped lay for the cooperative movement was beginning to decompose like cement mixed with too much water and not enough sand. The proclamations of unity with which the co-operators had launched the free-market movement in 1987 had turned into cries of spiteful discord by 1989. There was an adversarial quality to it all, and on conventions to restrain the growing junior-varsity mafioso tendencies of many cooperators. The movement needed to be relaunched, amid great fanfare and triumphant fellowship orchestrated to garner the support of the public and the government. So, in the greatest tradition the Soviet Union had to offer its revolutionaries, the cooperators of the U.S.S.R. rented Moscow's most acclaimed and distinguished building for nine thousand rubles and held a congress in the very rotunda where Lenin spoke. There was history in the Hall of Columns: the corpses of Stalin and Brezhnev had reclined there on public display, and there Khrushchev tried and convicted U-2 pilot Francis Gary Powers of capitalist espionage.

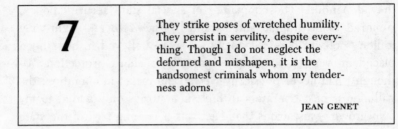

7

They strike poses of wretched humility.
They persist in servility, despite everything. Though I do not neglect the
deformed and misshapen, it is the
handsomest criminals whom my tender-
ness adorns.

JEAN GENET

SABINA ORUDJEVA hated Volodya Yakovlev: she hated
his style. She hated his lies. She hated his voice. She hated the
way in which his eyes slanted into an Asiatic leer whenever he
started cooking up a new deal. And when you asked Sabina Orudjeva why she hated Volodya Yakovlev so much, she said that he
did no good, adding that she, like Volodya Yakovlev, was a Pisces
and knew the difference between a good fish and a bad fish. Sabina
was like that, always describing people and events in animal terms.
Which was why she hesitated to attend the first Congress of the
Associations of Cooperatives of the Union of Soviet Socialist Republics. "It is going to be a hall full of bad fish and Yakovlev will
be there to rob everyone. Let us buy one of those spear guns for
protection."

As it turned out, the long-awaited cooperative congress that
took place under the crystal chandeliers in Moscow's Hall of Columns on June 30 and July 1, 1989, did include a speech that
denounced Yakovlev as a thief, forcing Yak to defend Fact's sale
of reprints of free government information for one hundred five
rubles each on the grounds that he was the "first Soviet student
of the Harvard University School of Business" and "understood

132

that market price was derived from demand and the expense of production."

"*One hundred and five rubles!*" Yuri Shchblenko shouted on the opening day of the congress, hundreds of heads turning to observe the confrontation taking place on the former dining and dance hall floor of the two-hundred-year-old, ex-aristocratic club. "*One hundred and five rubles!*"

"We pay a high price for paper and these very editions of which you complain are in a deficit," Yak retorted with loud, cynical amusement through a microphone on the other side of the stark white hall. The delegates laughed; they had just elected Yakovlev their Director for Informatics—the chief PR man for the Union of Joint Cooperatives of the U.S.S.R.

"One hundred and five rubles!" the Moldavian builder shot back, waving a pamphlet on Soviet cooperative law through the air. "I paid one hundred and five rubles at your booth downstairs for this. One hundred and five rubles."

"Turn the book over," Yak said, a humble smile on his face. "You will see the cost is printed. Only five rubles and fifty kopecks. That's the *official* price."

There was a brawny peasant woman mixing concrete out in front of the Hall of Columns on Pushkinskaya, and most of the wet cement picked up on the shoes of the two thousand cooperative delegates attending the congress could be found deposited in front of the sales booth Yak had set up at the foot of the stairway that led up to the main conference hall. Most of the delegates did not pay any attention to the price and, if they did, Shchblenko was the only one to complain publicly.* The delegates swarmed the booth

---

*It was never clear how much Fact actually charged for its publications, which included Fact-produced directories of cooperative restaurants and automobile garages, as well as numerous reprints of government-produced rules and regulations for cooperative law, banking, and taxation. Many of the cash transactions that took place at the booth appeared to be based on what the buyer could afford to pay. Sabina and I observed customers' paying a variety of amounts higher than the one listed on the cover. Some booklets had been printed without prices and many customers bought dozens of the same booklet. What was certain, and ironic, were the high prices being charged by the cooperator-delegates who resold their hoarded booklets after Fact exhausted its supply. In one such instance, a Georgian

like cripples at Lourdes; the miracle of accurate information in the Soviet Union had been always expensive in one way or another. Fact had helped organize the affair with Boris Yelagin, director of the Moscow Region of Cooperatives; Andrei Demetev, director of the Russian Republic Association of Cooperatives, and Andrei Federov, chairman of the Moscow City Organization of Cooperatives. Along with Yak, these were Sabina's "big dogs" of the cooperative movement. But Yak, as Sabina expected, wanted to take no part in the public glory of directing the congress from the stage.

Yak's place was downstairs, brashly selling information at the Fact booth or striding the hall as a capitalist prince with a bagful of tapes to make sure his Western recorders captured every word for transcription and sale by direct mail. Although Yak never spent a day at the Harvard School of Business, he knew what its textbooks said without ever having laid eyes on them; besides, what he was doing in the Soviet Union would fill the Harvard Coop with more management studies than its shelves could hold. Professor Marshall Goldman, Harvard's senior Sovietologist, had graciously invited Yak to attend a three-week course at the business school when he first visited the campus before flying off to hustle computers from Lorrie Grimes in Seattle. Yak eagerly agreed to return; but he never showed up or even called. There was no need to go again to Harvard: the Soviet heavyweights at America's universities were already suitably impressed with what Sabina called Yak's "craftiness amid the disorder" to send clients to his door. And the chaos of muddle and turmoil that afflicted the Soviet Union's assembled freemarketeers was such that the congress would have been just as appropriately overwhelmed had Yak told them that he studied free markets alongside the Doublemint chewing gum twins. "It doesn't frighten me that the state and cooperators are turning us into a third-world country in which to play with their lies and social experiments," Sabina said. "Of course the economic experiments aren't yet killing people in the streets. Talk, talk, talk. People will still stand in line for three days for food that runs out the moment

---

cooperator sold a Moscow cooperator three of Fact's one-hundred-twelve-page restaurant guides, with the cover price of one ruble, eighty-five kopecks each, for one hundred rubles.

they reach the counter. It's always been this way and the cooperators just care about themselves. If they can't have it they steal
it, if they can't steal it they destroy it. It's the only way to survive."

Over sausage and coffee in the Novosti foreign press center a
few days before the Soviet cooperators assembled in Moscow, Vladimir Tikhonov had expressed a hope that the passions of the
gathered freemarketeers might in some way eventually grow into
a vibrant organization to replace the Soviet Union's corrupt trade
unions and kindle a sense of national worth. Sitting in a creaky
chair in the dark and gloomy Novosti bar, the leader of the new
Nepmen and spiritual leader of the Soviet Union's approximately
one million cooperators glimpsed beyond *perestroika*. Ebullient,
alert, and tense about the possibilities to come from the cooperative
congress, Tikhonov wore the crimson pin of a People's Deputy
with the pride of what the words *narodny deputat* might someday
represent. More philosopher than politician, more Russian peasant
than Soviet patrician, the furrows in his face deepened with anger
at the thought of corrupt cooperators being in the majority, as the
state said and too many of the public believed. "They want to
believe this because very few of them actually understand what a
free market is," he explained, nervously twisting another cigarette
into an ashtray already filled with the residue of his anxiousness.

Tikhonov's idea to evolve cooperators into a major political
and economic force to replace the trade union was as sound in
theory as it was impossible in action. But the notion of using the
free market to penetrate the moribund All-Union Central Council
of Trade Unions was a key element in the ultimate success or failure
of Soviet economic reform. The All-Union Central Council of Trade
Unions was the Soviet superunion. Created after the Bolshevik
Revolution to "protect the interests of the working people," the
one-hundred-forty-million member union represented both blue
collar worker and white collar manager.

Stalin had merged the trade unions with the Ministry of Labor
in the 1930s to consolidate his power and turned the union hall
into a social insurance agency for loyal but useless Party members.
Collective bargaining was a farce, and the union's council became
the "depositing ground for failed Party members, who were placed

in the union as a last resort for a job," according to Gennadi Nikolaev, the deputy director of the Higher School of the Trade Union Movement. New members joined for the perks. At the top of the trade union pyramid was the powerful Central Council of Trade Unions, a conservative core-group that used the trade unions as a carnivorous institutional dinosaur to frustrate any form of free enterprise on the pretext that it was protecting the interests of the people.

Perestroika had given the union a second-rate role, but restructuring did not threaten to sap its power to crush free enterprise until a few weeks before the cooperative congress. Tikhanov knew the superunion was doomed from the moment he heard there would be a walkout of twenty thousand union members to start the Independent Association of Socialist Trade Unions.* Modeled on the Polish Solidarity Union, the Russians' *perestroika*-generated trade union was to be eventually run out of business by the state through the application of laws that prohibited their members from running for the Soviet parliament as union candidates. "We were trying to fight against the monopoly of the central council," explained Sergei Mangenel, one of the new union's leaders, "but the government did not allow any of our members to run for parliament because they claimed we did not have any fixed structure."

Although no one could have predicted exactly when or where it would happen, Tikhonov surmised on the eve of the cooperative congress that the combustible mixture of *perestroika* and angry workers would soon explode, forcing the state to rebuild the union along the lines of a Potemkin Village. When the two thousand three hundred delegates of the All-Union Central Council of Trade Unions assembled in October 1990 for their nineteenth congress,

---

*This was the first of many independent trade unions to emerge between 1988 and 1991. Another and more potentially powerful autonomous union was the Independent Trade Union of Miners, created in late 1990 by radical coal miners in the Donetsk, Ukraine, coal region. Throughout *perestroika*, coal miners had been the most unified labor group organizing protests and strikes. Their walkout in 1989 threatened to leave much of the country without fuel. The new union, with a potential membership of over two million miners, gave coal mine workers a new platform from which to enforce their demands of workers' rights, better housing facilities, and readily available supplies of food.

they discovered that it was to be the last—at least under the old name, just as Tikhonov had foreseen sixteen months earlier. In fact, it seemed as if Tikhonov might have written the script for what took place. The "newly elected" leadership of the renamed superunion said that if its members were not given their rights, they would take them, which would bring about a workers' disintegration that would be fatal for the country. This was a Potemkin Village on a truly grand scale because the newly elected leadership was the old leadership, as evidenced by union boss Vladimir Shcherbakov's conviction that the new trade union was going to be different because it had changed its name to the All-Union *Confederation* of Trade Unions, the first national body to use the word and therefore part of the free market. Gorbachev, who was sitting on the stage when all these dramatic changes took place, failed to mention his newly legalized parliamentary right to veto anything that the trade union did or anyone who did it.

Tikhonov wanted the democratic men and women of the first cooperative congress to be fearless and ambitious in going after Gorbachev and his double-faced policies. He hoped the fledgling freemarketeers, once assembled under one unified democratic banner, could be full of emotion without reverting to the old ways. "The newly elected people's deputies will not play a major role in helping the cooperative movement," Tikhonov rationalized. "We must do it ourselves because the most effective way of organizing political and economic democracy is through cooperatives. The question is obvious: do you want democracy or not? Those who want democracy support cooperatives; those who don't support democracy don't support cooperatives. This is the hot point of *perestroika*. Any attempts to strangle the cooperative movement are attempts to strangle *perestroika*."

Brutally handsome, flashing the tattoos of youthful indiscretion on both hands, this academic whose father's arrest had branded him a "son of an enemy of the people" wanted his cooperative children to birth an economic democracy that renounced the state's exclusive right to represent workers, and espoused a willingness to cooperate honestly with any group that represented the interests of the workers. "Once we do this," the sixty-five-year-old Tikhonov said, "the government will come back to the cooperators and tell us that we are not necessary for this because the official trade union has been restructured and is taking care of the workers and the cooperators. We will point to our workers, real workers, and say, 'No, it is not.' " But this was dizzying stuff, too much inside-the-Kremlin hardball for Tikhonov's contentious delegates to counter with any game plan of their own. By the end of their first raucous day, the delegates were having a hard enough time finding a place to eat in Moscow, let alone finding a ticket back home to the provinces tomorrow or getting a telephone call through to find out whether or not the cooperative they represented was still functioning.

The provincial delegates had been sleeping in cars and on floors, packed eight to a crude hotel room and three across atop the tables at the Guriya cooperative restaurant. The cooperators from Moscow and Leningrad, the hard-currency-rich nucleus of the movement, came with drivers and walked the Hall of Columns like the aristocrats whose ghosts haunted the perfectly preserved landmark. The tension between the dozens of various social classes and hundreds of ethnic groups represented in their ranks was thicker than the slabs of brown bread they stacked with kolbasa for lunch in the hall's mirrored dining room. Mingling up and down the hall's smoke-filled marble corridors were smaller groups of cooperators, and to a man their discussions centered on how to beat the system that Tikhonov had wanted them to change. If any unified theme emerged from these private conclaves it was that the Soviet economy was a problem so gnarled and tortuous that it could never be solved, only taken advantage of. Crooked cooperators had avoided Tikhonov's detection with what had seemed like ease: the man did not want to consider that cooperators were swindlers, builders of businesses on the narrow defiles of the old system. Trust was a matter of sincere revolutionary conviction, and Tikhonov presumed that cooperators, above all else, were revolutionaries who honestly risked their lives to bring, as he described it, "utility to the ruble and function to the economy." Tikhonov hated crime of any sort and, Sabina believed, the cooperative congress had elected him as its president for that very reason. "There is nothing in his past that anyone can hang him on," Sabina observed, not knowing that Tikhonov had committed one crime in his life. "I was sixteen years old, too young to fight in the Great Patriotic War," he said. "So I altered the six to an eight on my papers and joined the army." Individually, the cooperators trusted him, but it was the congress who would decide if the time was right to invest their collective faith and muscle in passing a resolution that would pledge cooperators to wiping out the corruption that gave the economy no hope and the ruble no cause.

The cooperative sector never had any confidence in the ruble because it was unable to provide the purchasing power necessary to supply the Western technology that made the difference between a cottage entrepreneur and an entrepreneurial economy. There was only so much a cooperative could do with its rubles. The co-op restaurant that wanted to buy a modern stove on which to cook its ruble-purchased food or the co-op clothing manufacturer who needed a new sewing machine on which to sew ruble-bought material invariably crashed into the hard-currency wall once it tried to expand. "If I had a new stove I could serve more customers," explained Madame Zoya, the owner of the Guriya Georgian restaurant, rapping her index finger on a magazine photograph of a twelve-burner American stove. "The state doesn't sell this stove, they will not allow me to exchange rubles to buy this stove from America, and I am forced to think up other ways to get it."

The commercial ruble rate, based on a Byzantine system of over two thousand coefficients, was dispensed only to state enterprises that did business with the West; a cooperator (or any Soviet traveler) with negotiations in the West was permitted to leave the country with less than two hundred dollars in his wallet. The reluctance of the Soviet Gosbank and Foreign Trade Bank to extend hard currency to cooperators induced the freemarketeers to go to the black market or to bribe their way into the good graces of Soviet bankers. Many of the foreign companies, unaware of the depth of the hard-currency disarray, rushed into *perestroika* only to discover that their Soviet partner could contribute nothing but rubles. It was the Western partner who supplied the capital, along with a great deal of effort.

"Dealing with the Russians was more than improvisation," explained Nabih Baaklini, a senior executive at Combustion Engineering, who had dealt with both the state and the cooperative sector in setting up his firm's joint venture with the Ministry of Petroleum. "Financial analysis, project accounting . . . you name it, they don't have it. Imagine the difficulty in trying to run a business without having your hands on the costs or an exchange rate."

Juggling absurdity was a daily event.* Signing a joint-venture contract legally required the foreign partner to set its finances at the official exchange rate of around one dollar sixty-five cents for one ruble, said Baaklini. The artificially inflated rate usually ended up costing the American side extra millions to purchase or invest in equipment or real estate that might be worth less than half the dollar price under normal circumstances. "Say the Soviets came up with a building priced at one million rubles that we feel isn't worth one six five million," explained Baaklini, describing the bargaining tactic that created over two thousand different dollar/ruble exchange coefficients. "First we evaluate the property in dollars, mentally converting that to rubles at whatever the new official rate is. Then we negotiate the ruble price, not the exchange rate, down to what we decided the property was worth. This was the greatest challenge of the joint venture. We make the estimates of their costs and get them to agree to that figure."

Despite the problems, the cooperators demanded a piece of

---

*The officially prescribed method of dealing with Western firms was (and remains) in a constant state of perplexing uncertainty and flux. Although Gorbachev entered 1991 decreeing that foreign businessmen could establish wholly owned subsidiaries on Soviet soil, with the right to take out long-term leases on property and land, no Western businessman in the Soviet Union was ready to bet that the free marketplace had replaced central planning, or that *perestroika* had replaced proscription. The future of an operational Soviet free-market economy was a riddle of gigantic proportions. "The Soviet Union is the only world power other than China that doesn't trade its own currency," explained John Minneman, Chase Manhattan Bank's Soviet and East European expert. "Therefore, both its short- and long-term economic growth are tied to the availability of foreign capital. The enigma is how they'll bring value to the ruble by backing it up with the goods and services that for the most part can be developed only with foreign capital they don't have."

the legitimate hard-currency, joint-venture action because, as Tik-honov said, "American businessmen are getting tired of spending their money on nothing. I want the cooperative movement to emerge strong from the congress. I want us to be able to show American businessmen that they should avoid doing business with the state apparatus. I really don't see anything positive in the future for a market economy unless the Western firms stop doing business with the corrupt state ministries and begin doing business with the cooperators. We are the true free-market sector."

"We are the free-market sector, but I don't believe the co-operators will last long," said Vasya Chichivadze, a thirty-four-year-old Georgian cooperator at the end of the congress's first day of meetings. Chichivadze, whose hardware co-op, Tsarkov, aptly took its name from a kindly bull in a Georgian fairy tale, echoed the fears and suspicions on the minds of every cooperator at the Moscow conference. "The cooperatives are a fairy tale because all of us keep our state jobs to fall back on if the movement fails. We use the connections, of course, but all of us are hungry dogs on chains. The state knows this and will not let us go because we will bite them. This congress is full of infiltrators. These people were told to come here posing as cooperators and Tikhanov doesn't un-derstand. We cannot get rid of these fake cooperators easily because they are now part of the movement, and too many real cooperators are in business just to steal money from the Americans. Tikhanov is a great man and he speaks of important things, but he is a man of the academy and removed from reality. Maybe our only hope is that we will get hungrier the longer the Politburo keeps us chained. Then the more savagely we will bite them when released. These are not the words of the academicians, I fear."

Tikhonov was an academic, a rare and honest member of a Russian intelligentsia that had long ago lost its ability to overcome the corruption of life in the Soviet Union. The Party had cheapened the scholarly rank of academic. It was a title and, like everything else of value in the Soviet Union, a product that was bought and sold at prices set by the Politburo. There were not many left like Tikhonov. He earned degrees in both history and economics at the same time, and not by filing enthusiastic studies on the victories of rural and city communists in their struggle to create Marxism. Tikhonov was the most feared kind of felon in the Soviet Union: he stole the truth from those who would hide it. "The only way the Party can convict criminals like Tikhonov," explained Trusishka, the senior official who worked for the Communist Party Central Committee, "is to hope the people will not listen to him."

A political convention in the Soviet Union has its own laws of action and reaction. Like American conventions, boasting comes with the territory. Praise is hurled, insults are thrown, and everything is puerile and prepackaged. But it was not until *perestroika* that rebuttals entered the fashion. Since there was only one party, the only praise had gone to those who were fulfilling the plan, the only insults to those who were getting in the way of the plan. Party pols in trouble with the Politburo or Central Committee knew it before they even entered the hall, and the chance of rebutting charges in public were slim. Gorbachev changed all that, which shocked the Soviet public and politicians. It was as though an annual corporate dinner dance had decided one year to switch from Mantovani to 2 Live Crew.

Questions to the chairman of a convention or a candidate running in a Party-rigged local election before Gorbachev were always written down for review and selection by Party officials. Speeches—heavy, canned, and boring—were manifestos long on ideology and short on ideas. Smiles were doled out sparingly and selectively. Applause was passionless. Traditions emerged from the Soviet political liturgy, however. The torpidity of conventions, campaign gatherings, and voting booths was such that the state provided well-stocked and inexpensively priced buffet tables of consumer delicacies with which to lure people. To this day, no Soviet political meeting or polling station is complete without a selection of sausage, orange juice, Pepsi, red and black caviar, Western cigarettes, beer, pastries, Vietnamese pineapple, and— in one Moscow district off the Arbat during the 1989 national parliamentary elections—home power tools. But just as the Russians had come to the new democratic political process expecting a supermarket shelf, they also came anticipating the procedural rules to be the same. The sight of Boris Yeltsin storming out of the Twenty-eighth Communist Party Conference, the sound of radical-democratic parliamentarians interrupting Gorbachev in the Supreme Soviet, and the insolence of a "comrade" shouting and not writing a criticism to an official were lewd breaches of the norms of Russian etiquette. The majority of delegates simply did not know how to respond. The blustery arguments that always followed these passionate eruptions helped undercut the popularity and functioning of grass-roots, participatory democracy as an alternative to the old system. These farcical melodramas were the biggest and bitterest ironies of Soviet democracy, the humor overshadowed by the reluctance of the characters ever to fully believe that democracy was real.

Frightened and disoriented, Soviet cooperators had come to Moscow thinking the first free-market congress would be the beginning of the cessation to the problems they faced from the state and the public. To this end the congress elected Vladimir Tikhonov as its president, gave him a Mercedes-Benz 500, and agreed to his call for a minute of silence for cooperators who had been killed by the "mafias, rackets, and the earthquake in Armenia." Tikhonov's election took only a few minutes, leaving the remainder of the two-day congress to be filled with shame, exasperation, confused multiple agendas, and the animosity and bewilderment of people who had never before been allowed to speak.

"*Perestroika* is only at half power!" thumped Korobken of the Moscow Cooperative Institute, during the close of the congress's final day. "The people are refused when asked to buy a plane ticket under the pretext that they speculate on the ticket. You cooperators know who you are! Uncivilized cooperators should not take advantage of this situation to make a lot of money off an empty market."

"Be quiet, comrade! The tax rates are too high!" snapped Ulumbekov of Uzbekistan. "The government does this on purpose to make us charge more money and anger consumers into violent confrontations. You Moscow and Leningrad cooperators think you are smart. You pay only in cash. Ahh, comrades, this engenders suspicions from both sides."

"Gorbachev and his ministers don't follow their own tax laws, comrades, so why should we? I say *zabastovka!* ["strike"] "Pay no taxes at all," retorted Shanel of Odessa to the clap of wild applause. "I say this congress march to Gorbachev and ask him to explain in public why the Council of Ministers is violating the cooperative charters and laws adopted by both them and the Supreme Soviet. *Zabastovka! Zabastovka! Zabastovka!*"

"Comrades, comrades, calm yourselves. I'm Comrade Glushenko. I'm also Father Nikodim and I bless this congress for all their good intentions. Let the Princess of Heaven help you with her name and spiritual support. But I'm not only a comrade and a priest of the Church. I'm the chairman of the Siberian Bee Honey Association, and *perestroika* doesn't work because the government is trying to build a new structure on an old foundation. This cannot be done with beehives and it cannot be done with governments."

"The first thing we need to do is teach each other democracy," interjected Zelanov of Komi . . . "Yes, yes," Tikhonov interrupted to more thunderous applause, "but the tax laws are still *graboi*." ("Ripoff" is the nearest English expression.)

"Yes!" says Chichivadze of Georgia. "Since we are a socialist country, the government doesn't want to see us rich. This is why they want to tax cooperators instead of providing us with incentives. Those cooperators who are accustomed to stealing from the state and the people don't want us to be unified. I'm not optimistic about our future and I'm not here for political reasons. I believe most real cooperators feel this way. We are here for business and our business is turning into a war."

"These are raw speeches," a woman retorts. "Let's hear from the Estonian delegation. Estonia is going to leave the Soviet Union, comrades. They have ideas."

"We appeal to you to ignore the new tax laws and adopt tax laws on a republic level," an Estonian delegate says, hollow and automatic. "We cooperators of Estonia are Estonians first and don't want to be involved in the other republics' struggle for new taxation laws or any other laws. We are independent . . ."

"You Estonians have milk, though," jabs a delegate from the Ukraine, too fast for the chair even to ask his name. "Comrades, in the Ukraine we have milk in only one region. I tried to find out why and discovered a cooperative of invalids who made fur hats and decided to give a fur coat to the best milk lady in the region. This is why we have milk."

"That's nothing, comrade," counters another Ukrainian co-operator, snatching up his countryman's microphone. "Comrades, I've been to New York City and find all the city's souvenirs are made in Hong Kong. I ask you, comrades, why don't we Soviets make New York souvenirs in our country and sell them in America for millions? I will tell you . . ."

"I have heard enough," declares the deep and calm voice of a man, rising from his chair to find a microphone.

". . . Ukrainians who want to make souvenirs for New York don't have the access to idle production facilities controlled by the government. This is why the Ukraine can't make souvenirs for New York tourists."

"I again want to bring up the question why Vladimir Yego-revich is reprinting editions of government decrees and charging so much money for them," cries Shchblenko . . . "Your question is now too emotional," snaps Yakovlev . . . "Comrades, comrades, comrades, please don't behave as badly as the Congress of the Communist Party and the first Congress of People's Deputies," says Tikhonov, tired and discouraged. "There was too much yelling and screaming and physical crying and we all disliked it very much and cooperators should not behave the same way as . . ." "I'm Comrade Glushenko, also known as Father Nikodim . . ."

"I have heard enough!" the deep voice roared over the public address system.

". . . the Princess of Heaven says . . ."

". . . comrades, we should not behave like . . ."

I said that I have heard enough," rumbled the deep peasant's voice again, the jabberwocky deafened by the new speaker pounding the microphone into his heavily callused hand.

"What has happened in this hall over the past two days is typical of a whorehouse," the man continued slowly, coolly, pausing only to sweep the room with distinguished dark eyes and a menacing snarl of gold teeth.

"Most of the delegates have left because of the stupidity of this gathering and its unrealistic discussions of issues that cost people their lives," the man continued, bowing his head respectfully at Tikhonov, as if to exclude him from what was to follow. "I am a cooperator and I am ashamed. Am I the only man in this hall who respects himself? Am I the only honest man? You have said nothing for two days, but I have listened. You are whores!"

"Who are you?" asked the chairman, the hall growing quiet, with every bloodshot eye in the place glued to the large man, every clogged ear trying to distinguish his difficult Russian.

"I am Ibragimov Hajibau Isak Oglu," he said, moving a clenched fist toward his burly chest. "I am the King of Zakatala."

8	Wrong decisions for the right reasons. Right decisions for the wrong reasons. They lead inexorably to the same ending. PETER GENT

IBRAGIMOV HAJIBAU ISAK OGLU heard the gunfire first. Involuntarily, his large body began to shudder as if the slug and buckshot were coming off the mountain and into the cab of the Niva 1600 jeep. The buckshot zipped off the rocks outside, dartlike, and Hajibau watched as his sheep fell into the river that dropped down into the Azerbaijani valley. Some fell from the gunfire, others drowned in the clear, rushing water; a dark, ugly shape. The force of the river knocked over two of Hajibau's shepherds, coating their clothing with sheep blood. Hajibau jumped underneath the battered Niva that had taken us the twelve miles up the center of the shallow river from Zakatala. The night was clear with a full moon; the distressed and dusty voices spat out a garbled patois of Russian and Azerbaijani. Hajibau, looking up, realized that the pellets were still coming. The shots were landing perhaps no more than three feet from the jeep, and slowly coming closer, as if the *kolkhozniki** were purposefully aiming at him. A shepherd dived into the Niva to cut the headlight beam.

---

*People who work on a *kolkhoz*—a state-owned and operated collective farm. Private and cooperative farmers are known as *chastniki*.

147

Dead and dying sheep were scattered on the rocks or floating down the river, their heads broken and bleeding. Other sheep, exhausted from being chased twenty miles across the mountains by the *kolkhozniki,* cascaded off a seven-foot cliff, crashing into the water. Some took the fall and remained alive. Others were impaled on sunken rocks. Only the goats made it down in one piece. Makhmakhod Zhakanzher, Cooperative Lazat's chief shepherd, shouted that more of Hajibau's one-hundred-head flock had been stoned to death by *kolkhozniki* who did not want cooperative sheep grazing on state-controlled pastures. Makhmakhod, his thick black hair caked in dry blood from a vertical gash in his forehead, had been hit by the stones, too. "I'm sorry, Hajibau," Makhmakhod repeated over and over, a feeble grip on his own shotgun. "There was nothing we could do. To shoot back would've meant death." Hajibau screamed something to him in Azerbaijani. "He told his shepherd to be strong," Sabina said as she tried to lift one of the wounded animals out of the current and onto a small rock island.

Matvei, another shepherd, appeared, sliding through the Niva's open passenger door, pressing against the side of the jeep for protection. More gunfire came this time. Isolated shots. Shepherds were taking cover behind the carcasses of dead sheep, while others tried to dredge the animals out of the rushing water and onto the rocks. Hajibau crawled from under the jeep on his fat belly to one of the fallen animals, shouting wildly into the moonlight, sheep blood flowing into his hands. Sheep continued to pour down the mountain and into the river, an avalanche of fur. When the level of the dead and injured had risen high enough, the rest of the flock stumbled over them to the safety of one of the river's small rock islands. The gunfire stopped. Hajibau wanted to ferry his sheep out of the water and onto the largest rock island, where they would be safe until dawn, when he would return with a fresh set of official documents allowing the flock to graze on government pastures. But those grasslands were twenty miles away. What was left of the Lazat sheep would be dead before they made it that far.

Matvei, running through thirty yards of knee-deep water from the cliff-fall to the outcrop of rock in the middle of the river, said he heard laughter from the hills. Humiliation, too. It was Matvei who had driven the twelve miles down the river to tell Hajibau of the chase that had started twenty-four hours before. Wounded from the hurled stones, Matvei had stumbled into Hajibau's office at midnight, his eyes glazed with fright, his small and gaunt body exhausted. He was sputtering wildly.

"Twenty men with papers from the Zakatala city council, signed by chairman Asim Samadov. Said it was forbidden for cooperative sheep to be on state land. Told them we had permission. Hajibau has documents. They attack us. We have only four shepherds, two dogs, and one gun. They drove us off, chased us over two mountains. Many animals dead."

"This was not supposed to happen!" Hajibau shrieked, running with Matvei to the Niva, clutching a fistful of cheap onionskin documents that guaranteed Lazat's cooperative sheep and cattle the right to forage on state lands.

Hajibau cursed himself after the gunfire subsided. It was one A.M., July 19, 1989, and, looking at the twenty-seven dead animals, Hajibau began to cry. While he sat sobbing into the night, the specter of Asim Samadov appeared to him—a figure that tormented his life. Hajibau had made up his mind to be a cooperator, and the dead sheep were part of the cost. But now the worst had happened and Samadov would feel retribution. Somehow Hajibau would see to it. "Samadov. *Ahee,*" Hajibau said, spitting out the Azerbaijani word for bear. "Vicious *ahee.* There is no way yet to slaughter them."

I had witnessed only forty-five seconds of what Hajibau and his shepherds were experiencing daily . . . forty-five seconds in *perestroika,* hard time for a cooperative farmer in the Communist-controlled mountains of the Soviet Republic of Azerbaijan, twelve hundred uncompromising miles from the speeches of Moscow. Three weeks after the cooperative congress in Moscow, Sabina and I traveled into the heart of Azerbaijan to visit what Hajibau said was an honest cooperative surrounded by corruption. Less than twenty-four hours after our arrival on Hajibau's mountain, I understood what Cooperative Lazat was up against and what the dream of freedom is made of.

"Even if I cannot resist the state, part of my dream has come true," Hajibau said softly on the drive back down the river to Zakatala, his eyes focused on the horizon. The dawn was up; the mountains became a rolling wall of green shrouded in vapors of blue. "From that mountain," he continued, sticking his hand out the Niva, "to that mountain I am the master. It is only I who feed them. When the state kills Hajibau for not joining in their corruptions and provocations, the people will remember Hajibau. My people used to fight their wars with daggers, now we fight them with sheep and pieces of useless paper. Hajibau will win. This is why the people call Hajibau the King of Zakatala."

Ibragimov Hajibau Isak Oglu walked in the way of Allah and flew in the face of the Communist Party of the Soviet Union for forty-five years. The son of peasants, Hajibau began working in Azerbaijan's tobacco fields as a youngster, handpicking leaf for over a quarter century. The Communist Party political officers who indoctrinated Zakatala's tobacco croppers never got through to Hajibau. "There is a right way and a wrong way to grow and cure tobacco," Hajibau said. "The commissars told us to grow crops 'Lenin's way.' This was the wrong way. I told them this was the reason behind continued food shortages. They told me to reread my Lenin and there would be no more food shortages. This is why Hajibau is now a cooperator. This is why Hajibau fights the criminal bureaucrats."

It was not easy to be anything in Zakatala, high in Azerbaijan's western mountains, at the end of a road strewn with brush fires, emaciated cattle, and visiting Vietnamese workers roasting road-kill dog over spits. Azerbaijan is a once-beautiful land turned to waste, smelling of cheaply manufactured gasoline from the refineries of Baku in the east and the stench of southerly-flowing streams polluted with chlorine used to massacre the fish to be sold on the market. Six years into *perestroika*, billboards extolling Marx and Lenin still decorate a ragged barrier of forests and great clouds that in better times resembled the Blue Ridge Mountains of Virginia. Seven million people live in Azerbaijan, with over one hundred thousand in the Zakatala area, a wide swath of real estate connecting with the Georgian border sixty miles east of Tbilisi. And, like every inch of Azerbaijan, Zakatala was ruthlessly controlled out of Baku by Ayaz Mutallibov, the latest in a long line of Azerbaijani Communist Party bosses.

Power in Azerbaijan is sold to those who pay and those who truckle to the caprices of the Baku leadership. It costs one million rubles to become a Communist Party secretary in Zakatala; five hundred thousand rubles to become chairman of the city council. A bribe of twenty thousand rubles buys one a pasture, which can be snatched away at any time and for any reason. Twenty thousand more rubles purchases five hectares of land. Fealty to Baku is part of the deal, and if the allegiance is underwritten with further kick-backs, a contract to grow and manufacture Zakatala's hard-currency-exportable rose oil is part of the package.

It cost Hajibau ten thousand rubles in bribes to start Lazat, a multiservice co-op of sixty people that incorporated farming, ranching, vacation cabins, and three outdoor restaurant kitchens set on a Zakatala mountainside. Hajibau spent three days walking the mountains alone to find a site for Lazat; and when he told the officials who took the ten thousand rubles from his hand of his discovery they thought him mad. "If I was successful," Hajibau said, "I knew they would come back for more and more and more. I was going to be successful and I wasn't going to give them any more.

"Seventy percent of Azerbaijani co-ops are run by criminals who bribe the state to stay in business or limit their production to maintain shortages," explained Hajibau, who began with one hundred twenty beehives, two thousand sheep, and five thousand chickens scattered throughout what he called friendly pastures. "The communists first came back to me about my chickens. Hajibau had more chickens than the state. They didn't like this. The criminals on the state farms sold the people five eggs for one ruble. Hajibau sold them fifteen eggs for one ruble. The communists said this was not good for them and told me to stop selling the people eggs they could afford and to destroy my chickens. Hajibau said no! The communists said give us more money. Hajibau said no! They came and burned down one of my chicken farms."

Hajibau continued to say no. Too often. One afternoon in the spring of 1989, thirty-five officials from Baku arrived at Lazat with a message for Hajibau. Demanding a free lunch for having to make the arduous eight-hour journey from the capital, the officials told Hajibau that he was causing too many problems. "We made them pay," recalled "Johnny" Agakishiyev, the co-chairman of Lazat. "They told us to become part of their mafia. Hajibau listened to them for a long time. I sat there watching, because the entire cooperative was afraid he would do something foolish. Hajibau looked at them with great strength and said, 'No. I have respect for the people. I will not be part of your provocations.' "

Two days later, thirty-six heavily armed and greatcoated soldiers encircled Lazat, frightening the children and forcing the co-op's adult staff and guests into one of the treehouse dining rooms at gunpoint. Agakishiyev hid under a desk in the office until he could phone Hajibau undetected. Hajibau, rushing up the mountain to confront his adversaries, stood in the center of the armed contingent and laughed at their Makharov pistols and slung Kalashnikovs. "These troops were from the Sixth Department of the Republic Ministry of the Interior Anti-Racketeering Department," Hajibau recounted, tormented by the scene. "They came to arrest me as a mafioso, but brought nothing with them to prove it. They took all my files, everything. I laugh while they demolish my office. Then Hajibau feeds them all. They say it is better food than what they must eat in Baku. One of them tells me a Party official is angry Hajibau sends two hundred letters and telegrams to Moscow complaining about corruption. This man warns Hajibau the troops will come back to arrest me. The official with them says to write no more letters because Baku uses the paper for the toilet.

"So I sent another telegram to KGB chief Vladimir Kryuchkov in Moscow, telling him of this provocation. I sent another to Soviet Attorney General Sukharev, and another to the Minister of the Interior," Hajibau said. The cable read:

The fifty-seven people of the Lazat Cooperative want to inform you of our worrisome situation. We suffered an attack of the so-called state racket police of the Azerbaijan Republic. The road was blocked. All employees and guests were held at gunpoint. When we demanded a warrant or a decision of the ministry, two KGB officers told us that we did not have the right to demand anything. They told us they had come on oral authority of the President of Azerbaijan and the Azerbaijan Ministry of the Interior. The siege lasted until late that night. They took our documents. They told us to try and be friends with the local Communist Party chief, the local militia, and the Zakatala city council. This is all a mystery. It was like a foreign video film. We are worried. Please find out about this matter.

"Everybody in Moscow sends their telegrams to the Baku KGB for action. Baku sends the letter to the Zakatala city council for action. The city council sends their KGB man to Lazat. He says, 'Hajibau, neither you nor your cooperative are needed in Zakatala,' and threatens me with arrest if I send any more telegrams. I told him to get off my mountain. This is *perestroika.*"

Hajibau had slept little the night before we went to visit the Zakatala city council to tell the story of the dead sheep. He was ashamed that his guests had to participate in saving his flock, angry that so many sheep had perished, and outraged by the innocent looks of the bureaucrats standing in front of him. The officials crowded over maps behind Asim Samadov's large desk and bobbed and fussed like hungry crows. The heat of the mountain summer drifted into the office gently from a uniformly gray morning sky. Samadov, the chairman of the Zakatala district executive committee, sweated uneasily in the heat. Magshev Hajibau Madiashev, Zakatala's deputy district chairman, and Suleyman Suleymánov, the chairman of the Agro-Industrial Committee of Zakatala, were well able to contain their impatience with Hajibau, Sabina, and me much better than with the muggy, fly-filled air. Hajibau had not even telephoned to say that we were coming. He said there would be no reply. Sabina telephoned instead. There was no reply. Hajibau was aware of the aches his body had suffered lifting sheep. The pain in his head returned with renewed vigor, it seemed, since his decision to stop drinking alcohol so that he could better battle the corruption of Zakatala.

"Tea—coffee, perhaps?" Samadov asked, gesturing to one of his subordinates. "Wine, Hajibau?"

Hajibau slapped his hands smartly, walked with giant steps

toward the desk, seized a stool, planted it with a thud before Suleymanov, the party bureaucrat responsible for dividing Zakatala's pastures among farmers. Hajibau plopped his huge girth down, staring at the outraged bureaucrat with deadly eyes. Suleymanov looked away, fingering the maps. Samadov, returning Hajibau's cold stare, steadily groped through the papers on his desk for various documents, fished out a yellowed piece of onionskin Hajibau had given him months ago, and waved it in front of the King's face like a dainty handkerchief. "This is not correct," Samadov said, smiling. "You are in trouble and you shouldn't carry on so. You are going to ruin yourself, as you have ruined your sheep."

"You scold like a hungry old grandmother," Hajibau said in a dispassionate voice, as if he had exhausted all his emotions. And with that he got up and paced slowly to the window that overlooked the surrounding mountains. The wooden floor shook the tiny Madiashev, vibrating from Hajibau's heavy step. For a brief moment Hajibau stood with his sweaty back to Samadov, looking down at the empty market across the square, then turned around and bore down upon his unwanted adversary. "Get off my mountain."

"Impudent fool," Suleymanov muttered, looking up from his maps. "When will you learn?"

Hajibau dropped off into deep thought as if he had forgotten his grievances against the men who had ordered the death of his sheep. "I know the rules," Hajibau said to the officials. "I went myself to the city hall! I wrote the proper letter! Suleymanov signed it. Samadov signed it. Now you do this to make me uneasy. But I am Hajibau, yes, and you cannot stop me."

"Hajibau, we will of course have a full investigation," Samadov said sweetly. "This should not have happened."

"It appears this is the fault of your shepherds," injected Suleymanov, tapping a compass on the maps, pointing a pencil at Hajibau. "Look here. Your shepherds crossed this line," said Suleymanov, shaking his head. "They should not have done that. You have inexperienced shepherds, Hajibau. The state shepherds know the mountains much better."

"No! No!" shouted Makhmakhod Zhakanzher, Lazat's chief

shepherd, who had been standing meekly in the corner, intently listening to the discussion. "You all know I have been a shepherd in these mountains for twenty years. These are lies, Hajibau."

"I know these are lies," said Hajibau, his face fervent with anger as four more Zakatala officials entered the room with huge folders full of ordinance survey maps. One of the men, leaning his elbows on the primitive conference table in the middle of the office, looked up at Samadov and asked if he should open the maps. Samadov fidgeted a no.

"The problem is a simple one," interjected Makhmakhod Damada, a top Party member and *kolkhoz* boss with ten thousand sheep, turning from his study of the folded sheaf bursting with the council's thick file on Hajibau. "My sheep don't have enough land to graze on, Hajibau. We all understand the importance of cooperatives, but your cooperative is registered as a catering cooperative. You have the authority to have sheep, but you don't have the authority to graze sheep. What do you think, Hajibau? Does Hajibau think he can just buy sheep and bring them to the mountain? Did Hajibau think where he was going to put his sheep before he bought them?

"You need to re-register your cooperative, Hajibau," Damada added, cautioning: "But maybe it would be smarter for you to develop other agricultural products."

"Yes, of course, comrade!" said Samadov, smugly nodding to Damada. "This is why you have problems, Hajibau. You are not properly registered."

"I've been properly registered for over one year," said Hajibau, pointing to the document in his hand. "You signed the document, and the *kolkhoz* farms are not using their land. The mountain is full of pasture and you will not let cooperatives use it unless they bribe you. Hajibau will not do this."

"Let me see that letter," Samadov snapped impatiently, moving quickly around his desk, apologizing to Sabina and me for the confusion. "I see, Hajibau. Well, this is not an official document. This is just a friendly letter from me to you. I want you all here to notice—particularly our guest from America and Sabina Sabitnova, the granddaughter of the great Azerbaijani leader and Communist Party member Sabit Orudjev—that this letter, although properly written, doesn't contain the official stamp necessary to make it truly legitimate for Hajibau's sheep to graze on the mountain. Nonetheless, an official investigation will take place, the council will pay for Hajibau's dead sheep, and his sheep will in the future be allowed entry to state pastures."

Walking over to Hajibau, Samadov placed a firm hand on his shoulder and smiled through stumpy teeth. "It's important, Hajibau, that our friend from America and the granddaughter of a Soviet hero understand the Communist Party of Azerbaijan and Zakatala is behind *perestroika*. We are all honest men." Samadov's dark eyes hooded. His teeth were stained and displayed a genuinely frightening smile. Almost at once, a bird flew in the window and landed on the maps with a faint scream. The men froze at the sound. Chuckling, Sabina whispered: "That is a bad sign in Azerbaijan. It means somebody is going to die."

"Everything you heard spoken by those officials was a deadly lie, so I'm not surprised the meeting ended with the visit of a bird," explained Dr. Hajibau Alikhanov, Zakatala's chief medical surgeon, commenting on the phenomenon that took place in Samadov's office. "They are very professional criminals. Hajibau is one of the few people here who don't violate the law. Hajibau's strength comes from his refusal to cater to the Party bosses. He does not lie."

Dr. Alikhanov lowered himself closer to the fire he had built alongside the river where Hajibau's sheep had lost their fight with the bureaucracy, and took a bite of some freshly slaughtered lamb. The sun was sinking. And Dr. Alikhanov sat, his face in his hands, looking at the ground and hating all this, the blunt bone gripped in his fingers no more useful in cutting flesh than the scalpels in his hospital. He begrudged his hands, skilled hands that greed and stupidity would not permit to save lives. With firm, satisfied features, he looked up to see Hajibau, off in the distance, handing out food to people who passed up and down the riverbed. Dr. Alikhanov was a poet, and like all poets of his nation, the great emptiness he felt in his heart was caused by a land whose rulers never gave its people the ability to be left alone. The Russians even had a word for it: *grust,* the melancholy that accompanies every Russian's success or failure.

Dr. Alikhanov's burden was the heavy, invisible chain of the state—a weight lifted only by the vitality of dreamers like Hajibau. "That Hajibau is alive represents that a shift to democracy is taking place in the Soviet Union," Dr. Alikhanov said, tossing the bone into the river. "But there's not enough food, even with Hajibau, to feed democracy. The problem will get worse. It's for the benefit of the local Party officials to maintain shortages. I don't understand this; as a doctor, mind you, I can't operate on people because I have neither the proper tools nor medicines. Even if I did have the equipment, many of my patients would be too weak to survive the procedures.

"However, as a forty-eight-year-old man who has lived under this system his entire life, I understand their need to destroy Hajibau and create shortages. The people who run my country are incompetent, and Hajibau shows this very clearly. *Perestroika* will not change this; corruption is a pathological condition without a known cure. Marx and Lenin were supposed to have made a fabulous society, but the corruption killed them, too. Hajibau is a marvel who can help the people. It's unbelievable what he has done, but when you behave like that you have a lot of enemies. Hajibau isn't always right in how he handles the bureaucrats. He causes scandals, but I'm coming to understand scandal is a price one must pay for democracy. Hajibau has been my friend for fifteen years and, as his doctor, I can tell you he is physically healthy. A bull. Mentally he's a little crazy, but much saner than the bureaucrats of Zakatala."

Dignity meant much to Hajibau. Pride, to the point of stubbornness, even more. He said he would not sleep nights if he trusted the lies spoken by the cooperators in Moscow's Hall of Columns. He trusted Vladimir Tikhonov, but the letters Lazat had sent asking the academic for help in defusing the bureaucracy had done nothing. He trusted Dr. Alikhanov, but he did not trust himself to find a solution to bureaucratic villainies through more diplomatic means. Sabina said Hajibau was a bull, too, and she did not regard his forceful approach as melodrama, or exaggerated or out of proportion in comparison to what he was up against. "The criminals know when they are fighting Hajibau," she said.

Hajibau proudly judged his life as a capitalist by the smiles he provided the Soviet families who paid four rubles fifty kopecks a day for room and board at Lazat. When the city council reneged on their promise to build a bridge across the ravine to Lazat because Hajibau would not give them forty thousand rubles, Hajibau built the bridge with four thousand of his own. Every year Lazat was fulfilling the quota of food it promised the state. The council failed to give him the "official stamps" necessary to double the ten thousand tons of meat he supplied between 1988 and 1990. "There are no vegetables in Zakatala," said Hajibau. "Again, the council refused to give me idle land to grow vegetables. I sent a cable to the Soviet Minister of Agriculture:

> Ungrounded opposition to the cooperatives in Azerbaijan has forced many of us to become bankrupt. Land is not being allocated and we are forced to slaughter sheep and cattle because there is no place for them to graze. Cooperative Lazat has lost one ton of cheese and two tons of wool for the people because of opposition. Please allocate land to Cooperative Lazat for vegetables and pasture. Please tell me of the measures you will take.

"The reply was a visit from Telman Orudjev,* a secretary of the Central Committee of the Communist Party of Azerbaijan. He asked me *why* I fed people," Hajibau continued, shaking his head between disgust and amazement. "He said to let people take care of themselves. 'Why have one thousand sheep, Hajibau? Raise only a hundred sheep and we will give you all the land you need.' Hajibau told him to get off the mountain."

It was strange, Hajibau said, that after finally explaining his plight—the "fate of all honest cooperators"—he would no longer wonder in more private moments if his battle was just. He said that fear stretched behind men like shadows, always trying to catch up and devour the one who gave it life. He found it blackly funny that the government bought food from the West while at the same time it killed his sheep because they were politically incorrect, prevented him from growing vegetables because the vegetable

*No relation to Sabina Orudjeva.

documents were not in order. The state and the Party wanted the people to live a life of disguise and bluff, amid all the old corruptions repackaged under the notion of *perestroika*. Yet through it all, triumphs and nightmares, Hajibau exuded a towering energy that shamed all those who believed the stolid impassiveness of the system was unassailable.

Hajibau's nonstop efforts to clean up Zakatala and the cooperative sector had reached Baku, and it was the unexpected suddenness and apparent irrationality of his movements to wipe out the shameless fixers and awesome bunglers that made Azerbaijan's top officials uneasy. They had firmly contained Hajibau, of course, but the recklessness with which he attacked the Apparat on the food issue made them uneasy, leaving them to wonder how many others might be inclined to adopt his tactics. "Hajibau is a great irritant to the officials in Baku," explained Alim Azimov, the director of the Bakcoop Bank, Azerbaijan's first commercial cooperative bank. "I lend Hajibau money for his ideas without any guarantees. He goes too far, but he has ideas and knowledge and that is all the collateral my bank requires.

"The loan policy of the Bakcoop Bank will sound foolish and amateurish to the great institutional banks in the West," said Azimov, who had directed the main finance department of the state's Baku Gosbank before starting his cooperative in 1988. "Credit without guarantees is madness only if there is collateral out there. There's nothing out here, and that is the tragedy of our history. I lend out money to make something, anything. Hajibau believes in his dreams. That is sufficient for money."

Money—specifically rubles—was not sufficient to complete a negotiation in the Soviet Union. There was always something else needed—bribes, favors, kickbacks, hard currency, or consumer goods were necessary for any of Azerbaijan's three thousand cooperatives to conceive a project. "The methodics of creating honest business when the state doesn't want honest business means you must do dishonest things in order to control the situation and bypass any sort of harassment the state might plan to use against you," explained Amir Mamedov, the chairman of the Azerbaijani delegation to the Cooperative Congress and a Bakcoop Bank customer.

"Great men like Hajibau and Alim do this at the cost of much personal suffering. We need rubles, but they are worthless without the state's permission to use them."

Although Azimov started the Bakcoop Bank with ten million rubles in capital, the bureaucracy prohibited him from lending any more than two hundred fifty thousand rubles, no matter how much money the bank had on deposit. Most of Azimov's clients required sums greater than that, however, forcing the thirty-seven-year-old banker to become the de facto comptroller of his client's cooperatives, paying "loan money" totaling millions of rubles directly to contractors to whom his ruble-capped borrowers were indebted. Azimov, who never knew whether or not the procedure was legal, did this because it was the only way for a cooperative banker to underwrite the free market in a nation of contradictory laws administered by corrupt bureaucrats through a cynical system of government. Depositors received one percent interest, borrowers were charged 10 percent interest, and the disparity of the figures was of no importance because revenue was essentially nil.

"Profit doesn't matter. The downside to lending honestly is the difficulty I encounter trying to prove to people that I'm not a crook. Cooperators learn Soviet reality quickly," Azimov added in measured tones. "There is definitely a war going on between the cooperators and the state. Tikhonov says there are many men like Hajibau, but I know that Hajibau is a general without much of an army. The least I can do is give him the rubles he needs to try to make all our lives better."

Hajibau had no illusion as to the ruble's worth without his toadying to the bureaucrats he needed to ply with hard currency. To the state, Hajibau was a peasant, a member of a half-caste lot unschooled in the matters of high finance and without enough education to handle hard currency effectively. There were provisions in Soviet law enabling men such as Hajibau to have hard currency, but the loopholes were wide and tyrannically enforced by the state banks to keep their unquestionable control over the flow of *valuta*—hard currency. The successes of cooperators, particularly rural cooperators operating outside the Moscow-Leningrad-Kiev axis, amazed and frightened the bosses at Gosbank and

Vneshekonombank—the Soviet bank for foreign trade and de facto controller of *valuta*. Vnesh never responded to Hajibau's letters and telegrams. Standing arms akimbo outside Vnesh's headquarters whenever he was in Moscow, Hajibau asked everyone leaving the bank for help to get inside because the guards would not let him past the steps.

The Bakcoop Bank was Hajibau's only link to the world of investment capital and he clung to Azimov for it. It was not easy for Azimov to lend money to Hajibau and other cooperators, but it was necessary—despite the threats to his family. "Part of my husband's job is to lobby officials so they will allow Alim to use the bank's money," described Aza Azimov, rubbing her thumb and index finger together, the Soviet signal for *blat*. "There is great discrimination against us. People on the street, I don't know them, come up and scream that Alim's loan to a cooperative bakery has taken bread from the mouths of the people or that Hajibau is a criminal. Cooperators everywhere in the Soviet Union are threatened like this. The state orders strangers to harass us, even our children. They tell us we will not live. They laugh at us.

"It's their laughter I cannot stand," she went on. "I hate the laughter."

Hajibau hated the laughter, too. He stood straight whenever it came, with fisted hands deep in the pockets of his pants, so as not to take them out and attack. The laughter was easier to take when he felt the solid ground of the mountain beneath his feet. Sometimes, when the bureaucrats came to Lazat, Hajibau greeted them in a fifteen-foot fleece cape lashed together from the skins of a dozen sheep. He said the cloak brought out his warrior spirit. He would stare stiffly at the bureaucrats, looking neither to the right nor to the left but at the eyes only. The bureaucrats laughed. Hajibau, his workers gathering around him in a crescent, continued to gaze into their eyes. Soon the Apparat replaced their hilarity with questions, demands, explanations, and good-humored warnings. Hajibau stared in silence, the absurdity of the spectacle overpowered by how he presently made the bureaucrats quiver, like children seeing a fairy-tale ogre come to life. Dr. Alikhanov, Alim Azimov, or whoever else happened to be visiting Lazat invariably entered the crescent—standing quietly, staring intently, watching the fury of the Apparat turn into sullen, festering silence. Sabina and I hesitated at first; then one summer night, abruptly, we walked the few yards down the hill to join the twenty-three people gathered around Hajibau. As Hajibau spoke, carefully punctuating each word with a scornful jerk of his head, he looked at the taller of the two officials who had come with an invitation to return to the council chamber and discuss the large number of Lazat chickens being sold in the market, his left eye open and wide, the right slanted and nasty-looking. Hajibau moved closer to the bureaucrat. The two men stood exactly opposite each other: one short, fat, and wearing red plastic sandals; the other tall, heavy, and sweating in the costume of a giant sheep.

"I am Hajibau and you know me," the King of Zakatala said, grabbing the documents, crumpling them in his hand and astounding the bureaucrat's face into perfect terror. "Get off my mountain."

9

> You can run with the pack, in the middle
> of the pack, but if you want to do some-
> thing, get to the edge and peel away.
>
> CLARENCE DARROW

GLASNOST HAD GIVEN the Soviet Union the opportu-
nity to experiment with over two hundred years of American ideas
and fashions, but no trend was visibly more popular than the white
go-go boots that suddenly appeared in Moscow shortly after Gorbachev became the Communist Party General Secretary. Although
the political significance of go-go boots was imperfectly understood—and the condition may have been the result of some quirky
countertrade deal with the director of Alabama's Dixie National
Baton Twirling Institute—the love between a Russian woman and
her go-go boots was a deadly serious affair, regardless of her size
or Russia's climatic conditions.

The white go-gos favored by the Soviet woman made her
resemble nothing so much as Chef Boy-Ar-Dee dressed as a drum
majorette: self-confidently poised, sloping calves shooting out the
bottoms of heavy overcoats and into their relics of the discotheque
years, Moscow's female *narod* thought it the height of style to slog
around in knee-high, Nancy Sinatra jobs made of cheap plastic and
pig hide which, when clean, glowed like exploding stellar matter.
Wearing white go-go boots in public was both tricky and dangerous,
however. Russian women preferred wearing their go-gos with Bul-

garian nylons and short skirts that looked more like Fruit of the Loom boxer shorts. It was never a pretty sight, particularly when winter caked the white boots with mud and snow, and especially when the rheumy-eyed Moscow militia began arresting the go-go women for indecent exposure during the summer months.

Covering this kind of sad and humiliating story in the Soviet press was a very special art, and one that Volodya Yakovlev excelled in when he worked at *Rabotnitsa*, a passive and meaningless Soviet woman's magazine. Knowing it would be hard to generate public support for go-go boots and short skirts in the essentially puritanical Soviet society, Yak decided to attack the problem from the shoe cream angle. Keeping shoes clean was a nightmare for anybody without the necessary connections to get shoe polish—especially white shoe polish. So Yak put on a pair of dirty white go-go boots and boxer shorts and proceeded to walk Moscow's streets searching for insights, until he got himself carried off and locked up like a common criminal. Stories that ended behind bars were not popular among Soviet bureaucrats with major ambitions and very keen memories. The editors at *Rabotnitsa* cringed and portrayed Yak as a blundering fool motivated by nothing more than a lust for publicity.

Yak had been trained to be a Soviet journalist, and by Russian standards was generally viewed as an embarrassment to the trade. Those who worked alongside Yak at *Rabotnitsa* agreed that when his charm and irony wore thin, Yak showed himself to be a harsh and arbitrary man who lived under the iron necessity of being right all the time. It was a severe description offered with malice and, in fact, with a certain bitter affection for Yak's ability to stretch the boundaries of what the government and the Party permitted Soviet journalists to get away with.

"Yakovlev's past instructs us about what he created at Fact," said a writer who worked with him at the Moscow newspaper *Sovetskaya Rossiya*. "His ideas were quite good, but he never had the ability to follow through on them. All of the young writers wanted to see *perestroika* work and were willing to take whatever risks were necessary to achieve change, but Yakovlev's energy was directed toward hustling and generating publicity for himself. He never failed to alienate his allies in the profession."

Soviet journalism was a crossroads of sorts for Yakovlev, however. Moscow's newspapers and magazines were safe houses for tired Party hacks and Golden Youth children. The editors were all politically approved, the staffs compliant with Party directives, and the canteens full of consumer goods unimaginable on the streets. The work was strange, lifeless, and often intolerable, but the hours were short and the perks made the Soviet newsroom a mainly nice place to be indentured in a society that was not likely to see democracy develop in the midst of an economic catastrophe. From outside the *perestroika* hothouse, any Soviet who bucked the system looked inspiring, so any individual who dared make the system uncomfortable with his work was a hero. The temptation was strong to see Yakovlev as a big proud fighter for *perestroika,* to exalt his extremism, admire his energy, and get behind his theatrical whimsy as a policy of resistance to the undoubtedly chauvinistic arguments and anachronistic political tendencies of the Soviet government. And this was exactly why Americans came to Fact's door. The gesture of sending rebels like Yakovlev a little business gave the Americans the impression they were genuinely supporting *perestroika.* Yak encouraged his Soviet critics because their reproaches only strengthened his own portrayal of Fact as being on the cutting edge of *perestroika.* This in turn washed away any fear a Western investor might have had about becoming an unexpected victim of *perestroika.*

Yak was leaning anxiously against his office wall the first time we discussed the riddles of his past, and his body tensed like a trap about to be sprung, his eyes as cold and sparkling as crushed ice. "I've spent my entire life proving to people that they are wrong," Yak said, with a puzzled look upward, lighting another Winston. "What do you expect *those* people to say about me?" he asked with hurried nervousness. "The communists thought everyone else was crazy but themselves. It was the only way they could think, the only way they could face themselves. For them I will always be wrong. Even if I wanted to, how could I make them believe me?" he asked rhetorically, quickly changing the subject with a deep and prolonged sigh.

Yakovlev believed his history of being a thorn in the side of the state authorities was entirely justifiable in the context of the future. By 1989 the Iron Curtain had gone down, but an Economic Curtain was going up and Yak had visions of becoming the impresario for the thousands of players who wanted to be on that stage. There was no need to disguise his failure as a state journalist, because the Americans who came to him for help saw such failure both as a willingness to take chances and a sort of free-market merit badge. The refrain ran in his head like a jingle: Yak was known to everybody in Moscow, Yak was the cooperative movement, Yak could do anything, Yak had the invitation letter from the Harvard University School of Business framed on his desk. And it worked. The spectacle of *perestroika* overwhelmed the flood of unprepared new visitors as they passed through the tobacco-stench of the strip-lit Sheremetyevo airport customs control hall and into the crowded and echoing arrival terminal with a sense of foreboding and weakness. Moscow numbed the mind from the moment the body crossed its threshold, and the best way to kill the sensation was to have a Yak-arranged Chaika limousine on the curb.

There was no smart consensus about where Yak was heading with it all. Most people saw him as just another one of those millionaire high-rolling cooperators who had come to see *perestroika* as a new way of running a con. He looked good, talked smooth, and kept the bureaucrats off his back. There was no longer anything really taboo about being a cooperator, not in Moscow, anyway, particularly when the ministry men were knocking on his door to ask for help in arranging trips to study Western business practices on Greek beaches and in Paris discotheques. Information and contacts were Fact's currencies and, although not always precise, they were often more accurate and readily available than those provided by the state. There were over two hundred people working at Fact by the autumn of 1989, and their daily dispatches from the Soviet Union's fifteen republics provided the cooperative with a continuous stream of information sold to such customers as the U.S. Embassy and the Soviet Council of Ministers. With the help of A Bunch of Guys Who Do Things, Fact had expanded to offices at Seventeen Good Highway with a ceiling allegedly lifted from the Yugoslavian Embassy. Yak's new office was safeguarded by iron-rodded windows that overlooked parking lots, playgrounds, and clumps of weeds. Everything was heavy: the drapes, the stationery, the coffee, and the ministerial men who arrived at strange hours, speaking ambiguous words in soft voices. Fact was a legitimate business, but only so long as its bureaucratic *zashchitniki** deemed it such, so long as its carpeted hallways and wood-paneled offices remained a railway station of American, Spanish, Greek, German, and French *biznessmeni* bearing gifts of *kompyuteri* to *finantsirovat* the operation. Pistol-packing guards dressed in Soviet Army camouflage gear protected the premises; Fact's lawyers erected the legal shield by splitting the cooperative into three separate businesses, each registered as a separately run cooperative under Yakovlev's supervision. Gleb Pavlovsky ran the Postfactom News Agency, Loshia Ivanoff managed the Postfactom Press, and Yakovlev officially struck his name as the editor-in-chief of *Commersant*—the first privately owned and independent newspaper since the revolution.

Yakovlev and I had first discussed starting a newspaper in July 1989: "It will be called *Commersant* and it will be the first business newspaper in the Soviet Union since the Bolsheviks closed down the original *Commersant* in 1917. The national economy will remain in a chaotic state for some time to come. The government says they want private ownership, of course, but only if there is no exploitation. Unfortunately, they have no definition of exploitation. *Commersant* will define this variant, too.

"Moscow doesn't have a real business newspaper," Yak explained. "There are more than enough ministerial publications, but the entire Soviet Union still doesn't have a business newspaper targeted at business people as a social group, regardless of what particular business they are in. The need for information, rather than the need for a political purpose, will be *Commersant*'s goal. This newspaper will not be a collective propagandist and agitator, but a vehicle for keeping people informed as promptly and as fully as possible. We will leave it to the reader to draw conclusions and take stands."

---

*In Russian slang, the officials who defend and protect an individual and/or his enterprise.

*Commersantъ** was designed to be the flagship of Yak's growing information empire. Every Russian who dealt with Yak, and who had any dealings with Fact, claimed he had been managing the enterprise solely by taking sly personal advantage of *perestroika*'s disorder. Recalling *Ogonyok* editor Vitali Korotich's early warning that no good would come out of his rogue reporter's cooperative, Yak's contemporaries looked at *Commersant* with immediate suspicion despite the fact that the newspaper did not have the hard currency, equipment, or resources to begin publication. Using "ъ" as the *Commersantъ* logo was an aggravating burlesque to many of Moscow's other young journalists, who were either trying to change the character of state publications or groping to find the financing necessary to start new ones. The idea of *Commersant* was not the problem, but Yakovlev's history as both a state journalist and a cooperator had the potential to be used by the West as a yardstick for the character and integrity of every Russian journalist.

Yak's former translator, Svet Raikov, had first acquainted his boss with the problem in December 1988. Raikov told Yak that his penchant for sensational publicity coupled with his history of conning Western businessmen could corrupt the entire free-market movement, leaving all the cooperators lumped together as hustlers and crooks because he was the movement's most visible and charismatic leader. "Yakovlev was going too far," Raikov said shortly before leaving Fact to start the Moscow Business Center. "He wasn't paying people, he wasn't returning calls, he was making promises and not following through on them, he was entering into deals and then disappearing . . . this will do none of us any good since there are only a limited number of Westerners who want to do business with us. There must be something we can do to calm Yakovlev down before he destroys us all. I have tried to speak to him about this problem, but he won't listen."

Raikov's premonition of tragedy and his criticism of Yakovlev's

*The official logo incorporates the banned Cyrillic "ъ" as a gesture of defiance against the Party, which outlawed the letter, or accent, in order to simplify Russian and limit the authority that the Orthodox Church had over the language until the Bolsheviks took control of the country.

approach to business, however, went only so far. Payoffs, kickbacks, and bribery were part of the system, and the ability to double-deal and successfully pull strings was part of Yakovlev's and Raikov's cooperative job description—but only insofar as the hustle did not alienate or jeopardize the Westerners with whom the cooperators did business. The Americans were extremely easy targets for Yak's brand of business because they believed Fact was a capitalistic enterprise marooned on the shores of a communist island.

The great myth of the cooperative movement, and the grand fantasy shared by too many of the Americans who came to deal with the Soviet free market, was that cooperators (as well as the restructuring ministries) were apprentice and accident-prone practitioners of capitalism when in reality they were experienced practitioners of sophisticated exploitationism. "Yakovlev makes deals without seeing anything but himself," Raikov observed, "and when things of his making go bad, he sees nothing whatsoever, no matter with whom he is dealing."

"Yakovlev got into trouble with the state because he is dishonest and unprincipled and he is a fellow who will get into trouble with his business for the same reasons," Sabina warned shortly before Yak started his search for financial backing for *Commersant*. "There is a Russian proverb that says these things are bred from the milk of the motherland, and these things do not change just because of *perestroika*."

But there were doubts whether *Commersant* would ever get off the ground. Yakovlev was having serious problems in securing the equipment necessary to start the newspaper. To be sure, I sincerely believed the *Commersant* project would be a savvy attempt to overcome the country's patchwork of laws, nationalities, and two hundred linguistic groups and lay a computerized foundation for the Russian version of Dow Jones, complete with newspapers, magazines, analyses of Soviet and Eastern European markets, and daily listings of Soviet stocks, bonds, currencies, and commodities that could all be sold to Western investors and financial data bases for hard currency. The harsh indictments leveled against Yakovlev had been noted, of course, but such was the risk all foreigners assumed from the moment they decided to try cracking the fearfully complex Soviet market. Yak was maddeningly enigmatic, but he was one of a handful of cooperators with a habit of catching the government by surprise and the guts to seize *perestroika*'s opportunities and then fight for them.

"It was also fun to be part of Russia's second revolution," Charles Bausman, Yakovlev's former partner, explained. "Dealing with Yakovlev was fun and exciting because he described doing business here as a struggle and never downplayed the possibility of everything falling apart at any moment. And I think Yakovlev played on this. He always left explanations suspended, something you'd never get away with in American business. But this was Russia and danger was part of the deal, so it was very easy for him to control the irritation of Fact's Western partners and clients by blaming his own screwups and inabilities on the government and the bureaucracy. There was no such thing as a balanced negative reaction to Yakovlev because he was an incorrigible guy who lived entirely on the edge, and it was the one character trait he shared with every American and European trying to do business in Moscow."

Dealing on the edge: the ability to cull profits from what the mainstream believed to be sucker situations. Quick returns from crazy circumstances: the corporate battlefield's version of the Congressional Medal of Honor. Although every businessman believed he possessed the right stuff to pull it off, there were very few who actually had "the gift," which American commodity traders liked to describe as the genius to juggle without arms. The MBA professors called it risk management. Thomas H. Billington called it the Race Group.

Tom Billington was a Midwestern farm boy who turned his knowledge of the grange into the world's largest privately owned commodity corporation by the time he was forty-two. Billington was not just a great trader; he was an extraordinary trader of unparalleled integrity and utter commitment to those who worked for him. He had built Race into a powerhouse of grain, cattle, stocks, bonds, fine art, exotic currency combinations, and every other financial instrument imaginable. He dined at the finest res-

171 / BEAR HUNTING WITH THE POLITBURO

taurants, owned the fanciest automobiles, and shuttled around the globe in private aircraft from the largest estate in Chicago's Oak Park district. Billington had the largest research department in the commodity business, the largest trading floors in Chicago, London, and New York, and the largest Monte Cristo Cuban cigars in his humidor.

Everything about Tom Billington was big, but nothing was bigger or more important to him than his appetite for learning. He attended classes on history and philosophy at a local community college and spent his weekends doing homework in between tap dancing and drum lessons. Billington visited farms, walked fields, and hung out with the men and women who grew or manufactured what he sold. The stranger the place, the odder the circumstances, the better Billington liked it because there was something new he could learn from the experience. Billington answered his own phone, poured his own booze, and set his own standards that made competitors uneasy. His greatest assets, however, were his eyes. Whereas most commodity traders perceived only the quick-hit of the deal, Billington focused on what was going on around the deal, using his knowledge of history, philosophy, sociology, and art to analyze the outcome and chart future courses. Although Race's bottom line was always the total at the end of the balance sheet, the figures that added up to the company's profits embraced more than numbers. Those who lived on the edge needed an edge, and the knowledge of culture and environment was Billington's head start on the competition.

Moscow was Tom Billington's kind of town, a city of potential with powerful undercurrents of risk, drama, and history; and the Soviet Union was Race's kind of environment, a marketplace of confusion tailor-made for the commodity business. Moreover, Billington realized that success in commodities—like Yakovlev's mastery of the Soviet Union—boiled down to one thing: the ability to correctly hedge a bet in a muddled and complex market. Billington had been helping the Soviet Union purchase grain for years when he made his second visit to Moscow in December 1988, to finalize an agreement to train state bureaucrats in the art of trading at his Chicago headquarters. But, as happened with every American busi-

nessman who came to Moscow, Billington's official Soviet hosts
failed to follow through on many of their promises for on-the-ground
support. There was nothing odd about the bureaucratic snafus that
greeted Billington's arrival, the screwups in transport, accommo-
dation, and meeting schedules the Russians called *mudestika*. Billington understood Soviet *mudestika* better than most visitors and
decided to use the failings of the official bureaucracy as an opportunity to check out the cooperative freemarketeers first hand. Yakovlev, who had been introduced to Billington through some
common friends, was more than happy to be his guide.

"You immediately knew these guys were pulling all kinds of
strings and angles to get their businesses started," Billington said,
describing his earliest impressions of what he saw at Fact. "And
they got things done that the government either couldn't do or
wouldn't do for you. And they delivered. Yakovlev is up against
two thousand years of Russian history—and he's pulling it off. He's
going to make a hell of a lot of mistakes, but that's natural for any
new business. The guy went off on his own to learn and to grow
and that's damned impressive in the Soviet market."

Billington gave Yakovlev an intensive four-day education in
the form and function of American big business. Yakovlev looked
upon this gesture as nothing short of a young gunfighter's being
given private lessons by Jesse James, but the Soviet bureaucrats
from the Ministry of Foreign Economic Relations, whom Billington
and his attorney Ed Weidenfeld had gone to Moscow to meet in
order to conclude Race's market training school deal, grew extremely apprehensive over the developing relationship between
the commodity cowboy from Chicago and the cooperative gunslin-
ger from Moscow. Billington, Weidenfeld, and Yakovlev were all
poignantly aware of the awkward situation percolating beneath the
surface, a predicament of power, politics, and the limits of *perestroika* that boiled over during the farewell banquet Fact hosted
for Billington in the Kolkhida cooperative café.

Billington enjoyed bringing together people from different
backgrounds, cultures, and professions, and had asked Race's official Soviet hosts to join the group for the Georgian dinner. Yak
agreed; but having no idea who these Soviet bureaucrats were or

exactly from where their power came, he grew duly alarmed at the prospect of dinner with anonymous officials. Bureaucrats and co-operators sharing a public table with an influential American businessman was unheard of, and Yak grasped the aesthetic and political dangers such an encounter might precipitate. People, no doubt powerful people, would hear of the encounter.

Climbing out of a fleet of Fact cars into the cold wind of a December Moscow night, Billington and Weidenfeld greeted their official Soviet sponsors as they walked up Ulitsa Kusinina to the restaurant from the nearby Polezhayavskaya Metro station. Immediately, the two bureaucrats grew nervous: the ministry was supposed to have afforded Billington transport and other unspecified services; they had failed to collect him upon his arrival at the airport and now they were watching him being delivered to a restaurant—by *kooperativshiki*. Trembling like parents witnessing their children humiliate them during an important ceremony, the bureaucrats shuffled uneasily into the restaurant alongside Fact's senior staff, where the entire group was confronted by three long tables blanketed with beef, pork, lamb, chicken, fish, sausage, soup, vegetables, fruit, chocolate, coffee, tea, ice cream, torte, pie, wine, whiskey, beer, and brandy.

"My God!" exclaimed one of the Soviet bureaucrats, staring with his mouth open at a rare repast worth thousands of rubles. "I've not seen such a table in years!"

"Don't you go to cooperatives?" Yak inquired with a taunting smile and a large sigh of relief.

"Well . . . no, I don't," muttered the startled official, whose salary was probably no more than three hundred rubles stuffed in a brown envelope at the end of every month.

The posture of the bureaucrats, who offered nothing but the simplest courtesies during the dinner, was apparently enough to satisfy Yakovlev of the evening's success. Yak had committed every ounce of his talent to providing Billington with a regal sendoff in return for the commodity trader's advice and encouragement. It was an impressive performance, not the least of which were the awe and apprehension of the men from the Ministry of Foreign Economic Relations. The bureaucrats looked violated, like those on the receiving end of a violent crime against which one had absolutely no defense. Remaining ruefully uncommunicative for most of the evening, the ministry officials spoke in the dubbed and monotone voices of actors trying not to be caught in their short-comings.

Steadily blinking in between numb stares at the cooperators, the "Chief Expert of the Main Administration for Economic Relations with Developed Capitalist Countries" and his sidekick, the "Deputy Head of the Main Administration for Economic Relations with Developed Capitalist Countries," devoured the food at a pell-mell pace and, in between each course, smoked every Western cigarette offered, the authority of the state as the sole arbiter of the economy evaporating with every puff. For the bureaucrats, the party ended with correctly executed smiles and goodbye-shakes of Billington's hand; walking to the Polezhayavskaya Metro alone together in the icy night, with lifted bottles of Yakovlev's Armenian brandy secreted under their coats, the ministry men missed the toasts of friendship and the invitation Billington gave Yakovlev to visit Chicago as soon as possible. Yak had done more than provide the Race group with the services the bureaucracy had pledged and failed to deliver on; he had come out of nowhere to simply outclass the Ministry of Foreign Economic Relations on its own turf and with one of its wealthiest and most influential partners.

Volodya Yakovlev had made his big move.

10

When we were fourteen, a group of us used to try to knock ourselves out. Organically. By taking twenty deep breaths, head held down between our legs, and then coming up real fast and blowing on our thumbs without letting out any air. Then all the blood would rush up or down, I don't know which, but it would rush somewhere, fast. And we would hope to pass out, but it never worked. Then we'd spin in circles until we all got so dizzy that we fell down. Then we went home.

SPALDING GRAY

AMIDSUMMER'S MOONLIGHT glistened off the titanium-skinned wings of Volodya Yakovlev's Pan American flight to Chicago eight months after he had put Tom Billington in the backseat of the old Moskvich for the snowy ride back to the Intourist Hotel. Yak had been smiling then, in the Soviet snow; but this was America and the chairman of Fact fidgeted in his aisle seat with uncharacteristic nervousness. The smoking light on the Kennedy–O'Hare shuttle had been off for thirty minutes and the tepid Styrofoam coffee Yak had been drinking since he left Moscow aboard Aeroflot over twenty hours before left him frazzled as we walked out the jetway behind a group of off-duty pilots. A well-dressed chauffeur took Yak's stuffed suitcase off the luggage carousel and directed his charge through an electronic door toward an elevator to the top floor of the field's high-rise parking garage. Yak stood in the dirty, graffiti-sprayed lift in silence, suspending all thought as he tried to decipher the exotically painted messages on the elevator's three walls.

"I guess I'm in America," Yak said, trying to figure why BEATRICE SUCKS ANY DICK and JULIO IS AN ASS HOLE.

"They use Rust-O-Leum," the driver said. "The message lasts longer. It's good paint."

"What's Rust-O-Leum?

"Russia, right, you're from Russia."

"I don't look like a communist, do I?"

"No, sir, you sure don't."

"Good!" Yak said, laughing. "Then maybe this will be a successful business trip."

"I wish you the best of luck, sir."

Yak needed it. Billington had agreed to discuss the possibility of Race's investing nearly five hundred thousand dollars in Fact, the money to be used to purchase the sophisticated equipment required to begin regular publication. Inside Yak's black leather and chrome-buckled briefcase, alongside the numerous encouraging Telexes he had received from Chicago, were the financial breakdown of *Commersant*, the Council of Ministers' authorization legitimizing the weekly tabloid as a "project of the U.S.S.R. Alliance of United Cooperatives," and fifty copies of *Commersant's* premier test issue in both English and Russian. Yak's staff had scrambled to write *Commersant's* stories when downtime allowed on Fact's overworked computers, which continued to churn out commercial and political information and statistics on the Soviet cooperatives and state-owned enterprises that Fact sold either raw or in pamphlet form to clients. *Commersant's* copy was typeset on government-owned equipment and printed on Finnish paper rolled through presses owned by the Soviet Army newspaper *Krasnaya Zvezda* (Red Star). On the front cover was a sketch of a winged foot depicting the rapid growth of Soviet joint ventures with Western corporations; on the back cover was a drawing of a giant tennis racket sticking out of the Moscow skyline, slapping the Earth. Sandwiched inside *Commersant's* twelve pages were stories on the state's banking monopoly, the causes of inflation, customs regulations, and the legal mechanics behind registering a joint venture.

"*Commersant* is just not just a paper," read the erratic but Citizen Kane–like Declaration of Principles Yak bannered across the centerfold of the first Russian-and-English-language edition. "The copy you're holding in your hands is not number zero, not even number one. However, it is also the 2,036th issue of the *Commersant*. The Presidium of the Alliance of United Cooperatives of the USSR decided to publish it as its own weekly just two months ago. But this newspaper has actually been around since 1909.

"Today's Soviet businessmen are people without a past. They are people without the weightiest argument in their favor—historical experience. Isn't this the root cause of many present troubles? A rootless tree is so tempting for a lumberjack. An alternative economy? Leaseholding? Cooperatives? Oh, that's an interesting beginning all right. One of many. A try. An experiment that won't be hard to stop by just pushing the lever back. This is our history. The history of latter-day Soviet businessmen. A terrible, hard, equivocal history. But is there anything in this society that hasn't had a difficult history? Politics? The cinema? Or maybe literature?

"The *Commersant* was published in Moscow between 1909 and 1917. It was a newspaper for business people, and many of its stories are still fit to print today after a little editing. So we decided against launching a completely new newspaper. We opted instead for resuming a publication suspended for reasons outside the editors' control. We also decided to stick to the old title and even kept the pre-revolutionary 'hard' accent sign at the end. Since the use of this letter is a matter of principle for the Editorial Board, we will keep it.

"I am not keen on looking for direct and cheap historical parallels. But look: sugar is rationed. And so is butter. Dressing yourself decently isn't all that simple. People need to be fed and clothed. They need to be relieved of the humiliating queues and adolescent wages. This is our task. This is a task for entrepreneurs. But we are not the first in this country to begin trying to tackle it by sober, realistic action rather than sloganeering. The coils of the historical spiral are long known to coincide. We do have a past after all."

Commersant was the final link in an astounding, not to mention implausible, chain of events never before seen in the Soviet Union. Yakovlev had published the first privately owned newspaper since Lenin assumed power and the Party took control of the nation's press. An amazing accomplishment of fearlessness, *Commersant* was all the more dangerous because the paper's future hinged entirely on whether or not Billington would underwrite the project in return for the opportunity to distribute the weekly and retain the rights to sell information provided by *Commersant* and the Postfactom News Service in the West. Nothing had been negotiated or signed, but as Yak climbed into the limo for the drive to Billington's Oak Park estate guest house, Fact and *Commersant* staffers back in Moscow were negotiating bribes with doormen to gain entrance into the International Hotel's Armand Hammer Business Center, where Yak had scheduled—and decided to miss—a morning launch party to introduce the capital's Western business community to the fully equipped "Soviet Business Weekly."

"And I don't have any money," Yak confided meekly as the limo accelerated down the Illinois interstate toward Oak Park, Billington's butler ringing on the backseat cellular phone to see what time the guests would arrive. "The Aeroflot people in Moscow made me give them my last two hundred dollars for overweight luggage."

The energetic voice of Bruce Springsteen, singing about being on a last-chance power drive because there was no place left to hide, blared out of the automobile's solid speaker system. It was an ironically apt anthem for Yak's arrival in Chicago. There was a belief widely held in many quarters of the cooperative movement that Yak, and Fact and *Commersant,* had gone to Chicago in desperation, a consequence of the cooperative's alienating and provoking potential Soviet hard-currency sources by flaunting its rubles while the overall economy crumbled. The popular analysis was limp. Although Fact's monthly cash flow was quickly approaching one million rubles, the kind of big bucks the cooperative needed to play in the international market were not to be found in the empty vaults of Soviet banks. Moreover, Yak realized that *Commersant* needed much more than money. The English-language edition, the engine of *Commersant*'s future hard currency through subscription sales in the West, required the talents of American-trained editors to repair the horrid reportage and bland translations provided by the Soviet personnel. For the Soviet staff, reporters so long under the thumb of Party censors at the state expurgation agency *Glavlit,* editing of *any* sort was tantamount to the most grievous political censorship. The rambling Russian-language *Com-*

mersant was a *Wall Street Journal* in comparison to the Communist Party daily *Pravda,* but judged by the standards and principles of American journalism, which Yakovlev claimed to accept, the English-language edition of *Commersant* resembled the result of a literacy experiment among baboons. The stories were monotonous, muddled, and unintelligible. The clutter was augmented by translators, who regularly misspelled words and gnarled grammatical structures which, themselves, were further complicated by the fact that Bolshevik grammarians abolished the direct use of the verb form "to be" in the present tense. The paper also broke some of the basic rules of journalism. It neglected to include quotes from the people it wrote about. The titles and affiliations of the people mentioned in Postfactom and *Commersant* dispatches were rarely given by reporters. Lead paragraphs often contained the names of as many as five people, with no means of identifying them or their role in the story. Enforcing elementary journalistic techniques on deadline—the removal of a comma, the rewriting of a sentence, or the spiking of a story—ignited precious hours of tumultuous political discussion and vicious argument that ended in threats, recriminations, and missed deadlines.

The American editors with whom Yak had spoken viewed *Commersant's* Tinkertoy journalism as a cultural-technical hurdle that could be conquered with time, training, and patience, because the one thing Fact did have was a singular access to information that no other government or private organization had. An alarming difficulty, however, was the tendency of the Postfactom/*Commersant* news staff to eagerly encourage and accept bribes from the people and businesses whose information it published. Payola was traditional. *Perestroika* further popularized as a means of making a bit more pocket money. Russian readers did not care because they were receiving information long denied to them by the state. Fact's Russian staff forthrightly confirmed the practice while in the same breath guiltlessly denying that the custom was a thorny problem for a free press—particularly for a business newspaper and a market news service designed to be sold in the West, where ability and accuracy would be assessed under an entirely different set of rules.

"There was no way the Russian staff would ever stop this practice," Charles Bausman explained, having fought the same *vzyatka* problem with Yakovlev at Fact and the Moscow Business Center. "Volodya and I had discussed the situation briefly when he made his first visit to the United States in December 1988. But all he did was watch television constantly, fascinated by cable and grisly horror movies. He spent his evenings buying combat knives, hunting knives, and Chinese flying stars at the stores on Times Square that catered to mercenaries. He'd return to the apartment to eat raw Oscar Mayer bacon and make espresso on my yuppie coffee machine until dawn.

"Volodya made an arrogant ass of himself on his first trip," Bausman said. "Everyone who worked for him back in Moscow hoped this visit with Billington would be different. He finally had the right clothes, because I had taken him to Moe Ginsburg to buy Italian wool slacks, a natty blazer, loafers, and a pair of Ralph Lauren eyeglasses that finally corrected his beady nearsightedness. Chicago was his big break, and although a lot of people wanted to see Billington tear him apart, there were just as many who wanted to see him pull off a deal with a guy of Billington's caliber because it might finally wise him up."

Yak nodded, studying the passing cars. The air was darkening as the limo slipped into Billington's driveway and Yak tapped the filter of a cigarette on top of his watch. "Yes," he said. Soviet journalistic standards and business practices were different, as was entering into a partnership with one of America's largest companies. New priorities, strange and awkward, were being revealed, and Fact might have to change, to become more beholden to unexpected American principles than its staff might want to accept. No matter how much high-tech American equipment Fact had at its disposal, it would be impossible to ignore the cultural price tag attached. Corruption—*only you Americans call it that, you never understand what other people might reasonably have in mind, we can't help wanting what we want when we've had nothing*—created symmetry and balance: it was normal and acceptable and hopeless to stop in a system that was growing more corrupt with each tick of the clock. "So—you think this will be a problem?" Yak asked heavily and then, answering his own question, "I do, too. I might as well admit it," he said. "You've no doubt guessed it for yourself. This will cause many problems, but not today."

Weighing the ethical and professional issues that challenged the successful distribution of *Commersant* in the West as his limo stopped in front of Billington's guest house, Yakovlev decided they were moot because what he needed were computers, printers, disks, telephones, intercoms, graphic reproduction machines, cameras, film, chemicals, batteries, pens, staplers, staples, paper clips, ink, computer design software programs, Russian-English word processing programs, computer networking systems, electrical power convertors, cables, lenses, extension cords, plugs, copying machines, large-format computer design monitors, direct satellite phone links to the West, answering machines, and—most important—hard-currency backup from Billington to repair any technical problems and to cover the purchase of spare parts.

"Equipment is the most important variant," Yak said, erecting the huge and heavy hand-carved chess set he had brought to Chicago as a gift for Billington, sapping his penultimate two hundred dollars. "*Commersant*'s success in America and in the Soviet Union depends entirely on having computers. These other matters are not variants until we have a newspaper."

"Hey, Volodya, how's business? How was the flight?" Billington asked in his rapid-fire staccato, bounding into the immaculately decorated living room of the old carriage house, wrapped in a white flannel bathrobe.

"Business is good; the flight was too long," Yak said, shaking Billington's hand.

"Yeah, you look beat." Billington laughed, heading out the door and across the lawn to the main house. "Get some sleep. Breakfast tomorrow around eight."

Stretched out in a patio chair overlooking his forty-two acres and gnawing on the tip of a Monte Cristo the following afternoon, Billington flipped through the Russian-and-English-language editions of *Commersant* and fired questions at Yak: How many copies did he intend to print? Where was he going to get ruble-priced newsprint? How would the paper be transmitted to the United

States? Would the weekly be able to sustain American journalistic standards? What kind of assurances were there that the state would not shut down Fact and *Commersant?* What kind of equipment was needed? Whom else had he been talking to about financing? What would Race's cut be? And, finally: "How much money do you need, Volodya?"

"Maybe five hundred thousand dollars," Yak said, describing the immense cost of starting a newspaper from scratch.

"That's a lot of money, Volodya," Billington said calmly, looking out at the multimillion-dollar Henry Moore sculptures that decorated his lawn. Billington was well aware of the games that Soviet culture had coerced Yak into playing so that he could create Fact. These were risks and, although the ethics Yak employed to take them might not survive close examination in the West, the fact that Yak had climbed out on a political and economic limb to get his business started impressed Billington. Billington knew that even Yak's harshest detractors never accused him of not having guts. Guts made fortunres. Guts built empires. And in the Soviet Union it was guts that got things done. Guts and cunning. *Shtruny* and *khitry.* Yak had both.

Billington understood the Soviet Union because he admitted that he did not understand the Soviet Union. "Somebody once told me that Chip Bohlen, the old U.S. Ambassador in Moscow, said there were two big lies in life never to be believed," Billington explained. "The first was 'I never get drunk on champagne' and the second was 'I know what's going to happen in the Soviet Union.'" Throughout his adult life, Billington had been able to comprehend the attitudes of the foreign countries in which Race operated because he surrounded himself with advisers whose most important qualification was an understanding of both the street and the market. The accepted, rational views of the Soviet Union from the ivory towers of academia and tunnel-visioned perspectives of the State Department were flawed because they never took a full register of what was actually going on for either personal or political reasons. Billington walked soybean fields and talked to cattle ranchers before studying the facts and figures offered by the experts. Likewise, in the Soviet Union, he wanted to rely on individuals who could see what was really going on behind the silhouettes presented by academic experts, television and newspaper reports, and U.S. government policy.

Three of the people Billington turned to for advice on Fact were known as his Russia Group, and they had firsthand knowledge of the Soviet Union. Ed Weidenfeld, Billington's Washington lawyer, cut through the murk of State, Defense, and Commerce Department Soviet policy doctrine with the precision of a veteran radar man picking cruise missiles out of cloud formations. Weidenfeld's encyclopedic knowledge of U.S.–Soviet trade restrictions, and his insider-takes on the congressional legislation and executive branch directives that sculpted America's Soviet posture, were buttressed by long and quiet friendships with senior Soviet officials in Washington and Moscow. The second member of Billington's troika was Sally Onesti, a doctoral candidate in Soviet studies from the W. Averell Harriman Institute for Advanced Study of the Soviet Union at Columbia University. Handsomely tall and very straightforward, Onesti was fluent in the Russian language and in the workings of the down-and-dirty mechanics of the Soviet political process. The final member of Billington's advisory panel was Robert Manoff, the former editor of the *Columbia Journalism Review* and *Harper's Magazine*, who had left the cut and slash of journalism to found and manage the Center for War, Peace, and the News Media, the distinguished Soviet-American media study institute at New York University.

Informally, the Russia Group provided counsel on the principle that *perestroika* was a possibility, not yet a reality, and they pulled no punches in advising Billington of the risks he assumed in any deal cut with Yakovlev. Weidenfeld outlined the technology-transfer problems, chief of which would be receiving the special government licenses needed to legally export much of the computerized networking equipment Yakovlev required, including systems with military and intelligence applications. Onesti briefed Billington on *perestroika*'s often senseless riot and disorder and the tendency of cooperators to latch on to Western businessmen like tapeworms hooking up to a nutritious digestive system. Manoff provided a synopsis of the vagaries of Soviet journalism and, warning of the ethical explosions and technical difficulties *Commersant* would encounter from the moment Yak declared the weekly a member of the free press, offered the free services of his center to search for and select American editors who could best breach the difficulties without repercussions for the final product or Race's reputation. The group's final consensus was that a deal of this magnitude with the Russians, particularly a cooperative, was an extremely perilous undertaking, but the dangers were outweighed by historic and potentially profitable results if the venture proved successful.

"Hey, Volodya, if I send you all this equipment, you're not going to go out and sell it on the black market, are you?" Billington queried, half mocking, half serious, and tapping the iconlike, page-eleven *Commersant* photograph of Roman Kudriavtsev's head captioned: *It is so difficult to run the business honestly.* Roman, who served as one of Billington's Fact-appointed Moscow guides, had been a guest at the Oak Park Estate a few weeks before Yak's arrival and had thrown the entire household staff into turmoil. The dentist to whom Billington had sent Roman to get his teeth fixed ended up pulling out a few unsalvageable molars. Returning to the estate a bloody mess of beer and novocaine, Roman proceeded to fall asleep atop each of the guest house's three beds, leaving a trail of pus, blood, and cotton balls on every sheet, bedspread, and piece of linen in the place. Roman had never seen so many rooms in his life, and there was enough beer in the refrigerator to keep him whacked for twenty-four hours a day. Billington had rightly gauged Roman's lunacy and hapless ignorance, the result of a life spent on the lower links in the Soviet food chain; and Billington could only shake his head and tell Roman to get a grip on reality when, a few hours before taking off with one of the estate's young drivers for his nightly trip to pick up "wanton women" in Chicago bars, he asked for a fleet of Chevrolets and Mercedes-Benzes and three dozen digital walkie-talkies plus cellular phones and a supply of nickel-cadmium batteries, with which to open the Moscow Business Center Courier Service.

"No, no, Tom," Yak laughed, his face exhaling smoke, and narrowing into a squint-eyed leer: Sabina's sure sign of impending disaster. "We need the equipment too much to do that."

"Uh-huh," Billington said, eyeing Yak with the hard look of a man who's heard it all before. "That wouldn't be a very bright thing to do, Volodya," he added soberly and then, his cautious business baritone rising a few octaves, "but I *like* this deal. I like this deal because the Soviet Union is a market with great potential, and information is the one commodity everyone who deals in it is going to need and be willing to pay for. I like this deal because all of your overheads in newsprint and accessing the information are costed in rubles once the equipment arrives. I don't want to be nickeled-and-dimed out of more hard currency down the road, like every other joint venture going on in the Soviet Union. This is important. . . .

"Volodya, you really need to go visit my dentist to get your teeth fixed," Billington said suddenly, repeating the offer he had been making all day.

"I hate dentists," Yak countered, with the full knowledge of what the visit had cost Roman, "and my teeth are beyond repair. All a dentist would do is make them worse."

"Okay, Volodya, it's crazy and it might work, so you got your-self four hundred thousand dollars," Billington said, nodding his head through a thick cloud of cigar smoke, a satisfied smile on his face. "You go inside and make a list of what you need and I'll get the lawyers to draw up the contracts.

"And Volodya, listen," Billington cautioned. "Don't get in over your head."

Yak was in too much ecstasy to hear. Yak never listened, maybe because Billington smiled a lot that cool summer afternoon, the brown eyes the softest element in features offset by long arms, broad shoulders, and the spring-box stride of a linebacker, or a lion. He wore only dark suits. The cut was British proper and it tended to make his body look uncomfortable when he laughed, which was often. Billington was the embodiment of a country boy "done good" and Yakovlev had come to him as the supplicant of a system at war. The relationship between Billington and Yakovlev was not only interesting in itself; unknown to Yak, it fed directly into the commodity profession's ability to see profit in chaos. Most commodity traders worship only the deal, not the product grown or manufactured from the commodity: it is evidence of the market's dependence on the profession of buying and selling. Billington, a farm boy, was different in that he passionately cared about farmers, soybeans, pork bellies, and everything else his company traded around the world. Billington encouraged people to accept responsibility for their dreams, and then, if the dream looked to be a good investment, backed up his energy with money. Fact had its new computers, but the deal had tapped a firestorm of energy that Yak had never understood or anticipated. Billington operated on an extraordinarily intense level, as did Yakovlev. The difference between the two players was that Billington always knew what he was doing.

To the sound of honking Canadian geese and a popped vintage champagne cork, U.S.–Soviet history was made on the patio of an Illinois estate: the first newspaper to be jointly owned and operated by an American and a Russian, the unique nature of the deal furthered by Billington's unwillingness ever to speak with newspaper people. Billington understood the massive problems that faced the project, and the possibility of the state's coming in and shutting down the operation without any warning and for any reason. The risks were high and uncontrollable, but the rewards of his union with Fact were potentially impressive. If the free market hit the Soviet Union as *perestroika* promised, then Race would be on the cutting edge of Russia's financial-information base and in an unrivaled position to market data to the West. It would also have the ability to negotiate the purchase of Soviet broadcasting and banking licenses, commodity and stock market exchange seats, and Soviet raw materials through the cooperative sector. The initial investment would be returned to Billington with a tidy profit through Race's sale of *Commersant* subscriptions to the West for around two hundred forty-five dollars a year, and through licensing agreements to distribute the Postfactom data base by way of Dow Jones or Reuters, both firms having expressed interest in negotiating terms to transmit Postfactom's rare information to their clients.

Yak grasped that Billington reckoned to use Fact as Race's Moscow outpost, and he was happy to oblige the man who was now both his American mentor and backer. And, although Billington never admitted it, Yak knew that the Chicago commodity trader saw a lot of himself as a young man in the *Commersant* project, fighting to start a business and kneading profits against all odds. "Yeah, I want to help these guys out," Billington explained after he concluded the deal. "These cooperators are people with brains who American businessmen might want to abandon because to work with them is to possibly alienate the governmental authorities. I don't see it that way. You've got to help out people who want to expand, you don't want to get in the way of people who want to grow."

The negotiations took less than twenty minutes, concluding with Billington presenting Yak with his Mont Blanc Diplomat, the initials "TB" etched in the pen's fat gold band. "That's for you to sign all your future deals with," Billington announced, sticking the black pen in Yak's shirt pocket at the end of the outdoor conference. "Let's go see what's in the kitchen, guys," Billington said, adding, "The big dog eats first."

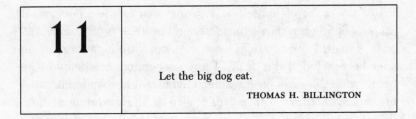

11

Let the big dog eat.

THOMAS H. BILLINGTON

RUSISHKA WAS at first drained by the wild news; then, his shambling figure draped over coffee and whipped egg whites a few days later at the Margarita Café, the young Politburo bureaucrat started going like mad with the usual selection of old apocalyptic images. There were those in Moscow, he said, including some prominent liberal politicians, who saw Yakovlev's overnight transformation into the Citizen Kane of the Soviet Union as a dark day for *perestroika*. Trusishka wondered how long it would be until Yak wormed his way onto the Oprah Winfrey show, because even Gorbachev had heard of the Fact–Race deal through his economic adviser Stanislav Shatalin. There was no shortage of criticism and an absolute glut of fear in the government corridors. Trusishka said quite a few people just laughed, but acute discomfort was the best way to describe the overall reaction of the Apparat. Even the allies of the cooperative movement on the Council of Ministers were privately joking about Yak's deficiencies even as they publicly hailed the importance of *Commersant* as another step to a truly functioning free market. "Why the criticism?" I asked. After all, Fact had been together for two years—an eternity for a Soviet cooperative and certainly long enough for Kremlin liberals to express some faith in Yak's ability to use *Commersant* and the Race deal as a powerful tool to help implement *perestroika.*

"That is a miscalculation," Trusishka divulged in the low, deep breath of the Soviet bureaucrat. "There's nothing I can really put my finger on. I don't think anyone is going to close down Fact, but there will be a conscientious review on many levels."

"Conscientious review? What does that mean!?" I asked. Four intense days with Tom Billington was plenty of time for even a Russian to learn just about anything he needed to know about business, especially the attitude needed to survive a deal with Race and win in the American market. Yakovlev's survival in Russia and America was a question of enlightened and overlapping self-interest for both governments. The success of *Commersant* would be a public relations coup, a solid example that Americans and Russians could work and financially profit together.

Trusishka and I had discussed the question of money and why hard cash was so important to the success of Soviet economic recovery. Since Gorbachev's election as General Secretary of the Communist Party in 1985, the state foreign trade bank, Vnesheconombank, had been pursuing cash like never before. During the Brezhnev years, the Kremlin paid cash for necessary imports that topped sixty million dollars. But Gorbachev was strapped for cash, so desperate that Vnesh bankers were aggressively seeking Western bank underwriting for foreign trade deals worth as little as one hundred thousand dollars—the very kind of small investment-capital cooperators needed to vitalize a true free market.* Gorbachev was so broke that the nickels and dimes cooperators like Yakovlev required to buy Western equipment were being used instead to

*"The credits and cash that American banks have extended to the Soviet Union since *perestroika* are usually tied to specific trade and investment deals," explained the Moscow director of a major American bank. "But for a Western bank or corporation to track down its capital to see if a loan is used for its specific purpose is costly, time-consuming, and impossible in the Soviet Union. We have tried to get official permission from the state to visit a number of sites to investigate whether the lent capital is really being used for its specific purpose. The answer is no nine times out of ten. The excuses we receive are that the area is a security zone, the people we want to see are not there, or the factory is a danger area not fit for amateurs. The most popular excuse is that there is no place for us to stay overnight."

service the state's debt load and purchase food from the West. Vnesh was unable to make small hard-currency loans to coopera- tors. Tom Billington was. So the consequences of the Oak Park meeting were serious, with the potential to be financially fatal to the entire cooperative movement. If Yakovlev failed to deliver the kind of product Race could market in the West, there was little chance that other American businessmen would dare to invest in the cooperative revolution.

"You and I, and I am sure Billington, agree that the success of this unique joint venture is of equal importance to both our governments and the Soviet free market," Trusishka said, "but you are wrong to assume that Yakovlev and others would see it in such terms because they care what happens to the cooperative move- ment. I dare say the naive believe Yakovlev merely makes money off the mafias when he is, in fact, the mafia. Yakovlev is one of those involved in shady dealings."

Trusishka, as usual, offered a dose of traumatizing reality as I returned to Moscow with Yakovlev. It always took a few days of hard ground-time to realize all over again that the U.S.S.R.—even with *perestroika*—was the unhappiest of contracts between citizen and government. The energy of the Race deal was positive and exciting until one crossed into Soviet air space. What hit hardest was the absolute inability of Russians to fathom the imperatives of individual integrity, social justice, and public service. Instead the U.S.S.R. offered only a struggle for money and power won by skillful shenanigans. A generalization, perhaps, but near enough to ring true. American and other Western diplomats irrepressibly said as much in private. Publicly they were more circumspect, of course. Most Soviet experts in the West were fearful of burning any bridge that linked their careers to the Kremlin's inside track. But it was a different story of "half-breeds" and "amateurs" told when one spent an evening at the Canadian Embassy's Friday night beer and hamburger party with U.S. State Department officials and American businessmen stationed in Moscow. Reality's ugly lump also showed itself when one tried to initiate an evenhanded discussion on the new spectrum of Soviet political thought with a nicotine-hungry Soviet People's Deputy three days after he had come to blows with tobacco kiosk vendors who refused to sell cigarettes without dollars. *Perestroika* was a scandal of fundamental falsity and slick hubris. For the Russians who wanted to stay in-country, the only way out of the mess was to sell out to a rich foreigner.

By the end of 1989, the pop excitement of *perestroika* had turned to vascular blowout, and not even Trusishka could see anything positive in *Commersant*'s pledge to help open the Soviet free market and unlock the floodgates of democracy. Yakovlev's adrenaline was pumping, however. Making money in the twilight zone was Yak's forte, and he did it by engaging his partners as both romantic collaborators and revolutionary peers in nothing short of transforming the Earth's richest and most misunderstood land mass into the world's largest industrial hypermarket, with *Commersant* positioned directly in front of the checkout counter. Yak did not have any pragmatic strategy. His flexible arrangements with government *zashchitniki* remained murky.* What Yak did have in abundance was the perception to mix black-market reality with the fundamentals of Soviet corruption. A few, like Hajibau down in Zakatala, tried to stay clean in their operations, but they were being hit very hard and then harder again. Despite the efforts of Vladimir Tikhonov, the Cooperative Congress had become arrogantly ridden with factions bogged down by the same mushy philosophies and gauzy policy justifications that defined and paralyzed Gorbachev's government. Their frivolous rivalries and competing ambitions mirrored the revolutionary French *Frondeurs*, the malcontent party that rebelled against Cardinal Mazarin and Louis

---

*Fact's single most important bureaucrat seemed to be Bela Petravitus, a Lithuanian in charge of advising the Council of Ministers and the Central Committee on cooperative policy. Petravitus, who many believed actually fashioned the cooperative laws and decrees of the government, was, concurrently, Fact's most welcomed and feared visitor. The only insight Fact's employees ever had into his motivations occurred when Yakovlev returned to the office one afternoon in a panic, asking everyone if they had access to women's nylon stockings. Petravitus's ulcer had reached such critical mass that he had been taken to the hospital, where nurses allegedly refused to attend to his needs without first being given hosiery. Almost all business in the cooperative stopped for twenty-four hours, returning to normal only after a cache of Western nylons had been found and delivered to Fact's ill *zashchitnik*.

XIV and who took their name from the word applied to children who threw stones and then ran away giggling as soon as the police arrived, only to throw more stones the moment the authorities turned their backs.

Corruption remained the driveshaft of the cooperative machine, just as it had been when Vitali Korotich first sent Yakovlev off in 1987 to investigate the free-market phenomenon for *Ogonyok*. By January 31, 1990, *perestroika* had created one thousand three hundred Soviet joint ventures with the West and only one, Combustion Engineering's deal with the Petroleum Ministry to manufacture factory control systems, had shown a profit. Moreover, the intoxicating cooperative wars of *perestroika*'s early years were supposed to have been fought against the creeping corruption of communism, but *perestroika* turned into one big abusive internal conflict, with few government or private sector operations caring about anything other than getting in on the action to enrich themselves. The Russian bear was not dead. Its wounds had not even proven fatal. Through their actions, both the cooperators and the state bureaucrats revealed that they had no program for real reform, no motive other than self-interest, no able or politically honest leaders, and no cohesion. Yak started Fact daring to be different, but his staff privately agreed that the most exciting things Yakovlev's mind ever did after his return from Chicago were lie, laugh, and create chaos that others ended up having to deal with.

But controlling chaos was the solution to making money out of the muddle that was the Soviet economy. Yak knew this. He had told Billington it was possible to make money out of the Soviet market if Fact and Race specialized in helping Western business cope with the world of *perestroika*. Billington agreed, but he made it clear that he wanted to see results.

"You get one chance, Volodya, so don't get in over your head," Billington had repeated over and over in Chicago.

Crates of sophisticated computers and newspaper-production gear started arriving in Moscow in early December 1989, so much high-tech that Soviet customs agents kept the stuff locked up for weeks because it was impossible for them to figure out exactly what the equipment did and why it was being shipped to a remote cooperative on Good Highway. The arrival of the equipment threw the co-op into a panic, causing Fact's chief fixer, Bela Alexandrovna Ivanov, to virtually live inside a car parked at the airport. Many items left the Sheremetyevo customs shed opened and damaged: Xerox machines arrived drenched in toner, computers mysteriously lacked the proper circuit boards, and assorted stationery articles appeared to have been pilfered. It was not a good start, because every second counted: Billington had given Yak until June 1990 to put together a marketable newspaper; otherwise the machinery would be hauled back to America.

Masterminding Race's end of the operation was Peggy Yott, a thirty-seven-year-old communications expert in charge of Race's instant global information system. Although Yott had never been to the Soviet Union, she did have the good fortune to be married to an Illinois bunko cop, who accompanied her and Billington to Moscow once the bulk of the equipment had been installed in *Commersant*'s office in February 1990. Immediately, Yott told herself that she would have to be careful. For her, Yakovlev's smile—Sabina's "leer"—was not the result of nearsightedness, but the look of a man who might well destroy everything around him simply out of amusement. Yott registered the perception dispassionately, but proceeded to conduct an inventory of the equipment in the office against a list of what was sent from Chicago. Yakovlev went ballistic.

"Volodya's a snake," Yott said four days and as many arguments into her first visit to Moscow. "There are a lot of people like him in the commodity business. There's also no doubt that he can get things done. If he wants to."

Yak wanted to. At first. He brought out the limos, ferrying Billington's group to the circus, the ballet, and Moscow's last old-fashioned Russian *banya* steambath. The highlight was the party Yak threw for Billington in one of the grandly gilded dining rooms at the Prague restaurant on the Arbat. There were wild gypsy dancers, plates of caviar and rare meats, and fist-sized tumblers of vodka and cognac downed with toasts of friendship. Yak, who had assembled the entire Fact staff for the occasion, ended the evening by presenting Billington with a six-thousand-ruble Russian shotgun as a gift with which to hunt bears. It was a beautiful weapon; but, as Billington's gunsmith later warned: "I wouldn't fire this if I were you. It has every chance of blowing up in your face."

Nonetheless, Billington and Yott were eager to be pioneers on the new frontier of U.S.–Soviet relations. Gorbachev had turned on the charm for business leaders such as Billington during a gathering at the Soviet Embassy in Washington a few months before the Race–Fact deal. The businessmen had left the ninety-minute session impressed by what they heard, looking favorably on expanding business with the Soviets. The eagerness of American business to enter the Soviet market was entirely the result of Gorbachev's calls for American companies to participate in joint ventures with Russians under new policies that relaxed a number of the inflexible conditions the Soviet government had established to protect itself. Foreign firms, for example, now had the opportunity to own more than 49 percent of a joint venture. Furthermore, Gorbachev had confessed to American businessmen that the Soviets were "too myopic in looking for results that would benefit the Soviet Union as against those who were the joint-venture partner." This statement, according to some of the American businessmen who attended the meeting, led many business leaders to believe that American companies would be given a more equal footing with their Soviet partners.

But Gorbachev spoke only about joint ventures between the state and the Western businesses; he never directly addressed joint ventures involving the cooperatives. The Council of Ministers retained broad regulatory authority over cooperatives, going so far in the spring of 1989 as to decree: "Cooperatives may not engage in the purchase of goods intended for resale for export." Just as no one at Fact was sure whether or not this decree included the purchase of news and information for sale to the West, they were just as certain that any problems the cooperative might have in this area would be best corrected through the continued sound application of the payoffs known as *vzyatka*.

Fact's Soviet attorneys advised Yakovlev that the most efficient temporary loophole, until the constantly changing laws were made more receptive, would be officially to register the cooperative's association with Race as a partnership under Soviet law and as a joint venture under American law. Although no one was certain of the move's legal ramifications if the authorities ever decided to crack down on the partnership, it did give Yakovlev a rather ambiguous opening to keep whatever hard currency might come of the association in the United States. As a matter of course, Billington agreed to investigate this option with his Chicago attorneys. But whenever the opportunity to press the issue presented itself, Yakovlev repeated, almost desperate: "The American-registered joint venture is the most important variant. We must have it."

Indeed, Yak spent an inordinate amount of time urging Billington—via Telex, fax, and telephone—to register their partnership as a joint venture in America. It was certainly odd, Yott thought, particularly since Yak had done absolutely nothing to repair *Commersant* during the six months from the time the deal was signed in Chicago in September 1989, until her arrival in Moscow. Eight issues were published between January and March 1990, and while the American editor hired by Billington's adviser Rob Manoff had yet to arrive, the English-language edition was getting worse with each passing week. Yott had transmitted nearly two hundred Telexes to Yakovlev, and his replies to questions about deadline schedules, transmission timetables, and the contents for the American launch in June, as well as the details on the proposed sale of Postfactom news to Reuters and Dow Jones, had been ambiguous, uncertain, and unsatisfactory.

"Most of the Telex traffic centered on when Billington was going to register the joint venture in America and when the rest of the equipment would arrive," Yott said. "This was the most important matter on Volodya's mind, when the most important matter on our mind was making *Commersant* readable. A lot of the equipment he needed had been held up by Commerce Department technology reviewers or by Soviet customs. But he had the computers and enough stuff to get the paper going; the paper was coming out, a fact which we felt was a major success, but the other equipment he needed was not necessary to repair the problems in the paper."

Billington had built Race into a powerful company because he knew how to delegate power and responsibility. Yott was the woman in charge of the Fact project. Somehow, Yakovlev never understood this, and his ignorance was underscored by his inability to perceive Yott's hands-on management style from the American end as anything but interference from a woman who did not understand business or the Soviet Union.

"Everyone at Race was very sensitive to Volodya's wishes," Yott explained. "I knew this was all new to him, and I realized the difficulties he and the Soviet Union were facing. We were prepared for major political, technical, and financial problems, but what we weren't prepared for was Volodya's aversion to helping us repair them. He actually thought that he was smarter than Billington, which was a major, major mistake."

Yakovlev, angry that Yott had failed to convince Billington to register the joint venture in America within eight weeks, was further enraged by Race's failure to deliver the large computer monitors and ancillary equipment necessary to design and transmit a newspaper electronically. These specialized pieces of hardware, along with a computer information sharing system called Ethernet, had never before been legally exported to the Soviet Union, and according to Yak, the only Soviet firm that had similar equipment was the Ministry of Defense, which customized the machinery's internal computer-chip structure for Star Wars–type applications. Billington, who categorically refused to ship equipment outside channels that did not take into account U.S. technology-transfer laws, had pressed Ed Weidenfeld to get Commerce Department authorization for the equipment to be shipped to Moscow, even if he had to lobby to change the law. Although Weidenfeld was ultimately successful, Yakovlev believed the delays to be part of a provocation directed against him by Yott in an effort to kill the deal. When the thirty-thousand-dollar monitors finally arrived, physically broken and without the computer chips to make them operate correctly, Yakovlev steadfastly believed that he was on the short end of a conspiracy and that Yott was either taking kickbacks from suppliers or purchasing inferior equipment to save Billington money.

"I'm sure of it," Yak said, throwing one of his flying stars into the door, asking me reproachfully if there was any way Yott could be exposed and removed. "There can be no other reason."

"You're crazy, Volodya," I said. "Billington doesn't operate that way and Yott would never dream of doing such a thing. Look at all the equipment you already have. There's absolutely no reason to think Yott is screwing you over. People like that have a limited life expectancy with Billington, and you better wise up, otherwise you're going to be one of them."

"There's no other reason!" Yak responded, supremely indifferent to the reality around him. "Why do we not have the joint venture? Why don't the monitors work? It's a provocation."

"You're on dangerous ground, Volodya," I warned sternly. "Something is blinding you and I don't know what it is. Your suspicions are unfounded and insulting. These things take time and lawyers. Over ninety percent of your equipment arrived in a little over two months. That's a confirmed miracle. Billington said that you could choose whatever equipment you wanted, but you went out and bought IBMs when every newspaper and graphic designer between Moscow and Chicago—including Fact's own art director—told you to get Apple computers and monitors because they're more efficient, easier to service, and more easily authorized by the Commerce Department."

"They are real shits," Yak said. "They do nothing."

"No, they're your friends and partners—and if you continue thinking like that they won't be for much longer. What's a piece of shit is *Commersant,* and you'd be better served putting your energy into making it a readable newspaper. You're supposed to launch this thing at the Bush-Gorbachev summit in June and that's only three months away."

12

> *Commersant* was like a pool hall, always
> filled with smoke and strange guys.
>
> BRAD DURHAM

BRAD DURHAM, jet-lagged and with a pocket of Bic pens leaking into his wrinkled khaki trousers, first caught sight of the Fact/*Commersant* offices through a heavy rain twenty minutes after clearing Soviet customs. Fact's staff stared at Durham's precise profile, which bore an uncanny resemblance to that of actor William Hurt, whose movie in grim appraisal of American journalism, *Broadcast News*, was making Moscow's underground video rounds. The Soviet Union to which Durham arrived in March 1990 was a nation nearing the threshold of a violent revolution. Wariness, about everyone and everything, was rampant. There was a national mistrust that could not be described in words: it had to be felt, and the doppelgänger of William Hurt's cheesy network reporter was under siege from the moment he arrived.

Rob Manoff had warned Durham of Fact's social and political turmoil in January, shortly after sifting through nearly two dozen résumés sent to him at New York University from around the United States to select *Commersant*'s American editor. Durham, a third-year law student at Suffolk University in Massachusetts, held a master's degree in journalism from Boston University. Durham had worked on the *Boston Phoenix* and had been the managing editor of *The World Paper*, a Boston-based periodical supplement produced as an insert for newspapers and magazines around the world. Fluent in German and with a working knowledge of Russian, the twenty-eight-year-old native Oklahoman told Manoff and Yott that it would be exciting to leave law school and *The World Paper* for one year to become involved in the genuinely radical experiment of *Commersant*, even though his salary would be paid entirely in rubles. Like all the other final candidates, Durham's editing skills were superb, and his written critique of *Commersant's* first few issues was a bull's-eye, accurately targeting the problems that needed to be remedied before the summit launch. For the next ten months, Durham would live in a series of Russian hotels and apartments arranged by Fact fixer Bela Alexandrovna, commuting to and from Good Highway in whatever taxi or private car he was able to flag down in the street. (Despite the increasing violence in and around Moscow among the private mafias and small-time thieves, it was still perfectly safe to follow local custom and accept rides from random citizen drivers who wanted to earn a few extra rubles.)

"Two things were clear immediately," Durham said at the end of his first day in Moscow, scattering the usual Western supplies of toothpaste and peanut butter across the floor of his room in the Hotel Mir. "*Commersant* could be a widely read and valuable tool in the West, but facing off with Russian intransigence will be a real challenge, with deadlines that will be crucifying. I'll need a competent staff and bushels of patience, and the energy to pull this off through a leviathan effort. All in all, my situation here is too good to be true, so I'm sure some travesty must be lurking."

Durham intended to reason with Yakovlev and the *Commersant* staff. If reason did not get results in time to meet deadlines, then Durham would assail Soviet sensibilities in the only manner proven to work. "I discovered very quickly that it was necessary to scream a bit if you wanted to be taken seriously," Durham observed at the end of his first week in Moscow. "Stand up, get in their face, and yell at them like you would a stubborn bulldog. A businesslike demeanor gets you nowhere here.

"The first issue was Volodya's refusal to do a routine layout of the whole paper before it was pasted up on the computer. I kept telling him it would be a good idea if we knew what stories were coming down the pike and where to put them in the paper, instead of being blindsided at the eleventh hour. So the proofreaders began huffing and puffing every time I asked for a story list. All they said was, 'It's a pity we don't have one.' "

Commersant's stories were bad, often spurious, and Yakovlev went into shock whenever Durham, in his position as the editor of the English-language edition or I, as Yakovlev's adviser, explained this to him. Each article was an exercise in abstraction and full of phrases such as "this theory of business is confirmed by objective information." Durham, who started describing himself as a "voodoo editor" at the end of his second week on the job, began to smoke out stories on his own for the English-language edition. "The most memorable thing about *Commersant* was how all the copy read like something out of a Marxist manual," Durham recalled, bleary-eyed, the Monday morning after he closed his second English-language edition. "I attacked the copy with a vengeance. The majority of copy published in the Russian-language edition was written as notes, not stories, so the translations came into our news department as notes, too. There was serious resistance when I tried to rearrange the copy, but I did it anyway. The English edition was my baby and it would succeed, or fail miserably, based on my decisions on how to handle the copy. It took me all night. The files kept coming in from the translators. Things were slightly surreal. Who would have known one month ago I would be watching the sun come up on a Sunday morning in Moscow, drinking cognac, having just edited an entire newspaper at a world-class pace with a vodka-sodden security guard fond of taking apart his pistol and whispering 'boobala' in my ear. Poor dolt was a moonlighting Soviet Green Beret.

"Whackos I can put up with, but this kind of writing has to go, and I'm going to have to teach them," Durham laughed. "But it isn't easy. At six A.M., a few minutes after we had closed the paper, I had a strategy session with Yak. Though I was completely spent, I still managed to get my dander worked up when he told me that I was to get no help for the American edition. I told him about the pathetic copy. There's this one guy, Igor Fine, who writes the 'Sports Line' column. No one at Fact has ever seen him because some professional wrestlers from Tashkent are after him at the moment because he wrote something about a Russian basketballer who drank too much champagne and was then knifed to death by some Uzbeks.

"There are things that just cannot be explained, like the Dreaded Sokolov, our chief political writer, who speaks in grunts nobody can understand, or why, on my fifth day in Moscow, I arrived to find my desk infested with mosquitoes. It's winter."

There were many events in and around Cooperative Fact that existed beyond the realm of explanation. Unreal occurrences were part of the *Commersant* experience. For instance, the Moscow sewage workers out on Good Highway, who, having somehow lost the lid of a manhole, sawed down a thirty-foot tree and dropped it down the open hole so cars would not plunge in. How do you lose a manhole cover?

Only a few weeks after he began work, Durham phoned my apartment at dawn one day to commiserate: "I think we're in for some trouble. *Pravda* slammed *Commersant* this morning, said the staff was making three times as much money as other cooperatives. And yesterday I went over to see the new U.S. Commercial Officer in Moscow. He told me that he thought the Russians were cute when he first arrived in the Soviet Union; now he thinks they should be used for genetic experimentation. I feel hung over, though I haven't touched a drop. What the hell have we gotten into?"

It was a good question to ask. The West's new political perception of the Soviet Union was light-years removed from what Durham and I were experiencing daily. "There are a lot of buffoons on the staff," Durham wrote in the diary he kept intermittently for the first few months of his stay in Moscow. "One of them came up to me drunk last night to confess that he's a 'capitalist.' It's considered to be hip and progressive to make some ribald pledge of allegiance to capitalism—long live the forbidden ideology!"

The approximately two thousand five hundred square feet of the Fact/*Commersant* office was supposed to be the center of the new-look, entrepreneurial Soviet Union. Nearly sixty people worked on *Commersant,* and one of the many weekly arguments among them was who would be granted the use of the byline "Maxim Pac Man" atop their copy. Yakovlev had organized the place along the lines of a video arcade in the sense that the machines, and not those who worked them, came first. The appearance of Durham, who would presumably give the office a more professional atmosphere, seemed fortunate; but *Bradchik,* as he had been nicknamed, was losing whatever little support he had hoped to gain from Yakovlev. "Volodya is not a real journalist but an egomaniac and a great Soviet businessman," Durham said, describing the recurring scene. "The paper needs work and the Yak spends most of his time playing Pac Man, as does the rest of the staff. 'Editing Pac Man, are you?' is what I say whenever I catch them. If *Commersant* fails it will be because of Pac Man. That's the reality of the place. The only one immune to the game is the Dreaded Sokolov, who feels that his time could be better spent at home with vodka."

The Russian staff was completely committed to the success of *Commersant*'s Russian-language edition, however. Yakovlev and his disciples had engraved a popular image of themselves as revolutionaries in the minds of *Commersant* readers. Virtually every reader was touched—from the kiosk hawkers who sold the paper around Moscow, to their customers who scooped up over 350,000 copies of *Commersant* within hours of its arrival on the streets on Monday morning. By Soviet standards, *Commersant* was unconventional, its unique personality, when judged alongside the listless official press, yielded both reader interest and staff loyalty. *Commersant*'s art director, Kit Golovanov, had worked for twelve years at the publishing house of the Communist Party Central Committee before coming to Fact. Yakovlev had lured Golovanov away from his state position with the promise of lots of high-tech design gear and computer software; unfortunately Yak had used Billington's money to purchase all the wrong equipment, causing Golovanov no end of technical problems. At first no one complained: *Commersant* was the angle many Russians spent years looking for, never to find. The French had a word for it, *attentisme,* the act of waiting for something to come along. "There was a lot of absolutely preposterous hustling. This was their chance and by God they were going to take it," Durham explained. "Andrei Vasiliev, one of the senior business editors, used the cooperative as a means of getting to Italy, from where he returned with a bagful of Fiat windshield wiper blades to sell in Moscow because they fit the Soviet Lada.

"Volodya's girlfriend, Ksenyia, was the manager of the American edition, and she stood behind the silliness without shame, unable to acknowledge that *Commersant's* stories were seriously flawed," Durham said. "Accuracy was most important and if our American distribution was to be realized, accuracy—not using the cooperative to get windshield wipers—had to be stressed."

The policy of Billington's Russia Group was to allow Durham full management control of the English-language edition. My role had evolved inasmuch as I no longer took an active part in the nuts-and-bolts editing of the American edition. Durham kept me advised of his progress in shaping the organization as the summit launch approached and, if the Russians interfered too much with him, I went in to negotiate a solution with Yakovlev. Yet Yak was unable to grasp the problems that had to be resolved. Always careful to not infringe upon the perks cooperative members enjoyed, Yak made a point to avoid participating in the moral and political conflicts that were developing as a result of Americans and Soviets working together.

Yet there were unique revelations taking place inside *Commersant,* prompting both Durham and me to take a fresh look at the wide-eyed observations being made in the West about *perestroika.* The *Commersant* political and economic writers spoke of Mikhail Gorbachev, Abel Aganbeygan, Stanislav Shatalin, and other leading restructurist economists and politicians as being right-wing. Whenever I asked political editor Sasha Fadin why his staff was so distrustful of *perestroika* (particularly since the disaffection came from people who were benefiting from the changes put into effect by the government) and how restructuring could be considered a totalitarian policy in light of Soviet history, I was told that I could never really understand the duplicitous nature of a communist politician, no matter the explanation, because I was an

American and easily fooled otherwise. Fadin's thinking was *per-estroika*'s hard bite; and the abundance of confusingly intimate and anecdotal evidence he and his staff presented to support the contention that *perestroika* was no more than a clever political intrigue was eventually confirmed by the growing right-wing slant of the Supreme Soviet, by Gorbachev's own attempts to limit personal and press freedoms and, most graphically, by the body count of citizens that would be taken on the streets of Latvia and Lithuania in January 1991. No one at Fact ever said it out loud, but there was no anticommunist alternative in the Soviet Union short of revolution.

Russian political and economic reformers, many Soviet pundits in the West argued, were learning about democracy and free markets from scratch. According to those individuals who subscribed to this "politically correct" posture when dealing with Soviets, it was unwise to provoke further disharmony by reproaching their rudimentary efforts. Such criticism, in light of Russia's political and cultural heritage, was considered inappropriate. The Soviets, too, systematically used this excuse as a buffer whenever fabricated incompetence revealed itself to be concocted cunning, often with tragicomic results. One afternoon a British entrepreneur visited Fact to tell us of the baby birch trees he was buying in the Karelia region to resell in London for one pound apiece. As the conversation progressed in English, it was plain the businessman had come to seek information from Fact's marketing advisory service consultants about selling extremely lucrative tours for foreigners to hunt pheasant in Uzbekistan. The *Commersant* experts thought it would be a good idea, but they thought he was talking about Uzbek peasants and continued the consultation along that line. After a few more minutes discussing the hard-currency profits that would come with organizing Uzbek peasant hunts, it was ruefully clear the misconception had absolutely nothing to do with the misinterpretation of language. Finally, when the distinctions were drawn between shooting pheasants and peasants, one of the *Commersant* experts exclaimed: "We can organize pheasants, too!"

I had become a part of Gorbachev's democratic incubator; and, like the Western leaders, who directed vast amounts of financial and technological assistance to Moscow in reward for the regime's apparent abandonment of the past, I had acquiesced to the wrong signals about Kremlin reformers and free-market cooperators from the very start of *perestroika*. I had come to Moscow wanting to believe in *perestroika*. Like many of the other Western correspondents who grew beleaguered trying to report objectively on the increasingly apparent absurdity of the "new" Communist Party applying *perestroika* as an alternative to the society the "old" Communist Party had created, I tended to depersonalize the struggle as much as possible as a reporter, only to find myself personalizing it more than any of my colleagues once I became a cooperator.

The political reformers, in particular, paraded *perestroika* and the cooperative movement as the microcosm of the future Soviet free-market society. *Perestroika* was to set the tone for the co-ops, which in turn were supposed to serve as models for other Russians. But *perestroika* opened a Pandora's box of hostilities and, as far as the public was concerned, the cooperators did more to further pauperize the economy than to enrich it. Honest cooperators were the Nowhere Men in the zany mélange of new Soviet society; and, as Sabina had told me upon our return to Moscow from Zakatala in the summer of 1989, a precise, razor-sharp line of divergence endured between the Yakovlevs and the Hajibaus of the movement. Sabina's picture was not pretty: cooperators saw *perestroika* only as an opportunity to gain power in a country where they feared the consequences if they failed. "You must be Russian to see the canvas," she said.

"The longer you try to live as a Russian, the better you will understand the realities no one other than a Russian will accept about this country," instructed Fadin, who had learned his English behind bars, reading "every word" Kurt Vonnegut ever wrote while serving a long jail sentence on charges of political subversion for possessing a banned copy of *Doctor Zhivago* during the Brezhnev years.

Many of the discussions Durham and I had with the *Commersant* political staff took place in the Cuban Room, *Fact's* Havana-trimmed political news bureau, so named because Fadin was always asking Durham for a "bottle of Cuban room [rum]."

Well-educated, full of street-savvy, and often wearing U.S. Army uniforms, Fadin's political staff rarely mixed with the rest of the cooperative's members, emerging like moles in the dark from the Cuban Room only to eat lunch in the Fact kitchen or to scamper out the door for secret meetings with government sources. Not even Yakovlev could control the autonomy and attitude of the boys in the Cuban Room and, maybe because of it, their writing and insights into what was taking place in the country were the best thing *Commersant* had to offer its readers.

Yakovlev knew it, too, and he began to use the information the political department developed in over a hundred Soviet cities as the basis for selling political risk investment analysis to Westerners who wanted to establish businesses in the country. Durham made sure that the same information ran in the English-language edition, alongside "The Consumer Basket"—the first accurate survey of what necessary items cost the average Soviet in relation to an item's availability and its cost in both state and black-market prices. Another of Durham's innovations was a ruble chart, which treated in a serious manner the fluctuations in the value of the ruble against hard currencies. The ruble chart was an irreverent and groundbreaking effort that analyzed both figures and fluctuations in black-market ruble prices as gauged against real increases and decreases in the cost of Western goods on the street.*

---

*In January 1991 Prime Minister Valentin Pavlov announced that bank withdrawals by Soviet citizens would be limited to five hundred rubles a month, and that fifty- and hundred-ruble notes would be withdrawn from circulation and no longer be valid legal tender. The decree, the first to be issued by Gorbachev's newly formed cabinet of conservative-leaning ministers, was designed to undermine the black market. The Ministry of Finance gave Soviet citizens one week in which to swap large notes for small notes at state banks, but very few banks seemed to want the useless tender. Moscow traffic police said motorists were actively seeking them out to deliberately violate laws to pay spot fines with large banknotes, getting change in smaller bills. Thousands went to train stations to buy tickets that could be partially refunded, and others wired themselves money orders. In a uniquely sardonic Russian way, Gorbachev's ploy to shut down the black market and halt inflation was a case of doing too much too late and with absolutely no consideration of the consequences. The new law, aimed at reducing "speculation, corruption, smuggling, forgery, and unearned income" and at "normalizing the monetary situation and the consumer market," sparked a panic that turned into a great boon for the black market: moneychangers, who gave all comers fifteen rubles cash for every hundred-ruble note, and around three rubles for every fifty-ruble note, paid bank workers a vigorish of between twenty and twenty-

"I knew we were making headway when a Belgian Embassy official told me two months into the job that thirty percent of the English-language edition was correct, but only twenty percent of the Russian-language edition was correct," Durham said during one of our biweekly review sessions. "I'm *Commersant's* Mr. Ten Percent."

Every Monday morning at precisely six A.M., uniformed officers from the *Red Star* would arrive at Fact to collect the *Commersant* layout for printing at the military press situated across the street from the cooperative. If the English-language edition was not ready for its ten-thousand-copy Moscow print run, the Soviet Army charged Yakovlev ten rubles for every minute he made the paper late on press. The week after becoming Mr. Ten Percent, Durham, who had been docked eight hundred rubles in late penalties by the end of his third month, nearly annoyed the government into closing the cooperative down because he gave a *Red Star* colonel a photo of Defense Minister Dmitri Yazov and KGB chief Vladimir Kryshkof with a caption that implicated them too directly as putschists in an attempted coup. Word traveled quickly. "Everybody assumed I was trying to get them thrown into Lubyanka prison," Durham said of the commotion. "The guys in the Cuban Room were the only ones who sympathized with my situation because it was their story that, when translated, said these guys were in cahoots to topple the government. Needless to say, the caption lost something in the translation and the editing process. Sasha Fadin said it posed an interesting dilemma because the Red Star press was controlled by Yazov, and Yakovlev had to call a general to tell him to stop printing the paper because *Commersant* had mistakenly printed that his boss was involved in a plot against Gorbachev."

Twelve months later, the story proved true.

As Durham and I slowly guided the Soviet staff toward

---

five rubles to make the legitimate exchange. Moreover, very few street speculators ever did currency deals using fifty- and hundred-ruble notes. Black-market transactions were usually handled with ten- and twenty-five ruble notes, as were always the legal dollar-for-ruble transactions in the state foreign-trade bank. Although there was no way to confirm my observation, the big bills the government wanted to get rid of were held almost exclusively as life savings by older Russians, who found it more convenient to stash large bills.

mastering the techniques required to create a readable English-language newspaper, there was also a backward slide into the primary problem we were trying to suppress: corruption. There was nothing clandestine or abnormal about the payoffs, the *vzyatka* and *blat* Fact used to get things done. To be sure, the savvy exercise of *vzyatka* and *blat* had been advantageous to Fact's great success in surviving the bureaucracy, and because of it no higher ethical ground existed for Yakovlev to put a halt to the time-honored Soviet tradition. Legitimate or not, given the circumstances, corruption posed serious problems for Fact as soon as it had entered into a partnership with the Race Group—and especially since the product of the partnership was the Soviet Union's first independent newspaper that, at least on its pages, was professing enlightened values.

"What was so curious about the corruption was that the staff, the readers, and everybody else knew it was going on," Durham explained. "It was certainly unacceptable and potentially crippling, but if people knew about it, so what? It was a non-issue issue for the Russian-language-edition staff, but a serious issue for the English-language-edition staff. Once Sasha Fadin offered me two thousand rubles to print a ridiculous Russian-edition story about a commercial bank in Siberia because the bank believed that was the way in which to get a story on their activities in front of a Western audience with money to invest. When I tried to talk him out of it, my efforts struck him as an anathema, as they did other members of the staff."

Durham and I attempted to ensure that the edition on its way to America remained clean, but with English-language *Commersant* dependent on the Russian staff for copy, there was no way for us to be sure by exactly what means our stories made it into print. The snowballing question of corruption was of no importance to Yakovlev, who, as the popularity of *Commersant* grew in the Soviet Union, refused to even discuss the matter. Domestically, *Commersant* was rising to heights of rotten glory, with Yak ballooning in power as the arbiter of Soviet free-market morality. This was not to say that *Commersant* and Fact did not perform important functions within the country. However, every consequential social, economic, and political step Yakovlev took was undercut by the

ever-growing need of his cooperative to employ and accept corruption as a matter of course. The honest Russians I knew, people
like Sabina and Hajibau, expressed distaste; but, at the same time,
hesitatingly admitted that the only way to erase corruption—the
single most profound obstacle to a functioning democracy in the
Soviet Union—was, short of a full-bore revolution, to become part
of the corruption and all that it represented. This was the conundrum of *perestroika*, the paradox of the cooperative movement,
and the great Möbius strip that wrapped itself around daily Russian
life with no beginning and no end.

I had grappled with this issue from the day I first arrived in
Moscow in 1984 as a reporter for *Harper's Magazine*. Six years
later, the profound problem remained as difficult to describe as it
was to solve. Durham, who had been confronting the paradox daily
for only eight weeks, expressed its impact on him and on Soviet
society in his personal journal. "I learned a great Russian phrase
today—*kuterma putimiza*. It means a mess. It describes perfectly
what the corruption has done to this cooperative and to this country."

13

> Few things are sadder than the truly monstrous.
>
> NATHANAEL WEST

IT WAS THE DECELERATION of events at *Commersant* that spurred Tom Billington to fly Yakovlev to New York for a meeting with him and members of Russia Group, twelve days before the 1990 Memorial Day weekend Bush-Gorbachev summit in Washington. The direct telephone line between Fact and Race had yet to be installed, reducing communications to the archaic method of Telex. Over three hundred Telexes had been transmitted to Moscow from Chicago, and many of them went without response. The operation was beginning to develop a frightening momentum: Peggy Yott was asking for status reports; Yak countered with requests for more equipment. The partnership was evolving along the lines of suspicion and half-knowledge, and Billington had hoped it was due to the distance and time difference between the two points. Bundles of *Commersant* were arriving weekly in Chicago, but the paper's copy and design were both looking progressively worse. Members of Russia Group, including Manoff and a number of professors from major American journalism schools, daily newspaper editors, and television news network producers, had couriered critiques of *Commersant* to Moscow for Yakovlev to study and act upon. I had pressed the quality issue with Yakovlev, too, but he was deaf to everything except news about when the next load of equipment would be sent from Chicago.

Yakovlev arrived in New York with *Commersant* art director Nikita "Kit" Golovanov. Both men were tired from the Aeroflot flight and angry that Widenfeld had yet to cut the red tape that would allow more promised equipment to arrive in Moscow. Billington and his advisers, more concerned with the poor quality of *Commersant,* were in no mood to haggle about the legal status of further deliveries. Russia Group told Billington that it would be a mistake to launch *Commersant* in time for the Memorial Day weekend summit. Rob Manoff was particularly worried. Two weeks before Yak flew to New York, Manoff had been waiting in his office off Washington Square for a scheduled meeting with Gleb Pavlovsky, the director of Fact's Postfactom News Service. Pavlovsky and Manoff were supposed to discuss writing the prospectus to be used to sell Postfactom data to both Dow Jones and Reuters, as well as the details of a meeting with a Dow Jones representative that Race would help set up. Pavlovsky, who had been sleeping in a series of Manhattan crash pads without telephones, never showed up at New York University. He did, however, try to sell the Postfactom data base to Dow Jones on his own without any introduction, prospectus, or the knowledge of Race. Wandering around lower Manhattan on his first trip to the United States, Pavlovsky was apparently strolling unannounced into offices and trying to cut deals to sell Race-controlled information without the knowledge of anyone at Race or in the Russia Group. The former Soviet dissident refused to tell Manoff or any other member of Russia Group with whom he was speaking or into what kind of negotiations he had entered.

"There's nothing I can do," Yakovlev told me when Russia Group was first confronted with Pavlovsky's activities in New York. "Gleb is in charge of Postfactom and I must allow him the space to do what he thinks is best."

"Wise up," I told Volodya, enraged. "Pavlovsky's actions in New York were not only stupid, they were in violation of Fact's contract with Race. Race controls the rights to Postfactom information everywhere outside the Soviet Union, and it's self-defeating for you to allow Gleb to roam around New York trying to sell the data base without the assistance and contacts of Race. This is insanity; there's no other way to describe it."

"Mister Tom Billington doesn't control the sale of Postfactom news in the West," Yakovlev responded, forgetting the Fact–Race contract, which he had signed. "Mister Tom Billington doesn't care about this deal anymore." Then, suddenly, he was laughing. "You worry too much."

Billington, though irritated by the news of Pavlovsky's stupidity, was more concerned with the status of *Commersant* and requested that Manoff attend the New York meeting with Yakovlev. But Manoff had to leave for Moscow on New York University business, and, more critical to the *Commersant* project, to review the paper's editorial situation firsthand with Durham, who was working twenty-hour days with the Russian staff in hopes of creating a miracle before the summit. The hastily arranged meeting between Billington and Yakovlev took place in Race's executive dining room in the World Financial Center, twenty-two stories above Wall Street and twenty-two light-years away from anything Yak could have ever imagined. Billington, having brought Yott and graphic designer Ken Vanderveen with him from Chicago to discuss *Commersant*'s specific problems, had also asked a number of newspaper editors and American television news executives to participate in the Russia Group briefing.

Some of the individuals at the meeting asked that their names not be used and I have honored their requests. However, I am not breaching any trust in informing the reader that these advisers included some of America's leading newspaper and television executives. None of them had any financial or professional links to Race or *Commersant;* they attended the meeting because of their personal desire to see *perestroika* succeed, a goal they felt might be enhanced through lending their respective professional advice to the Soviet Union's first independently owned newspaper.

Over a lunch of grilled fish and new potatoes, the talk was so direct and to the point that Yakovlev and Golovanov had the stomach only to drink coffee and suck cigarettes. For the next three hours they were hammered on everything from the responsibilities of a newspaper to the most marketable trends in graphic design. Golovanov, who was on his first trip to America, slumped lower in his seat at every word, unable to answer why *Commersant* looked so clumsy and amateurish. Yakovlev, too, was speechless. *Yes*, he admitted, nerves cracking, after Russia Group's new members explained the absolute necessity for clear news writing and eye-catching design, many of the people on *Commersant's* staff were not up to American journalistic par, but the criticisms he had listened to were presumptuous and destructive.

"No, they are not," one of the network news executives said sternly. "*Commersant* is not going to go anywhere in this state," he added, waving a copy of the English-language edition in the air. "You may be able to sell millions of them in the Russian language, but this is not Russia!"

"Look at this," he said, leaning across the table, as if to make distinct, unmistakable, each of his critical points.

Yak looked at the issues of *Commersant* shoved across the glass table and fidgeted in his seat, pretending to study them—a trick of pretense. I could hear the echoes of his words to me over the past six months. *Really, it's like that, is it? Well, you need me because it's my paper when it comes down to the final analysis.*

"These people know what they are talking about, Volodya," Billington said calmly, fatherly. "Listen to them. They all want to help."

"You know Soviet journalists, my journalists, are very talented people," Yak said, leaning back in his chair, regaining his composure. *They don't realize the staff is made of political and economic specialists, not journalists. I trained these people to be journalists myself!* "The problems you mention are questions of style and it is not a problem for us to imitate American writing style. They will write in whatever style I tell them to write. They will design in whatever style I tell them to design, and—"

"Volodya, you've been doing that for the past three months and the writing has become more bureaucratic and Brad has not received any support," I interjected. "We need another American editor and we need you to hire staff translators with journalism experience for the English-language edition. The ones you have now are only part time, and you don't even listen to them. You're not listening to what Durham is telling you and I don't believe you're listening to what the people at this table are telling you. There's no way *Commersant* can be launched in America in eleven days. And to spend the money necessary to sell subscriptions to the kind of paper you're producing now is disaster."

"No, no, no, you are all wrong!" Yak said without any suggestion of support from around the table. He looked across at Yott, who, tapping a pencil and sipping tomato juice . . . *I hate tomatoes* . . . sat quietly watching Yak begin to unravel. "I said the paper would be ready for American distribution by the summit— and it *will* be ready by the summit!"

"I don't think you understand," another executive said reluctantly, almost primly, to avoid infuriating Yak even further. "We all agree that we want to make a big impact with the first issue and that you can't afford to make even one mistake in the paper. One mistake and people won't subscribe. Surely you understand this? You only get *one shot* in this business, so it had better be good."

Yakovlev paused, then looked at each face in the room, their words but white noise to his plans. It was impossible for him to relax into the satisfaction of authority he used so effectively to pull Moscow's strings. Business—American business—was real, dull, and earnest. Of course Yak had approved the hiring of an American editor and the restructuring of parts of the newspaper to accommodate American tastes and values. But many on the Russian staff, as Durham had discovered, did not like being rehearsed.

"Over three hundred fifty thousand people buy the Russian edition every week," Yakovlev said, pressing his fingers together into a steeple. His face narrowed, then he added, "And the Americans will buy it, too, because the information is unavailable elsewhere."

"It's stupid," Billington said gruffly. "Haven't you been listening? Let's spend more time fixing the paper up and then launch it in the late fall. I don't have a problem putting back the deadline."

"Yes, Tom, I've been listening, but I don't accept your reasoning; everyone seems pleased with what has happened at this meeting. We need to distribute now."

"Look, Volodya," Billington said, grimacing and then raising his hands in an admission. "It's your decision and I'm not going to stop you, but everybody at this table thinks you are wrong. Let's wait until the fall."

"Yes, Tom, it's my decision and I want to do it. Now."

"But Volodya," I said, attempting to bring Yak to his senses, "the summit is exactly eleven days away and you don't even have any copy ready for the special summit issue you want to do. You've got nearly five grand worth of cameras and the paper hasn't had more than three photos in the past three months. And just who is going to set up the distribution and public relations backup you're going to need eleven days from now in Washington? This is hardly enough time for us to get the State Department to issue another visa for you to get back in time, and the deadline to apply for credentials to be at the summit is forty-eight hours from now."

"It's not a problem!" Yak shot back indignantly.

Billington nodded. "Who's gonna pay for it, Volodya? I'm not."

"*I'm* going to pay for it."

"You got the money?" Billington asked automatically, now realizing that prevarication was, for Yakovlev, his secret self. *I'm going to prove to Mister Tom Billington that he is wrong, just like I've spent my life proving everybody in Moscow wrong.*

"Yes, I have the money," Yak said, putting his hand up to remove his glasses because he was sweating around the eyes.

"Okay, Volodya," Billington said, unable to resist being amused by the scene as he concluded the meeting. "You got such a fucking hard-on for this thing to happen that you better do it. But you're in over your head and I'm not going to get you out."

"What's a hard-on?"

Ten minutes later, Golovanov, who had not uttered a single word while Russia Group savaged his primitive design of *Commersant,* was airborne in a chopper on his way to catch Billington's jet for the ride to a private Illinois airfield and a meeting with a Chicago design team. Time was so short that Golovanov had not been able to go across the street to pick up his clothes from the hotel. "Don't worry," Vanderveen said as the two graphic designers rushed out the door to the helipad with Billington. "I think my underwear will fit you."

Yakovlev remained in the dining room and pushed the piled *Commersants* away from him, the persistent nightmare of the past few hours flashing against the lids of his closed eyes. He could see it clearly, as if he were back in his office on Good Highway, across the street from the Red Army newspaper. Distribution. *American* distribution. That was the key to the success of *Commersant* in the West. Or so Yak presumed. The fact that *Commersant* was in no condition to be distributed in America did not factor into Yak's thinking because in the whole complex of reasons for the failure of the Soviet economy the most fundamental had been the collapse of distribution and transportation systems.

What Yak lacked as a newspaper editor was more than compensated for by his awareness of the importance of distribution and his ability to organize. The Soviet Union was a military economy designed to raise the military strength and political influence of the state over all else. Even with *perestroika,* the defense industries still accounted for 55 percent of all industrial production, and the key to their power was effective distribution. The Soviet people were poor and on the verge of revolution because the economy had been designed to serve a military-industrial complex which for more than sixty years had consumed most of the country's resources. Soviet agriculture, for example, never recovered from the destruction of its peasant culture and Stalin's reapplication of serfdom in the shape of collective farms ill-equipped for dispersing food over one-sixth of the world's surface. The success of *Commersant* in Moscow and Leningrad, the chief industrial centers of Sverdlovsk, Perm, and Chelyabinks, and other big cities like Volgograd and Vladivostok was a direct result of a good distribution system coordinated with access to newsprint and presses owned by the military. *Commersant*'s quality, so crucial to Russia Group as the necessary first step to establishing an effective U.S. distribution network, was of pointless importance in the Soviet Union because delivering information, or any product, was infinitely more consequential to success than how the information was packaged.

"You should not be worried about our success in the United States," Yakovlev said, opening his eyes to meet Yott as she entered the room. *"The New York Times* has taken a subscription to *Commersant,"* he said proudly. "I believe I sent you a Telex on this?"

"That has absolutely nothing to do with *Commersant* selling in the United States, Volodya," Yott explained, growing irate. "There's so little information published in Moscow in English as it is, that all of the American newspaper bureaus there will buy subscriptions."

"I think it's quite good for us," Yak said, using *The New York Times'* subscription as a lawyer would use evidence to prove his analysis correct.

"You just don't get it, do you?" Yott said in final exasperation. "You just don't get it."

Yak got up from the chair, galvanized by his current of thought, and went to the window. He looked down from the twenty-second floor, along the busy streets of the world's financial center. "I do get it, Peggy. I do get it."

Yakovlev grabbed a cab uptown to Fifty-ninth Street for a council with Peter Martin, the president of Peter Martin Associates, one of New York's preeminent public relations firms. The cab bucked wildly in the muggy late-afternoon traffic, further enervating Yak, making him barely able to remember any of the specifics discussed over lunch, or how he intended to muffle Russia Group's grim appraisal of *Commersant* from the ears of the man he was about to hire as *Commersant's* American director of press and public relations. His stomach twisted with coffee, and his head needed painkilling. For Yak, Russia Group had treated him as a powerless businessman; Yott wanted to humiliate him, treat him with contempt. Russia Group no longer wanted to help. Their recriminations had proved that, he decided. In his way of thinking there was no other explanation for their behavior.

The further uptown the old yellow Checker moved, the further Yak dismissed the observations offered by some of America's most brilliant media executives: Yak was in a silent rage. Billington had been deferential, almost silent, once Yak had made up his mind to pay for and proceed with *Commersant's* debut. Temptation was the black hole of the commodity-trading business, the trap Billington had seen too many big-time bean brokers fall into and not be able to climb out of. Yak was in over his head, and Billington realized it. Now it was up to Peter Martin to teach him how to swim with the sharks.

Only one thought was playing through Yakovlev's head: *I'll show Mister Tom Billington.*

<table>
<tr>
<td>

14

</td>
<td>

The tasks of the Party are . . . to be cautious and not allow our country to be drawn into conflicts by warmongers who are accustomed to have others pull the chestnuts out of the fire for them.

JOSEF STALIN

</td>
</tr>
</table>

I IMPLORED YAKOVLEV to meet with Peter Martin because he had been asked to accomplish the impossible before. Jamaican Prime Minister Michael Manley had sought the help of the "Associates" when his island nation had lost millions of tourist and American-aid dollars in the mid-seventies as a consequence of politically motivated street violence and a love affair with Fidel Castro. It was Martin's Jamaican campaign that put the country back on the vacation and State Department map. Seagrams, the multinational liquor giant, had come to Martin's ninth-floor office to discover if his team could assess wine coolers while at the same time reposturing the company so that its advertising was more in tune with the national safe-drinking/safe-driving campaign. Seagrams' sales subsequently boomed. When no American tourists were going to Greece it was Martin who brought them back; and when the U.S. Virgin Islands were no more than a pit stop on the cruise-ship circuit, it was Martin who used television to transform the American territory into the Caribbean's hippest hideaway (until 1989, when Hurricane Hugo's hundred-fifty-miles-per-hour winds and the surge of looters who followed hammered the place back into vacation obscurity).

Martin had handled American political campaigns, foreign-government accounts, and a host of products that ranged from Plax antitartar dental rinse to a Louisiana petrochemical refinery. His associates were all young men and women versed in politics and current affairs—two attributes Martin held in higher esteem than the ability of any individual associate to market an idea or product. Chairing meetings with clients in his trademark ten-gallon Stetson or flying off to West Africa to convince prime ministers not to lease their land to toxic-waste dumpers, the fifty-nine-year-old public relations man from Connecticut had the rare talent to manage dope-smoking reggae bands and cigar-chewing oil company execs with style and without quarrel. And, in a profession built on stretched truths, Martin had a reputation grounded in honesty, selectivity, and pro bono work. Martin never liked to admit it, but he had turned down the multimillion-dollar Nestlé account in the 1970s when he discovered the company was dumping substandard baby formula in Africa and other underdeveloped nations. There was an apocryphal story making the rounds of Madison Avenue that Martin had forfeited millions by refusing to recast the character of Drexel Burnham Lambert executive Michael R. Milken because the jailed junkbondsman balked at getting rid of his curly black toupee.

"That's not a true story," Martin insisted upon meeting Yakovlev for the first time. "But I would have advised Milken to lose the toupee had I taken the account.

"So, Volodya, what's *your* problem?" Martin asked, biting into a late-afternoon bagel.

After listening to Yakovlev's description of the situation, Martin said, "You don't have eleven days to put out a paper. You have eight days—and I have even less time to organize American television and print-media coverage of the launch. You'd better leave for Moscow tomorrow night and get the paper together. Eight days! This is totally crazy and insane, and I love it.

"But I want to tell you," Martin added earnestly, studying the *Commersant*s Yak had given him, "the advice Billington and the others gave you is correct. It would be better to wait until we have a more solid product to sell. The idea for *Commersant* is one of the best I've ever heard, but the product is not up to the standard of the idea. I suggest we wait until the next summit meeting. This will give me more time to organize an effective campaign and you the time to put together a better product."

Yak brushed aside the observation immediately. He began to wander Martin's office, finally sitting down on the couch, trying to arrange his body in a relaxed position. Yak was antsy, and it was difficult for him to sit still. He got up again, this time precisely pacing the room like someone preparing himself to be executed, Martin thought.

"Relax, Volodya," Martin declared, looking kindly at his new client. "Dead men don't look good on television."

Martin had been drawn into the Fact matrix late, but he immediately took command. It was a precise, visionary moment for the PR man; he, like the other members of Russia Group, felt the irresistible urge to contribute to the shaping of history. Now Martin had been put in charge of making the mold. Although his client's English was good and his product a brilliant candidate for television coverage, Yak himself needed coaching to be an effective salesman on television. He needed to be calmed. "I'm going to teach you how to look on-camera before you leave for Moscow."

"Oh my God, no," Yak crackled, pacing off tiny squares on Martin's carpet.

"Oh yes, Volodya; you need to look good, and speak quickly, clearly, and directly to the issue at hand, which is the unique nature of *Commersant* and the opportunities for American businessmen in the Soviet Union. You'll be lucky to have even fifteen seconds of your message broadcast by the networks, so you have to say it all in fifteen seconds—no, let's make it ten.

"Are you in any danger back in Moscow for publishing this paper?" Martin asked. "You know, is there any chance that you might be arrested for publishing something in *Commersant?*"

"Yes, of course; just showing up at the office is dangerous."

"Good. Then we'll bill you that way. Jai," Martin called, gesturing a pencil toward Jai Imbrey, one of his account execs, "are you getting all this: crusading Russian journalist who, with his staff, risks his life to put out the Soviet Union's only independent newspaper.

"Our second-most-important angle, our best angle is that *Commersant* is the Soviet Union's only independently owned newspaper," Martin added. "This is worth a lot of mileage. Third. We have this summit being billed as the *business summit*, and *Commersant* is the business paper . . . Angela," Martin yelled from his office to his secretary, "get me Robert at State and Jeff at the White House. I want to see if we can arrange for Yak to present a copy of *Commersant* to Gorbachev and Bush. Volodya, do you know anyone on Gorby's staff who can get us in with him? You know, what we really need is a photo of Gorbachev with *Commersant*— better yet, let's get Gorby to present a copy to Bush. Who do you know?"

Yak began to fidget. He had never expected this. "Well . . . Stanislav Shatalin, a member of Gorbachev's Presidential Council, is going to the summit. I can ask him. It's politically difficult, but I think it might be possible—"

"Gotta do it," Martin cut in quickly. "It's critical, and he's gotta physically hand it to Bush with the explanation that *Commersant* is the first independent newspaper, and an example of the free-market system that he wants all these American business leaders to invest in. Photo-ops like that take a lot of time to arrange and you haven't given me the time to deal effectively with our contacts at State and in the White House, so I'm gonna leave this one with you. It's a natural mix because from everything I've read about the Soviet Union, you guys at *Commersant* are the only ones who're taking full advantage of *glasnost* and *perestroika*, at least in a way free-press-thinking Americans can relate to. You're the point man and *Commersant* is the draw. What are you gonna put in the summit issue?"

"I don't know yet because it hasn't been written," Yak said, unruffled.

"What!"

"This is not a problem, Peter. My staff can put it together in a few days."

"We're thin on quality here as it is," Martin cautioned, flicking his thumb and index finger through *Commersant*'s pages, "but you think we can overcome the problem for the summit. Okay. I'll accept that for now. But you understand, Volodya, if the paper doesn't improve immediately with the first copy distributed in America after the special summit issue, all of this will have been for nothing—and I'm not cheap."

"How much?" Yak asked.

"Sixty thousand dollars, maybe more," Martin said, looking Yak straight in the eye. "Half now, the other half at the end of the summit. Four percent carrying charge for every month that you're late. And I don't take rubles. But you have the money? Right?"

"I'll be back in Moscow in forty-eight hours and I will have the bank transfer the first half to your account."

"Then let's draw up the papers," Martin said. He looked at Yak and saw the undisguised flicker of excitement in his slanting eyes. Before his meeting with Yak, Martin had been fully briefed on how Fact walked the thin line between the Soviet black market and the free market, as well as on the reluctance of Russia Group to go ahead with the project, and Yott's concerns about Yakovlev's ability to operate in the United States without Billington's financial backing. "Billington is not going to pay for this, you know," Martin added in the dead, sudden calm of the moment. *Mister Tom Billington.* It was as if Martin had turned on some spigot in his Russian client. At first, a drop; then a nonstop flow. "I can pay for it, Peter," Yak snapped. "There's more than adequate hard currency in the Vnesheconombank account. I don't need Mister Tom Billington for this."

"Okay then," Martin said, shaking Yakovlev's hand. "Let's make history . . . Jai, get the printer on the phone, and I want you to write up some *Commersant* press releases and a bio of Yak. Angela, call our attorney and have him get us legally registered as the Yak's American agent, then phone the Madison Hotel in Washington and get us four rooms for the summit. And you, Volodya, get your ass back to Moscow on the next plane out. We have one week to arrange a nationwide launch of a major newspaper that you haven't even written yet."

Or, more accurately, a newspaper that Brad Durham had not put together yet and, given the events that were taking place in Moscow as Yak flew back to the capital, might not have the opportunity to put together.

Shortly before leaving for Manhattan, Yakovlev gave Durham

the news that he might not be a legal alien in the Soviet Union. "It was one of those very strange, very Russian conversations," Durham explained. "Yak says that I'm having visa problems but that I'm not having visa problems. But any way I look at it, I have a problem."

The Soviet government was trying to solve the problem of people who lived outside Moscow coming into town to shop for dwindling supplies of simple food items. The government would soon be distributing food-rationing cards to all Muscovites, and Durham, who was paid in rubles and forced to shop in city stores that would no longer sell food to nonresidents, was about to find himself categorized as a non-Muscovite left at the mercy of the bureaucracy and the black market. "The good news is I'm going to be spending more time at McDonald's," Durham said, adding, "the bad news is the last time I was there the man in front of me began eating off the floor and one of the Soviet attendants told me that all the restaurant's toilet seats had been stolen by customers."

The neighborhood where Durham and his girlfriend, Suzan Tobler, lived during the height of Soviet food shortages was typical of the other crumbling neighborhoods and concrete apartment blocks lived in by average Soviets from Riga to Vladivostok. The sidewalks and alleys through these poorly constructed complexes— when there were sidewalks and alleys instead of dirt paths—were full of treacherous holes, and the only greenery was the menacing weeds that grew out of the litter-scarred soil. The geometry of a Soviet apartment, small and narrow, was made more compact by the stench of rotting garbage and pet urine that collected in the hallways and wafted up stairwells and elevator shafts. Apartment doors were thick and heavy, secured from the outside world by a series of jerry-rigged bolts and locks, the complexity of which would have confused Willie Sutton.

Although one of Fact's ubiquitous fixers sorted out Durham's residency problems, he almost never made it back to the office in time to hear Yakovlev's plans for the Bush-Gorbachev summit. Suzan Tobler had raised the issue of how long Durham intended to stay at *Commersant* and live in the squalor provided by the cooperative. The ensuing fight caused the neighbors to summon the police, who put the arguing couple in the back of a paddy wagon for a ride to the station house, the ride that launched *Commersant's* American debut.

"As soon as we arrived at the station some eerie-looking cop tried to coax Suzan into a back room for a private interrogation," Durham explained. "We were having none of that, of course. Suzan calmed down when one of the cops feebly said we could go if we gave him dollars. I offered him rubles and he said no. Finally, they drove us back to Fact in an ambulance. I walk into the office and *They're Here* . . . back from America, like the monsters from the movie *Poltergeist*. Volodya called me into his office to say we're going to do two English-language papers in five days, the weekly edition and a special summit paper. He's wild-eyed and in no mood for compromise. He wanted all new copy and I told him it was impossible. He finally agreed to using half new articles, half previously run ones. It was a savage argument. I told him the pegging of the launch to the political shindig surrounding the summit wasn't important and that there wasn't enough time to properly lash together such an important edition. He agreed, but insisted it was all Race's idea and the company wouldn't budge on changing the date because Billington wants results.

"Fadin comes in to tell me the Russian staff believes the American edition will be a disaster, that nobody cared about it, and that Yakovlev was essentially running a game," Durham continued. "This isn't what you want to hear on deadline, so I told him to spread the word there would be a big hard-currency bonus for the Ruskies if it was a success. It was a total lie, of course. I spent the next four days at the office, editing, rewriting copy, and napping on Yak's couch. Then, twenty-four hours before deadline, Volodya's voice came over the intercom system to say the issue needed to be ready in five hours! I barged into his office and exploded. He stopped playing Pac Man long enough to complain about my killing his summit issue cover story about a crocodile lying next to a pond surrounded by flowers and how this related to all the different exchange rates for the ruble. I went back to the job. I forget what time we finished the issue, but I do remember catching a ride with Tanya, the Fact lawyer, to bring some of the papers to the airport for shipment to America before going home to Suzan. The front tire exploded on the way. It was raining outside, and every truck that passed hit a pothole and soaked me with mud and water. The jack didn't work. I simply wanted to sleep. Two English-language issues in five days had been enough. Suzan was gone when I got home and I had left my key at the office. I collapsed on the doorstep certain the neighbors were going to call the police again."

| 15 | I woke up last night dreaming about what we accomplished at the Geneva summit. Ladies and gentlemen, boys and girls of all ages, welcome to the Moscow Circus.

PAVEL MAMAYEV |

TOM BILLINGTON had come a long way from the morning in 1969 when he walked, petrified, into the Chicago Mercantile Exchange pit as a fresh-faced broker for Jason F. Race Company to trade beans and bellies. It took him nearly ten years of butting heads and bucking odds to begin what the commodity world called the Race mystique, a charisma of profits built on the doubling of beef prices between late 1977 and early 1979. Trading cattle futures was Billington's forte and he amassed such huge positions that few traders dared bet against him. Billington's might in the business world was built on lean, too. He kept the company profitable by running an operation that demanded all employees, including top executives, contribute to earnings. If an office did not make money, heads went rolling. But Billington always gave his talented and highly motivated managers plenty of time, usually two years, to produce profits. If he was not satisfied with the take at that point, he either disbanded the subsidiary or sold it. "Billington is not an empire builder," Yott explained. "He wants results."

It was late when Yakovlev arrived in Washington for the summit, and his arms were tired from carrying hundreds of wire-bundled *Special Summit Issue Commersants* down from New York aboard the Trump Shuttle. Durham had pulled it off, and Yak had sent the "results of Fact's labor" to Chicago for Billington to review before Yakovlev hastily left Moscow to meet up with Peter Martin in Washington. The twelve-page tabloid was finally beginning to take on a personality. *Commersant*'s articles and graphics were far from perfect, but the issue reflected Durham's handiwork, including stories on real and black-market ruble values and an upbeat account of the newly legalized political parties. The issue had been wrapped around the summit, specifically addressing the economic and bilateral trade issues that Gorbachev and Bush would be discussing over the Memorial Day weekend. *Commersant*'s two-page centerfold contained a moving photograph of a young boy sitting on a train and wearing a Bolshevik *budyonovka* (the turnip-like cap emblazoned with a red star that was worn by Trotsky's Red Guards during the revolution); the caption asked: "Will he come to see the results of the summit?"

"In a country that is only now beginning to cut its teeth on the wisdom of the free market, bewilderment is understandable," Durham wrote in *Commersant*'s first exclusively English-language edition for the American market. "*Perestroika* is like the country which changes from driving on the right side of the road to driving on the left. Gradually. *Commersant* attempts to direct traffic. Written exclusively by Soviet journalists, economists, entrepreneurs, dissidents, and even former employees of the Communist Party Central Committee, the only common thread running throughout the staff is a rather healthy appetite for commerce. Most business journalists are certain that their subject, the economy, will still be standing in the morning when they rise. Not so in the Soviet Union, where business journalists live with a degree of uncertainty that would instill a wave of panic of the Wall Street variety in their Western counterparts. Thus, there is a sense of mission at *Commersant*, not just coverage but participation in the forging of Soviet business institutions."

After handing a few thousand copies of *Commersant* to Jai Imbrey, the Peter Martin Associates' executive charged with setting up media interviews, Yak had been too tired to see anything when he checked into the Madison Hotel on the eve of the seventh modern superpower summit, grateful and impressed that the desk clerk had treated him with all the speed and custom due to a diplomat. All of that changed the next morning, however, shortly after Yak went downstairs to unwind over a triple-espresso in the Madison's antique-filled lobby alongside dozens of Soviet and American security agents. Summit day dawned hot: First there was the prick of early-morning mugginess seeping up from Washington's concrete-covered marshlands, followed by the clamor of air conditioners cranking out steady streams of frosty haze to cut the heat, and then the sight of Gorbachev's entire delegation swarming the front desk like hungry mosquitos, checking into the hotel.

"Not bad, huh?" Martin said, sidling up to his client for a strategy session on the following day's breakfast press conference at the National Press Club. "We're staying at the same hotel as the Soviet delegation, and there's talk going around that Gorbachev might be staying at the Madison too," Martin added with sly satisfaction, and then, quickly: "What about Shatalin? Have you spoken with Shatalin about getting *Commersant* to Gorbachev?"

Yakovlev's eyes turned hollow. "We're in the *same* hotel as the Soviet delegation!? *Gorbachev!* Oh my God! And we've put copies of *Commersant* under every door in the hotel?!"

Perplexed, Martin turned around in his chair to look at the Soviet delegation with Yakovlev. Among the throng were nine prominent members of the Central Committee, and three of them sat on the Politburo. To a man, the assembled Russians returned Yak's horrified and hollow stare.

"I'd never seen anything like it in forty years of public relations," Martin said, chuckling as he watched Yakovlev freeze. "The Soviets are actually physically frightened that Yakovlev was in the same hotel as them. Some of them are actually shaking whenever they looked at him. This is an auspicious start to the summit."

Almost immediately after registering, unknown members of Gorbachev's delegation and Presidential Council dispatched their aides to the front desk to make sure that the name Vladimir Yegorevich Yakovlev had not been included in the rota of official Soviet guests to prevent entry to closed floors. (As it was later discovered, many members of the Madison's staff, as well as Amer-

ican security agents, were under the impression that Vladimir Yegorevich Yakovlev—the Yak—was either Politburo member
Alexander Nikolayevich Yakovlev or his son. The two men are not
related.)

"It's obvious these guys are the old-style Soviet bosses," Martin observed, after a hotel secretary informed him of their endeavor
to exclude Yak's name from the official list, "and they thought this
summit was their party. Now it's being crashed and they don't like
it at all, do they, Volodya?"

"No, Peter," Yak said, stunned at the turn of events, "they
don't like it at all."

"Good," Martin coached, slapping his client on the back, asking no further questions. "You're the future of the Soviet Union,
those men are the past. Now let's show the American public the
difference."

Yak hesitated, then added: "It will be more difficult to make
the Soviets here see the difference."

Superpower summit meetings are mainly private affairs, with
not much news for journalists. There is a lot of waiting on line for
special "pool" passes with which to cover photo opportunities
agreed upon by both sides. The Soviet delegation, in particular,
had a history of using summit meetings as an opportunity to get
in front of the camera in between shopping trips to stock up on
Western goods. Soviet summiteers smelled of Brut, filled their
Gore-Tex duffel bags with goodies bought in dollars. They were
all members of the Communist Party—a fact that the networks'
news readers never seemed to touch upon when they lined up the
Soviets to speak glowingly of *glasnost* and *perestroika* on Sunday
morning television. It was a strategy that had begun when Ronald
Reagan first met Gorbachev in Geneva and which only built up
steam after George Bush became president. Pavel Mamayev, the
former English-language ringmaster of the Moscow Circus, who
headed up the Soviets' new-look press center at the 1985 Geneva
summit, called the *perestroika* public relations team "Madison Avenue Moscow" and wondered aloud if an American Express card
in Raisa Gorbachova's hand would change the world. Since Geneva,
the traveling PR team that accompanied Gorbachev had been the
Westernized elite of Moscow's cultural and scientific communities.

They sucked on Marlboros and Salems; many chewed thoughtfully on the tips of designer eyeglasses, others removed their jackets alongside Dan Rather to reveal the Ralph Lauren polo ponies embroidered on the shirts they had selected at Macy's annual Whale of a Sale.

These men and women were *perestroika*'s account executives, but although they were expert at talking about the results of Gorbachevian democracy, they never once brought with them anyone who was not a member of the Communist Party high command. They were fully versed in the arithmetic of nuclear death and possessed a savvy and sometimes frightening understanding of Patrick Ewing's rebound average, but for all their talk about democracy and basketball stats, they were never quite able or willing actually to show American television viewers the results of *perestroika* in the form of a Vladimir Tikhonov or Volodya Yakovlev. To be sure, displaying a flesh-and-blood *perestroichik* alongside them on MacNeil-Lehrer would have been both dangerous and foolish: dangerous because he would go for Gorbachev's throat; foolish because the Moscow PR flacks might lose further trips to the West.

What the Soviets had done at every summit, however, was to go to great lengths to script Gorbachev as the friendly uncle. Indeed, it was easier for them to make Americans like Gorbachev than it was to make the Russians like him. The American news show bookers, whom the Soviets liked to refer to as "those cute little women," and the anchormen, whom the Soviets called the "shapers of the American conscience," never realized how adept the men who shaped Gorbachev were at hitching him and *perestroika* a ride on the Nielsen Ratings. Gorbachev's team first did this in Geneva, where they tested the weaponry of PR instead of the weaponry of war. Although their propaganda was met at first with cynicism, the warmth with which the Soviets packaged their spiel seduced the American media into their love affair with *perestroika*. So good was the Soviet PR machine that its former chief spokesman, Gennadi Gerasimov, now the Soviet ambassador to Portugal, was the first foreigner to win the U.S. National Association of Government Communicators' Communicator of the Year Award.

It had been a downhill ride for the Kremlin PR express after

Geneva, even when it was nearly derailed by sixty-mile-an-hour storm winds in Malta's Marsaxlokk Bay during the December 1989 summit. Gorbachev and Bush found themselves stranded in a storm—on a ship in a port. Communism had lost four East European countries in six months, more were ready to topple, and the summit seemed to be heading for a bust. Gorbachev desperately needed to ship out of Malta with something to cheer the folks back home. Despite the great PR campaign abroad, *perestroika* was tired news in Moscow, and the liberty it was supposed to have bestowed on the Soviet Union remained an elusive prize. Unlike the Eastern Europeans, who took to the streets against the old order, the Communist Party bosses were still too frightened to call their system's bluff. Until 1989 the people of Gorbachev's Eastern satellites had never opted out of the system Stalin had forced on them, but—cunningly—they never worked *with* it, either. Eastern Europe used the system's strength to turn it back on itself. This was the one thing the Soviets had yet to do, and the big question at Malta was whether or not they possessed the character to peacefully overthrow their reformed oppressors.

Malta was a dream come true for Gorbachev because Bush pledged to help the Soviet Union become a real part of the world economy. All the talk of nuclear and conventional weapons disarmament looked good on paper, but it was not as critical to Gorbachev as were GATT* observer status, relaxed controls on

---

*GATT, or the General Agreement on Tariffs and Trade, is the international roundtable for global tariff bargaining, a kind of high-stakes poker game in which larger industrial nations (often referred to as the Big GATT Cats) use trade barriers, import tariffs, and the abolition of preferential trade agreements as chips to raise or call third-world countries into reducing their levels of taxes and tariffs. Founded in January 1948 and headquartered in Geneva, GATT has received scant public attention because its negotiations historically have been conducted behind closed doors and hidden from the probes of citizen groups or elected officials. The Soviets had been seeking a chair at the GATT table for years because the GATT Cats had been rigging the game so that the industrial nations could extend and tighten their control of the world economy by downgrading the "development principle." The development principle allowed third-world members exemptions or privileges, such as more time, to comply with GATT obligations. Soviet economists, aware that their country was essentially a third-world economy, wanted, at the very least, observer status to monitor the thinking of the exclusive GATT Cat group. The Cats wanted GATT to become a kind of global fiscal police to enforce

shipments of advanced Western technology, and White House encouragement for hefty U.S. investment in the Soviet Union. Gorbachev wanted to collect democracy's dowry; Gerasimov had flown him into Malta as the Simon Bolívar of the Balkans and sent him home as the Franklin Roosevelt of the Steppes, paving his way to Washington seven months later as the Steven Jobs of Communist Party entrepreneurialism. This was exciting stuff and everybody gulped it down like champagne at a wedding reception. Somehow along the way the West forgot that Gorbachev had yet to divorce his old wife.

The men who had accompanied Gorbachev to his six previous superpower summits arrived at the Madison Hotel in Washington expecting to sing the same tune about their Party chairman, the man whom Gorbachev adviser and freelance cooperator Georgi Arbatov described as a "dedicated leader who realized the economic model of communism didn't work and needed some reorganization." Of course, Gorbachev failed to bring along any real cooperators, or any supporters of Boris Yeltsin or constituents of any of the new democratic parties, the ones who were pleading with Gorbachev to junk the "reorganized" communist economic model immediately, lest he further exacerbate the possibility of civil war.

And there was certainly no one put in front of a network camera who did not have a Communist Party membership card in his pocket . . . which was exactly why the dozens of officials who accompanied Gorbachev viewed Yakovlev as an unwanted picture at an exhibition, while Martin hovered around him with casual authority, telling his client to kick them where it hurts. Yak's face looked like it had been doused with Clorox. *Results. Mister Tom Billington wants results. I'm going to be arrested.*

The nasty looks Martin saw on the faces of the official dele-

---

new rules that would maximize unrestricted operations of multinational corporations. The Soviets were specifically interested in observing and helping to formulate an evolving policy that was allowing multinationals in the third world to be treated like locally owned mom-and-pop stores, subject to minimal state controls. Soviet leaders were caught between two stools on this issue because on the one hand Russia needed Western investment, while on the other they were terrified of abdicating control of their national economy to foreign enterprises.

gation, coupled with the dozens of interviews Jai Imbrey had lined up for Yak, confirmed the success of *Commersant,* but only if Yak knew how to play it so that Shatalin would set up the photo opportunity with Bush and Gorbachev. And Yak was not looking too good. In between radio and television interviews, he returned to the Madison's lobby, where he sat in silence, staring coldly at the Soviet delegates, who refused to acknowledge his presence, and waiting for the arrival of Shatalin.

Academician Stanislav Sergeyevich Shatalin, the president of the popular professional Moscow soccer team, Spartak, was the most eccentric major-league communist on Gorbachev's Presidential Council. Born in 1934 outside Leningrad, the Kremlin economist got his first big break when Brezhnev tapped him to head the State Committee for Science and Technology at Moscow University in the mid-sixties. This position led the Party to dub him the father of "the theory and methodology of balanced socialist economic growth," for which he was awarded the U.S.S.R. State Prize. Official accolades for his ineffective economic models notwithstanding, Shatalin consistently exercised his razor-sharp tongue to press for a free-market economy. One popular Shatalin story centered on the day when, as the Deputy Director of the Central Economics and Mathematical Institute, he cut short an important fiscal-policy aide to Brezhnev with the line: "Do you have any thoughts of your own, other than those of Marx, Engels, Lenin, and Stalin? If not, sit down." Most of his staff at the institute got up and left. After the group filed one of the earliest reports on the declining efficiency of the economy, some six staff members emigrated to the United States.

Such impertinence tested the limits of Party tolerance, which gave Shatalin the reputation of being a systematic humiliator of communist economic policy until Gorbachev brought him into the *perestroika* pack. In front of the summit cameras, Gorbachev was blending Shatalin's budgetary and fiscal ideas with those of other economists to concoct a new-fashioned economy, one that the American bankers and businessmen he was to meet with in Washington, Minneapolis, and San Francisco might see as worthy of investment. Privately, Shatalin was sitting in his room heavy into an Old Fashioned—long on the bourbon, light on the ice, and easily available from his mini-bar.

It was two A.M. when Yak finally had his meeting with Shatalin, who had arrived some twelve hours earlier with Gorbachev at Andrews Air Force Base, walking off Comrade One with the extra bale of *Commersants* that Yak had asked him to bring from Moscow. Shatalin had spent the afternoon and evening with Gorbachev and his advisers at the Soviet Embassy, and the rambling, drunken report he gave Yakovlev was not encouraging.

"Shatalin told me that Gorbachev is really angry that we're here," Yak explained tensely to Martin over coffee in the lobby the following morning. "There's no hope for us to get a photo of Gorbachev with *Commersant*. They want us to leave town. Now. Before the summit gets started.

"I think we should leave for New York immediately," Yak said, slumping further into his armchair. "We can do interviews in New York, yes? There are already enough *Commersants* in Washington. Too many *Commersants*."

"Hey, Volodya, fuck them, you know!" Martin declared, furious that a bunch of men who "look like they wear long underwear all year long" were trying to run him out of town. "You told me when I first met you in New York that we were going out on the edge with *Commersant*. Well, here we are and they don't like us one bit. Too bad. You're in their league now, Volodya, so start looking the part. I understand the risk you're taking with this, but it's gotta be taken if *Commersant* is going to be successful. . . ."

"Peter, we have a problem—actually a couple of problems," Imbrey said, running across the lobby from the deskphone. "A number of hotels, some of them where members of the Soviet delegation are staying, are now refusing to distribute *Commersant* as they promised."

"Shit," Yak said, lighting a cigarette, asking if he could go have a coffee. *Results*.

"No, sit here," Martin snapped, his body tightening. "Jai, we paid these people to distribute *Commersant*, right?"

Imbrey nodded. "They want to give us the money back."

"I'm going to the telephone!" Martin announced, picking up

his cowboy hat and pulling a small book of extremely private White House and Senate phone numbers out of his pocket. "You stay here, Jai, and no, Volodya, we are not leaving Washington. Jai, he has interviews scheduled with ABC, NBC, CNN, CBS, and a dozen newspapers and radio stations. Stick with the Yak like glue. I don't want him getting lost in the crowd.

"You're going to *every* interview, Volodya," Martin said, pointing his big white Stetson in Yak's face. "*Every* interview."

Martin hesitated before walking across the lobby to make his phone calls, studying the faces of the official Soviet summiteers who milled around the front desk. It was an eerie countenance of blankness, animation, and frustration that met his stony stare. The look of the bear.

16

> When imaginations begin to skid out of
> control so do events.
>
> GENERAL ALEXANDER M. HAIG, JR.

YAKOVLEV FLEW BACK to Moscow a happy man with a hoarse voice and enough press coverage to fill a thirty-minute videotape and forty-page scrapbook. Peter Martin had been right in convincing him to remain in Washington for the duration of the summit, even though Shatalin had continued to urge him to leave town for his own good. The Yak had entered the Big Time, prime time; and the Kremlin was for the moment in the process of dealing with more ominous issues (starvation and revolution being principal among them) than disciplining a renegade cooperative director whose American partner was one of the world's leading grain and beef brokers.

Peggy Yott's phone had been ringing off the hook with potential subscribers, advertisers, *and* investors. Peter Martin's office was under siege with media queries, many of the reporters asking where they could find the Yak for follow-up stories on Moscow's "crusading journalist." Rob Manoff was ecstatic: Brad Durham was beginning to make headway with *Commersant*'s Russian staff. The paper was not flawless, but it was improving, and faster than anybody imagined. Although *Commersant* did not receive as much media coverage as Gorbachev, no one had expected the paper and its editor to be accommodated in the same news articles as Gorbachev, and certainly not broadcast in television bites overlaid with video of the Soviet leader. Like the rest of Russia Group, Billington, too, had been impressed with *Commersant*'s American debut. But his excitement over the advertising queries and subscription checks that were beginning to flow in to Chicago was muted by whether or not Yak had the desire to polish *Commersant* into a product that could outlast the fickleness of the American newspaper and magazine market—a market of which Yak had no understanding.

Billington did not seek surrogate control of Fact, but he demanded that Yott be kept apprised of any potential new investors and the status of improvements taking place in the paper. Although Billington's staff had sent consultants and technicians to Moscow to arrange for equipment installation and repair and to give editorial advice, few people at Fact had expected so many Americans to be looking over their shoulders. This was no "enlightened self-interest" on Billington's part, but his way of helping a company, and a newspaper, that needed all the help available. Yakovlev treated Billington's envoys with respect, but he did nothing to gainsay the fact that many of his Russian staff viewed Billington's assistance as a form of corporate neocolonialism. Durham, for example, needed Yakovlev's blessing to attend editorial meetings with the Russian staff. Yak never gave it, leaving Durham to patch together the English-language edition without any foreknowledge of what stories were going to be in it. More critical to *Commersant*'s long-term health was Yakovlev's refusal to lobby the Russian staff to seek Durham's editorial council and direction on stories. Lots of good stories applicable to both the Russian- and English-language editions were going uncovered, and every story that came across from the translators needed to be re-reported and rewritten extensively. Durham was questioning detail, not substance, and Yakovlev resisted seeing the difference.

The process of legitimization was being facilitated only by the blessing-in-disguise visits *Commersant*'s Russian reporters made to the American Edition Room to share food and stories with Durham. Since Yak had rebuffed all of Durham's attempts to sit in on editorial meetings, the spontaneous encounters with the Russian reporters in the American Room were the only opportunity Durham had to discuss upcoming stories and impart direction on how they might be reported and written. Conducted over beer, which Durham paid for in his own dollars at Moscow's hard-currency stores, and in between savage games of Nerf basketball, these impulsive and unplanned gatherings turned into *Commersant*'s most decisive editorial meetings and were responsible for the improvements being seen in Chicago. This was Durham's private war of attrition and, as time went by, more and more of the staff began to seek his organizational brilliance before tackling a story. Time was running out, however.

Yakovlev and Billington agreed that *Commersant* would begin to accept American subscription money immediately after the summit. North American distribution was scheduled to begin sometime in September 1990. Moreover, Billington understood that Race was in no position to handle the nuts and bolts of marketing a newspaper, so he began a search for a company that could handle sales and distribution once the paper arrived in Chicago over the direct satellite link from Race's London office. The plan was for Yakovlev to transmit the English-language *Commersant* by modem every Sunday night over the direct phone line Race had installed between Good Highway and London. Once the copy arrived in London, Race's people would bounce it off the satellite to the company's West Jackson Boulevard office in Chicago, whence it would be sent to the printer by Monday morning. The system, sharp and tight, was set up by Yott and took full advantage of Race's ultramodern international communications network.

But despite Yott's Herculean efforts to make the system work effectively, Yakovlev continued to disregard her daily Telexes on subjects from the types of business stories American industry was interested in to what specific computer software Moscow would be using to transmit *Commersant* to Chicago. Scheduled tests of the tricky and sophisticated system never came to pass, Yakovlev claiming the dry runs had never been arranged. Chicago's Telexes to Durham requesting information on the status of the paper mysteriously never arrived in *Commersant*'s American Room.

Peter Martin's flurry of Telexes went unanswered, too. It was a little over four months after the summit and Yak still owed Martin thirty-four thousand dollars for his work. Yak refused to discuss the issue with Martin. Finally, Yak contacted Martin to say it was Billington who owed the balance. He told Martin to contact Yott, who would be happy to send the check along to New York. Martin knew full well this was not the case and, calling Yott in Chicago, informed her of Yak's increasingly queer posture. Martin and Yott agreed: the scene was beginning to turn ugly, and for no reason. Yak had the cash to pay Martin and Race's commitment to go ahead with the American launch.

Yakovlev neglected to show up for meetings Billington had scheduled for him in Moscow with American business leaders seeking information on the Soviet market. The white phone, the direct line between Moscow and London, sat like a paperweight on the desk of Yakovlev's secretary with the receiver taped to its body. No one in the office had any idea how to use it. And, although bundles of *Commersant* arrived weekly in Chicago by courier, Yakovlev had failed to draw up the letter Race needed to cash the sixty-one thousand dollars' worth of subscription checks collecting dust in Yott's desk drawer. Billington was concerned, principally because Yak had failed to pay Martin and other American suppliers who were beginning to come out of the woodwork for money owed in the wake of Yak's numerous appearances in the newspapers and on television. Meeting one's financial commitments was the bedrock of the commodity business; honoring debts on time made or destroyed a trader's reputation. For men of Billington's caliber, money was a barometer to evaluate an individual's honesty.

"Volodya is a deadbeat. End of story," Martin said after calling his bank for the third time in as many months to see if the money that Yakovlev said he sent had arrived. "He's not even contacted me to arrange a repayment schedule. I just receive Telexes saying the money is in my bank and that I should go look for it. Bald-faced lies."

"I don't understand what's happening," Yott added. "I know you have to think somewhat like a Russian when dealing with them, but Volodya's acting as if we're not interested in the project anymore and that he has to run off with everything Race has given him before we take it back. He's not very smart. Billington loves this project, and everybody at Race who's involved in it is willing to go the extra mile to make it successful. We have one employee in London ready to come into the office every Sunday night to transmit *Commersant* to Chicago because he's so into being a part of it."

"I have no idea what's going on," Durham explained, exhausted but grateful that Billington had agreed to underwrite the transport costs of sending another American editor to help him out in Moscow. "I spend sixty-hour weekends repairing the Soviet reportage and the rest of the time trying to train these guys. This is M*A*S*H journalism; I must let bad stories go into the paper so I have the time to save the critical cases."

"I don't need Mister Tom Billington anymore," Yakovlev said thirteen months after he had gone to Oak Park, begging for investment capital. There was no gratitude in his low and monotonous voice, no willingness to mask the spite that came out of his eyes. "I was so desperate for equipment last year that I would have signed a deal with anybody.

"Race has the right to distribute only English-language *Commersant* in the United States," he added, blind or oblivious to his contract with Race that gave Billington the exclusive right to market everything produced by Fact in English or in Russian everywhere in the world except the Soviet Union. "Mister Billington gets his newspapers and he can do with them what he wishes. I *needed* Race for the American-registered joint venture, but now I no longer need them and the contract is no longer valid."

It had all built in slow increments, like molehills that end up becoming one very treacherous mountain. Yott had Telexed Yakovlev with the good news that Race's attorneys had drawn up the joint-venture papers. There was no reply. Then Yak started making quick trips to Paris and holding odd meetings in Moscow with unidentified French businessmen. Yott and Martin began receiving reports of Russian- and English-language *Commersants* trickling onto newsstands in New York; this information followed by accounts of Fact directors entering into independent distribution negotiations with companies in Australia and Europe. Durham's success in creating a readable and increasingly popular English-language edition was being undercut by Russian staffers, who took bribes in cash and goods to place stories exclusively in the edition to be sold in America. Phones went dead, Telexes went unanswered, and attempts to reach Yakovlev about the payment of past debts and the plotting of future strategies were met with the cool response that he was out of town.

Yak's personal behavior upset Russia Group as much as the unnecessarily adversarial posture he was taking. Every member had heard different stories—tempestuous tales—about Yak since the summit through contacts in Moscow and over the grapevine. Race had created no conventions to restrain Yakovlev's desire to expand the business. In fact, Billington wanted to help in any way possible. "I've never seen Billington be so sympathetic to the requests and goals of a partner," explained a senior Race executive. "The whole company wanted to help this guy Yakovlev and encourage him whenever possible."

Yak had undergone a transformation in the three months after the summit, a metamorphosis from confederate to conspirator that was directly linked to the ever-changing face of the Kremlin's confused policy toward implementing the free-enterprise system. Simply put, cooperators were no longer chic, and joint ventures had lost their shine. Cooperative Union President Vladimir Tikhonov's effort to generate public support of cooperatives had been an abysmal failure. Indeed, cooperators such as Yakovlev were beginning to discover—like the state trade ministries before them—that the *valuta* pie had only so many slices. Sources in the State Statistics Committee had informed a member of the *Commersant* staff that a report to be released in early 1991 would show joint ventures contributing a pathetic 0.2 percent to the gross national product, doing little to increase the flow of Western investment into the Soviet Union or to fulfill Gorbachev's pledge that Western technology and management skill would sate ravenous consumers and arouse the economy. Joint ventures and their cooperative cousins devolved into such a morass of bribery, financial manipulation, and importation of electronic equipment and computer hardware for sale on the black market that within days of the State Statistic Committee's report Gorbachev pleaded personally for a hundred billion dollars in economic aid from the democratic world on the grounds that the investment would bolster global security. The ruble, to which easy access in 1988 spelled free-market success, was losing value with each passing hour. Those of us intimately involved in the cooperative movement knew the state was preparing to alter the official exchange rate from 5.7 rubles to 27.6 rubles per dollar* and that it was hard currency, not rubles, that would be needed to survive the 1990s. Nobody understood this better than Yakovlev, who had pushed Billington for a U.S.-registered joint venture that Cooperative Fact could wield to develop business outside Soviet law.

The conundrum that faced Fact (as well as the other early cooperatives that had grown prosperous since the movement's birth in 1987) was how best to keep alive the limited hard-currency channel it had opened with Race under old cooperative decrees while at the same time taking unlimited advantage of new joint-stock-company laws that allowed individuals more leeway to create profitable hard-currency deals with the West. This was a particularly vexing problem for Yakovlev because *Kooperativ Fakt* was contractually obliged to provide Race with its entire product output. *Commersant*'s average monthly Soviet sales were one million five hundred thousand rubles (two million four hundred thousand dollars at the official 1990 exchange rate), giving Yakovlev an after-tax profit of five hundred thousand rubles (eight hundred thousand dollars) or an amazing 33 percent profit margin. These were impressive ledgers to throw at prospective clients and investors, but only if Race could somehow be removed from the new joint-stock-company game, allowing Yakovlev the room to maneuver without any interference from Billington. Yakovlev's solution to the *valuta* enigma was to secretly transform *Kooperativ Fakt* into Joint-Stock Company Fact with the sweep of the Mont Blanc Billington had presented him as a gift.

Russia Group's doubts about Yakovlev's commitment to keep-

---

*The new exchange rate, which became official in April 1991, caused a panic at Moscow banks, where there were not enough rubles to accommodate those who wanted to exchange foreign currency. The new official rate was so good that moneychangers on the Arbat set a lower rate of twenty-five rubles to the dollar to oblige the foreigners who were turned away by the empty banks.

ing *Commersant* alive in the United States deepened whenever any of them had the opportunity to speak in person with Yak. Yak's strength was his energy, and it was beginning to sag under the annoyance he displayed whenever Billington's name entered the conversation.

"Mister Billington can have anything he wants from Cooperative Fact," Yakovlev declared with belligerent smugness when I first accused him of double-dealing in the summer of 1990. Sitting on the long gray sofa in Fact's office, arguing loudly and drinking the endless cups of coffee wheeled into us atop a nicotine-stained tray, Yak refused to explain why he thought Billington was treating him unfairly, except to say: "There's no longer a Cooperative Fact. It's Joint-Stock Company Fact. There's absolutely nothing to worry about. I have intentions of shutting down *Commersant* and starting a brand-new business publication."

"What about the staff?" I asked Yak during one of our discussions on the future of *Commersant*. "Where are they going to go?"

"They can find other jobs easily enough."

"What about the contract with Race?" I asked, stunned that Yak was considering the closure of *Commersant* a few weeks away from its American subscription launch, and without informing Billington, who had retained enough confidence in the new-look English-language edition to hire a marketing company.

"There's no Cooperative Fact anymore. And if there's no more Cooperative Fact there is no more *Commersant* and no more Mister Billington. We also need to get rid of Brad. He isn't working out. You will fire him."

Durham, who had specialized in the study of international contracts while at law school and then mastered the bare-knuckled techniques necessary to stop Yakovlev from inventing stories at *Commersant*, exploded upon hearing the news. "This is first-semester, no, first-day law-school stuff! You can't just change the name of a company to void it of contractual obligations! Yak's gone totally delirious. He acts as if he's pulled off a sophisticated big-business coup, and I'm worried because his stupidity has put everything we've done here in serious jeopardy," Durham raged on. Hundred-hour work weeks and a steady diet of Russian food and constant pressure to create a transformed *Commersant* had left him chronically fatigued and in ill-health. "Many staff members have left already over Yak's low credibility. He no longer cares about the paper. He refuses to admit that what he's done is potentially criminal."

The criminality of Yak's behavior was an issue the lawyers could sort out later if it reached that point. Yak did not care: he was strutting around Moscow, telling all who would listen about a new distribution deal that would award Fact more equipment and better global exposure, with no mention that it was Billington's money and commitment to founding a comprehensive and accurate English-language *Commersant* that was generating all of Fact's press in the West. In Paris, *Commersant* had become the darling of the French business community through articles written in the business newspaper *La Tribune de l'Expansion* and the biweekly business magazine *L'Expansion,* both publications of the privately owned French publishing empire ruled by Jean-Louis Servan-Schreiber.

Servan-Schreiber, who had met Yakovlev through the journalist who had filed the glowing report on *Commersant* and Co-operative Fact, invited the young publisher to Paris to discuss, as Servan-Schreiber explained, *L'Expansion's* becoming involved in "developing Western markets and distribution channels." Yak arrived in Paris with a nod and a smile and without any mention of Race's exact involvement in Fact. "Race isn't a problem," Yak told Servan-Schreiber.

Peter Martin fired the first ballistic fax from New York:

Please be advised that we have some very real concerns about Mr. Yakovlev's morals and business ethics. We launched the English version of Commersant *in the U.S. during the Bush/Gorbachev summit. Mr. Yakovlev entered into a legal, proper and binding contract with us. The American expression is that he "skipped town" without paying the $35,000 and we are taking appropriate legal action against him and* Commersant *in this country, so that any and all business dealings done by him and/or on behalf of Fact will be dealt with through the U.S. and French legal systems. Mr. Yakovlev has strewn* *the American landscape with legitimate debts that he has dishonored from other suppliers. I also understand Mr. Yakovlev is endeavoring to sell you property which is not rightly his, specifically Race's world-wide rights to Fact information. As head of an international PR agency, from time to time, I have come across ne'er-do-wells of Mr. Yakovlev's ilk. I have found it most beneficial to disassociate myself with them as sooner or later they will foul every deal in which they become involved.*

At first Race's attorneys fired a couple of warning letters over the French bow and advised a member of Russia Group to inform Yakovlev, who anxiously pressed for a meeting with Billington once news of the secret French deal leaked out, not to arrive in Chicago unless he had a cashier's check for eight hundred thousand dollars in his pocket. Yak certainly had the money. According to Yak, in the spring of 1991, Servan-Schreiber paid Yakovlev close to $3.5 million for a 40 percent stake in *Commersant* and the right to channel the paper's news reports and data base through *Groupe Expansion's Euroexpansione* economic information network of nine dailies, twelve weeklies, and ten periodicals. Through an offshore holding company owned by *Groupe Expansion* in France, Handelsblatt in Germany, Class Editori in Italy, and Dow Jones in the United States, *Euroexpansione* information flowed into fifteen countries, reflecting a combined circulation of 2.5 million copies. "The Soviet Union," Servan-Schreiber told me excitedly, "has a great future for our company because we are the leading network of European business, financial, and stock market publications.

"The letters from Martin and Race are strange because we're not entering into an agreement with Cooperative Fact, but with Joint Stock Company Fact and *Commersant*," he explained, perplexed over the flurry of warning letters that kept arriving at his office. "I don't believe Cooperative Fact exists anymore. I have read the contract between Fact and Race, and the contract only applies to the distribution of *Commersant* in the United States, which remains in the hands of Race."

Servan-Schreiber did not recognize Race's legal control of Fact/*Commersant* information beyond the Soviet border because

247 / BEAR HUNTING WITH THE POLITBURO

Yakovlev had apparently never shown the French publisher (nor Charles Meyer, Fact's French attorney in the *Groupe Expansion* negotiations) the third appendix to the three-part contract. It was the codicil that specified Race as the sole owner and distributor of Fact/*Commersant* information outside the Soviet Union, although the signed agreement could obviously be contested in court. "It was very surprising and hard to believe," said Jean de Hauteclocque, the attorney retained by Billington in Paris to negotiate an out-of-court settlement between Race and Yakovlev. "I sat reading the pertinent clauses to Meyer as he scanned the contract. He kept asking from where was I reading. I told him the contract. Meyer swallowed hard. He was absolutely stunned by the revelation. I'm sure it was the first time that he, or Servan-Schreiber for that matter, had ever heard of it.

"Meyer took the contract, had his secretary make a copy, and said that he'd get back to me on it," Hauteclocque added.

Forty-eight hours before the lawyers had compared contracts in Meyer's office, Servan-Schreiber hosted a sunset gala in the dazzling pastel marble plaza of the Banque Populaire building to formally announce a stock purchase that was an odds-on bet to keep him in the courts of at least five countries for years to come. A graphic statue of a naked woman with no arms that looked to be an avant-garde rendering of Justice Without Balance stared down on Servan-Schreiber's hundred guests from the center of the brightly polished hall. *Groupe Expansion* employees costumed as Cossack dancers and Moscow Circus bear handlers glided around the statue, offering champagne and canapés to French politicians and business leaders, members of the prestigious Académie Française, and the Soviet Ambassador to France. Volodya Yakovlev was late, and when he finally walked through the huge glass door, anxiously fingering a Japanese shuriken, Servan-Schreiber pulled a pocket comb from his striped jacket and ran it through his hair before he spoke.

"Economic information is one of democracy's weapons," Servan-Schreiber told the crowd, his eyes shining like pink pearls ready to be plucked. "This is why we have decided to buy into *Commersant*. What a joyful event it is to have our Russian friend among us. Vladimir is now a colleague and friend who has come in from the cold."

A shapeless smile crossed Yak's face.

There was irony in Yakovlev's role in perpetuating Servan-Schreiber's fantasy. Yak had said it all before to Billington, and to me for the nearly three years I worked alongside him as a cooperator. Servan-Schreiber was the latest in a long line of Moscow newcomers, and the thrill of dealing in the *perestroika* revolution distracted him from cross-checking the information Yak had provided about Fact's legal status and its relationship with Race, as well as the street-legal tactics needed to conduct business under *perestroika*. Martin's letters calling Yak a deadbeat and the questions being asked by Race's attorneys were easily explained. This was *Gorbachev's* Moscow, after all. Yak brought out Bela Alexandrovna and the Chaika limos, the circus bears and the Bolshoi dancers, sturgeon steaks from the Caspian and rare herbs from Georgia. Moscow was clean and clear and caviar smooth. A zinc day, a time when anything was possible.

17

A civil war is inevitable. We have only to
organize it as painlessly as possible.

LEON TROTSKY

IT WAS NEW YEAR'S DAY 1991 and the military coup d'état that trumped Mikhail Sergeyevich Gorbachev was still eight months away. Soviet Foreign Minister Eduard Shevardnadze had abandoned the political ring because he feared the coming "dictatorship." Gorbachev and Yeltsin agonized on prime time like two World Wide Wrestling Federation superstars; and the new Russian prime minister, Ivan Silayev, told the fans that peasants working on state farms would not be forced to buy private plots of land, but that the new land-ownership law would give them "even restitution" from the repressions of the past. Curiously, "Land for the Peasants!" was the chief slogan of the Bolshevik Revolution; the double entendre of Silayev's statement to the Russian legislature was not lost on anybody in the fifteen rapidly deteriorating Soviet republics.

New Year's Day was cold and hungry in Moscow, but it dawned with the pledge of the Kremlin to scrap major chunks of its nuclear and conventional arsenals—a new decade which made the West politically complacent about the Soviets ever again gearing up their war economy. But the Bolshevik Revolution that grew into the combat economy of the Cold War was based not on ideology but on food and land; specifically, the ownership of land and what was grown upon it. The *perestroika* revolution, too, was based on private property: precisely, the hope of millions of Soviet citizens, thousands of cooperators, and dozens of ethnic minority groups to own their own businesses and to manage their own affairs. "If the republics split off from the union," Gorbachev said, as hastily arranged emergency supplies of Western food and medicine arrived in the Soviet Union, guarded by armed troops to resist black-marketeer raiding parties, "we will have war, real war, and one that would be terrible not only for the country, but for the entire world."

There were only nine years until the new century, but Gorbachev and his advisers were still mired in discussing nineteenth-century forms of private property such as hundred-year leases in lieu of ownership, centrally controlled stock ventures, and limited rights of political self-determination. Private property that could be bought and sold by individuals, Gorbachev told the conservative cliques, was "inappropriate" because "people just won't accept it." At the same time, Stanislav Shatalin, the free-market voice on Gorbachev's now dissolved Presidential Council, told the country that Gorbachev "does not see private property as some kind of devil." However, Shatalin resigned as Gorbachev's chief economic adviser in January 1991 and a few weeks later was excommunicated from the Communist Party because he had "lost links with the Party," according to the Central Committee.

Perestroika was approaching its sixth anniversary and nobody was in the mood for celebration, despite promises of more Western credits to ease the anguish of restructuring. The new year unfolded without food and with indications that Soviet banks would not be able to fulfill their long-term financial obligations without more credit from the West. Although the Bush administration pledged to guarantee 98 percent of any new bank loans made to the Soviet Union, American financial institutions refused to underwrite further financing of the U.S.S.R. It was an unusual position for the banks to take amid White House enthusiasm because only a small portion of a bank's own money is at risk when credits are largely protected by the U.S. government. Wall Street's message was clear: President Bush's desire to prop up the stability of Gorbachev was no reflection of Moscow's ability to repay.

The mood was the same in Western Europe, where Sweden and Norway readied plans to set up emergency refugee camps and reinforce border security because of concern that tens of thousands of Soviets would take advantage of eased travel restrictions and flee economic catastrophe before a military crackdown. "A worst, worst case scenario with a great emigration, like wolf packs welling over the border, is not something we regard as possible," said Bjorn Blokhus, the Norwegian Foreign Ministry spokesman, as his country began unrolling more barbed wire.

Meanwhile, the Soviet Union's fifteen republics continued to fracture. Many of the nationalist groups were stockpiling arms and supplies. *Vremya*, Soviet television's official evening news show, began a segment that rounded up the number of Lenin monuments around the country under physical attack.

Vladimir Tikhonov, now popularly known as the "Cooperative Father," continued to rail against the bureaucracy and the central planners, but the Cooperative Congress never reconvened for a second session. The golden days of the cooperatives were over. The early cooperators, the new-age Nepmen who pledged to bring the free market to the Soviet Union, were disappearing behind joint-stock company laws and decrees that further thwarted any likelihood of a grass-roots entrepreneurial system. The official rota claimed five million people working in cooperatives—and the government and the people were blaming them for buying scarce goods to be resold at higher prices. The truth was that honest cooperators sold goods at more realistic prices than the artificial prices in state-subsidized stores—which had no food for sale, anyway. On April 1, 1991, the Kremlin doubled, tripled and, in some instances, quadrupled the price of food and other consumer goods. It was the beginning of uncontrollable inflation—a bloating of fear the Party tried to justify by saying it took eight years after the Revolution of 1917 to destroy private property in industry and thirteen years in agriculture, therefore it would take the Party more than a few years to reverse it all.

The coup was now four months away.

"Gorbachev is now *everything*—the British queen and the American president," said Vitali Korotich, who remained the editor of *Ogonyok* and a People's Deputy from Kharkov, still committed to preventing another revolution despite odds that soon overwhelmed him, his magazine, and his country. "But having the powers on paper isn't enough to solve the country's problems . . . at the beginning of 1990, we expected a Marshall Plan, but at the end of the year we were faced with martial law."

Food speculation reached pandemic proportions, with black marketeering so widespread that Russians were organizing "lynch mobs" to patrol stores and food centers. It was another echo of 1917—when "worker control" enforcement posses were set up by Lenin to ride roughshod over the country with the imprimatur of the Bolsheviks—as were the series of terse decrees issued by Gorbachev, giving the military greater sanction to use force in dealing with attacks on Kremlin authority. It was lock-and-load time, and most lingering doubts were dashed when Gorbachev, teetering to the whims of the repressive right wing, sacked energetic liberal Soviet Interior Minister Vadim Bakatin in favor of archconservative Boris Pugo, the former KGB boss in the Baltic republic of Latvia.

Gorbachev gave General Boris Gromov, the former commander of Soviet troops in Afghanistan, control of the one million two hundred thousand soldiers and police at the disposal of the Ministry of Interior. Within hours of Gorbachev's progressive "political solution," Gromov's troops and tanks took instant political advantage of global media attention on the war in Iraq and Kuwait to invade the Baltic republics of Latvia and Lithuania and to position themselves on the streets of the other thirteen republics to enforce martial law. Columns of Soviet armor rolled south into the republics of Armenia, Georgia, and Azerbaijan to smash ragtag bands of armed nationalists once the Red Army paratroopers flushed the guerrillas out of their mountain redoubts. Hard-line decrees to control the masses were issued with a flurry of fear; the KGB was given authority to examine and investigate "without hindrance" the cash, equipment, properties, and account books of all domestic *and* foreign businesses and joint ventures in the Soviet Union. "I'm convinced that in the long run, what you are seeing now in the Soviet Union will prove more important historically than the war in the Persian Gulf," mused the popular Lithuanian parliamentarian Algimantas Cekoulis.

"The Russian bear is not dead," Vitali Korotich told me, "but revolution is not inevitable."

Colonel Viktor Alksnis, a leader of the equally popular hardline parliamentary faction *Soyuz*, warned that the "situation in the army is comparable to the way it was in 1917." Members of the radical Democratic Union were waiting for the revolution to come, too, with the lack of food and the introduction of ration cards making their hunger strikes all the more simple. Many DUs, like their nemesis Colonel Alksnis, said blood revolution was inevitable because "Gorbachev 1991" mirrored "Kerensky 1917," the year when the army deserted Alexander Kerensky's feeble democratic government to save Russia by joining either Lenin's Bolsheviks or the ill-fated "Army of Iron Discipline" run by the doomed militarist Cossack General Lavr Kornilov.

Three weeks before the August 19 military coup d'état that required Mikhail Gorbachev to "undergo medical treatment" under the armed supervision of Communist Party "plotters" at his Crimean vacation dacha in Foros, Boris Yeltsin had ordered Communist Party organizations out of workplaces, schools, and government offices. Gorbachev was in London at the time, the first Soviet ruler ever to be invited to a Group of Seven economic summit, where he asked Western leaders for money they did not possess to finance a Soviet economic recovery plan that he did not have. The expert economic advisors to the Western leaders showered Gorbachev with statistics that revealed his country's 1991 GNP to be down 17.7 percent, oil revenues depressed by 15.5 percent, and inflation skyrocketing over 100 percent. Gorbachev went home to Moscow empty handed, embarrassed, but with a photo album of pictures that proved him now one of the club. Soviet hardliners in the military and the police, their frustration boiling over into Stalinist rhetoric, called on "healthy forces" to save the U.S.S.R. from "humiliation" and "fratricidal war" being brought on by "those people who do not love this country, who enslave themselves to foreign patrons and go looking for advice and blessings from across the seas."

The fuse was then lit for former Politburo liberal Alexander

N. Yakovlev, the intellectual guru behind *perestroika*, to resign as Gorbachev's political manager on August 16, warning that "the party leadership, in contradiction to its own declarations, is ridding itself of the democratic wing and is preparing for social revenge and state coup." Yakovlev's departure, seventy-six hours before the August 19 coup d'état, signaled the full dispersal of the team that had begun the *perestroika* experiment. Various political factions spent the weekend before the coup attacking each other: hardliners published a screed accusing former Foreign Minister turned independent democrat Eduard Shevardnadze of leading the country to defeat "in an undeclared, unfought third world war"; left-wing communists countered that there was no future for a Communist Party mired in dogmatic Marxism-Leninism. Others wanted to customize the party along the lines of France's Social Democrats, while still others pushed for a political course akin to the blundering political strategies of the left wing of the American Democratic Party in the 1970s.

Extravagant confusion spread like sap during the hot August hours that led up to Gorbachev's arrest by the head of his personal KGB guard, with party leaders of every political hue demanding plenums, extraordinary congresses, and worker roundtables to search for Marxist motivation and collective revelation. In the republics, Communist Party bosses haplessly advised the *narod* to review Lenin's *Collected Works* for inspiration to stop the *perestroika* revolution from turning the country into the loose confederation of independent states that would come with the signing of a new union treaty on August 20. Desperate, they searched for a harbinger with the wizardry to stop the sovereignty movement. Then, on August 1, *Air Force One* set down in the Ukrainian city of Kiev. Speaking in front of the Ukrainian parliament on his way back to the U.S. from a superpower summit in Moscow, the leader of the free world publicly condemned the single-minded pursuit of emancipation. "Freedom," President George Bush announced to the astonishment of Ukrainian liberation leaders, "is not the same as independence."

At the same moment, a few hundred miles to the north, the Lithuanian parliament was holding an emergency session to discuss the execution-style killing of six nationalist border guards, the latest in over twenty similar raids carried out against the three Baltic republics by the KGB. "The aggressive actions of the U.S.S.R. are being escalated," a Lithuanian parliament spokeswoman said grimly of the midnight attack, which had occurred only hours before Bush, in a somewhat literary attempt to sooth the strains between Kremlin hardliners and the republics, would quote an old Ukrainian proverb that says: "When you enter a great enterprise, free your soul from weakness."

"Bush came here as a messenger for Gorbachev," said Ivan Drach, a writer and the chairman of the Ukrainian independence group Rukh.

"The troops came here to kill us with bullets," said Lithuanian Interior Minister Marionus Misiukonis.

Back in Moscow, *Vremya* announced its annual mid-August warning about "a real threat of famine" while the Interior Ministry sent its elite black-beret troops to restore order in the Urals town of Nizhni Tagil after the arrival of twelve thousand pairs of Italian sneakers provoked three days of riots at a local factory.

Red Army tanks, acting under the orders of eight high-ranking Soviet officials who had all been appointed to their posts by Mikhail Gorbachev, rolled into Moscow at around one in the morning on August 19. They were about five hours late. The coup d'état had started at four A.M. Gorbachev had been arrested some twelve hours earlier than that.

"Fellow countrymen! Citizens of the Soviet Union! A mortal danger hangs over our great homeland," a sunrise spokesman for the military coup boomed over the state-controlled radio, accompanied by the sour strains of a symphonic dirge. "This is the result of a deliberate action by those who are carrying out a coup and reaching out toward an unbridled personal dictatorship. Unless we take urgent and resolute measures to stabilize the economy, we shall face famine and a new turn of the spiral of improvement. Only the irresponsible can put their hope in help from abroad. No handouts will solve our problems. We will cleanse the streets of our cities of criminal elements and put an end to the tyranny of those who plunder the people's assets."

The new ruling Committee of Eight (headed by U.S.S.R. Vice-President Gennadi Yanayev and including KGB boss Vladimir Kryuchkov, Interior Minister Boris Pugo, Defense Minister Dmitri Yazov, Defense Council Chairman Oleg Baklanov, Farmer's Union chief Vladimir Starodubtsev, Soviet Prime Minister Valentin Pavlov, and Alexander Tizyakov, a little man with the big title of President of the Association of State Enterprises and Industrial, Construction, Transport, and Communication Facilities of the U.S.S.R.) usurped Gorbachev's popularly disliked government on August 19 by ordering fellow plotters in the state news wire service TASS to transmit two urgent medical bulletins at six-fifteen A.M.

In view of Mikhail Sergeyevich Gorbachev's inability for health reasons to perform the duties of the U.S.S.R. president and of transfer of the U.S.S.R. president's power, in keeping with Paragraph 7, Article 127, of the U.S.S.R. Constitution, to U.S.S.R. Vice-President Gennadi Ivanovich Yanayev.

With the aim of overcoming the profound and comprehensive crisis, political, ethnic and civil strife, chaos and anarchy that threaten the lives and security of the Soviet Union's citizens and the sovereignty, territory integrity, freedom and independence of the fatherland.

Proceeding from the results of the nationwide referendum on the preservation of the Union of Soviet Socialist Republics.

And guided by the vital interests of all ethnic groups living in our fatherland and all Soviet people.

We resolve:

1. In accordance with paragraph 3, Article 127, of the U.S.S.R. Constitution and Article 2 of the U.S.S.R. law On the Legal Regime of a State Emergency and with demands by broad popular masses to adopt the most decisive measures to prevent society from sliding into national catastrophe and ensure law and order, to declare a state of emergency in some parts of the Soviet Union for six months from 0400 Moscow time on August 19, 1991.

2. To establish that the Constitution and laws of the U.S.S.R. have unconditional priority throughout the territory of the U.S.S.R.

3. To form a State Committee for the State of Emergency in the U.S.S.R. in order to run the country and effectively exercise the state-of-emergency regime consisting of: O. D. Baklanov, V. A.

Kryuchkov, V. S. Pavlov, B. K. Pugo, V. A. Starodubtsev, A. I. Yizyakov, D. T. Yazov, G. I. Yanayev.

4. To establish that the U.S.S.R. State Committee for the State of Emergency's decisions are mandatory for unswerving fulfillment by all agencies of power and administration, officials and citizens throughout the territory of the U.S.S.R.

In connection with the inability for health reasons by Mikhail Sergeyevich Gorbachev to perform his duties as U.S.S.R. president, I have assumed the duties of the U.S.S.R. president from August 19, 1991, on the basis of Article 127 (7) of the U.S.S.R. Constitution.
Gennadi I. Yanayev
Vice-President of the U.S.S.R.
August 18, 1991

The idea behind the charter that authorized the coup (signed by Yanayev, Pavlov, and Baklanov) obviously had been circulated among the leading members of the Soviet Apparat long before TASS announced the state of emergency, and it was apparently legitimate enough for a factory in Pskov to freight two hundred fifty thousand handcuffs to Moscow, a party-controlled typesetting plant to whip up a boxcar load of preprinted arrest forms, and to have the KGB place Gorbachev under house arrest. "Mikhail Sergeyevich is now on vacation and recuperating from health problems," chief putschist Gennadi Yanayev lied to the nation in classical SovSpeak later that day. "He's undergoing treatment in the south of our country. He's very tired after all these years, and he will need some time to get better. We hope that after he is restored to health he will be able to resume his position."

Gorbachev had succumbed to a particularly foul Soviet virus with no known cure or visible effects beyond humiliation and repugnance. Soviet bureaucrats, a group uniquely susceptible to the often fatal condition, know the disease as *Yshol Po Sostoyaniyu Zdorova*—retired for reasons of health. And the ailment was spreading. Transmitting a weak signal from inside the Russian parliament building, the underground loyalist radio station Echo broadcast on August 20 that Pavlov ("severe fluctuation of hypertension"), Yazov ("cardiac difficulties"), and Kryuchkov ("high blood pressure") had all "taken ill" and were no longer members of the ruling committee.

Rumor wafted through the chaotic Russian Republic high-rise—that very special kind of Soviet rumor always decorated with wisps of truth impossible to unravel. One armed defender told me that there would be internal coup problems because Yazov, Kryuch-kov, and Pavlov had never put their signatures to the adventure; the rest of the hardline clique had only told the public that the feared ultraconservative trio was part of the plot. The Committee of Eight never wheeled out Yazov, Kryuchkov, or Pavlov to speak publicly in favor of the coup. Such a move is right out of the Kremlin playbook: it allowed the ringleaders to preempt any denial the men might make for responsibility in the coup, as well as eliminated their personalities from the action and actual power; the premise was, "Listen, you're involved with the coup by dint of your rep-utations, and nobody is ever going to believe anything different."

But no matter the political games, the ruling committee's armor continued to rumble into Moscow from the surrounding districts, much of it moving down the Minsk highway and across the Kalinin Bridge past the loyalist stronghold inside the Russian Parliament building to take up positions around Lenin's tomb in Red Square and to prevent demonstrators' entry inside the Sa-dovaya Ring road. On the outside of the Sadovaya Ring, a huge, helium-filled barrage balloon, trailing the white, blue, and red Russian tricolor, aptly floated over the nineteen-story Belyi Dom, as tens of thousands of demonstrators gathered in the pouring rain in the Belyi Dom's parking lot. Atop the coup-sent tanks, the sharp, dark eyes of the turret gunners were nervous, but also unthinkingly loyal to their commanders, or so all of Moscow feared. There were no tanks in Leningrad. Mayor Anatoli Sobchak had made a deal with the commanders to keep them out of town. Tanks sent from one Baltic barracks to secure the Estonian capital of Tallinn got lost, arriving in the seaport city three hours late, unaware that a coup was under way.

Bravely descending from his heavily bunkered office and clam-bering atop a tank to call for nationwide strikes and demonstrations and to say that state-controlled collective farmers were allowing the harvest to rot in the fields, Boris Yeltsin told the invaders: "Soldiers! Officers! Generals! The clouds of terror and dictatorship are gathering over the whole country. They must not be allowed to bring eternal night. In this tragic moment for Russia, I appeal to you: do not allow yourself to be ensnared in a net of lies and promises and demagogic calls to military duty. Think of your loved ones, your friends, your people!"

Less than two miles away in the Kremlin, the junta decreed the closure of all banks, much-lowered food prices, and the stocking of state shops with provisions. Stalin had used similar tactics to build his power base in the 1930s, albeit with more professional ruthlessness; yet, as Muscovites angrily jumped atop tanks cruising along the Sadovaya Ring, I grimly recalled what Stalin's former translator Valentin Berezhkov had warned me of in 1988: "Russians need the fear of punishment over them to accomplish anything. Remove the punishment and you've removed the desire; put food on the shelves for two weeks and *perestroika* will be forgotten."

"As long as there's a piece of cheese in the refrigerator," Sabina Orudjeva warned a few hours after the coup began, "the average Russian believes that he's doing very well, and this may cause us problems." To make sure that dairy products did not cause problems in areas where there was enough cheese, the junta had Soviet warships isolate the Baltic coast and paratroopers land in Estonia. The leaders of the republics of Estonia, Lithuania, Latvia, Moldavia, and the Ukraine refused to recognize the new government, and their citizens took to the streets delcaring independence.

The enigmatic State Committee for the State of Emergency in the U.S.S.R., conspicuously lacking—or neglecting—to announce any authorization or support from their collaborators in the Communist Party or on its Central Committee, seized Soviet television and had its announcers brand everyone demonstrating against the junta a "drunken hooligan." The unreported news was not funny: the junta had also seized the secret nuclear weapon codes and keys necessary to launch the Soviet doomsday arsenal, and the ease with which they had done this guaranteed that Western banks would be using a new standard to determine the quality of a borrower's collateral and to fix the terms of the loan.

All independent publications, including *Commersant*, were shut down and ordered to "reapply" to the Interior Ministry for permission to publish again. The editors and writers of *Commersant* spent the daylight hours of August 19 and 20 in the streets gathering information and their nights atop the barricades. Yak moved offices to a secret location in central Moscow to begin publishing an underground *Commersant*. Tanks surrounded the building, their commanders unaware of what was going on inside. "We expect the KGB at any moment," Yak said as he orchestrated *Commersant*'s first night coverage of the coup. "But we will not be muzzled."

"The so-called order promised by these self-proclaimed saviors will bring the fatherland suppression of dissent, handcuffs, concentration camps and night arrests," Yeltsin said of the junta in a videotaped message on the morning of August 20. "All this can only evoke one feeling among normal people—contempt."

That night, the junta imposed an eleven P.M. to five A.M. curfew that Moscow ignored, igniting the coup's only fierce battle between the army and the demonstrators. A few elements of the 106th Guards Airborne armored division, backed by a smattering of paramilitary MVD and KGB and troopers from General Boris Gromov's black berets, drove through a crowd to smash a barricade of Moscow buses trimmed with Pizza Hut billboards to advertise the raw and effective communist power known as *strakh*: fear.

Commersant reporters were on the scene, oblivious to the danger. The training Brad Durham had given them in the absolute necessity of speed in the news business was combining with their own sense of extreme urgency to do whatever necessary to defend the Belyi Dom. A direct line was established between a street-corner pay phone and *Commersant*'s editorial redoubt. Yak heard the sounds of gunfire and the screams of the crowd over the line as the reporters filed their stories. For the moment forgetting the impending legal action against Fact/*Commersant*, Billington called me from Chicago in half query, total command: "Fuck 'em! We are publishing, right?!"

Hurling stones, rocks, and Molotov cocktails, the Russian resistance counterattacked the light armor of the mechanized unit head on with planks and iron bars as the vehicles encountered difficulty breaching loyalist fortifications less than a hundred yards from the U.S. Commerce Department Commercial Section office building on the Tchaikovsky Street arc of the Sadovaya Ring. The gunners, using their tanks and APCs to ram and reram the yellow buses and electric trams to create a passage, grew frustrated and opened up on the resistance with automatic weapons. The demonstrators scattered through a salvo of gunfire and ricocheting bullets to hide behind concerete traffic berms atop the entry to the Tchaikovsky Street traffic tunnel and down into the underground pedestrian subway on both sides of the Kalinin/Tchaikovsky intersection. Running hard through a rainstorm, other protestors scrambled fifty feet to the left of a U.S. Commercial Office window display of Michael Jackson drinking Pepsi Cola and down the two-hundred-yard side road that skirts the U.S. Embassy and falls out on the white marble of the Russian Republic Parliament. Shouting "Yeltsin! Yeltsin! Yeltsin!" they fearlessly joined ten armored vehicles from the Tamanskaya and Tula armored divisions and Kantamorovski division paratroopers loyal to the Russian Republic to tighten the phalanx around the Belyi Dom for the night. Sleep was wet and fitful for many of twenty thousand barricaded loyalists camped out on the Belyi Dom's lawn and parking lot. More rumors—this time, a nightmare of non-Russian-speaking, siege-busting KGB Dzerzhinsky division troops from Soviet Central Asia coming to butcher the demonstrators outside and engage in hand-to-hand combat with the no-nonsense Afghan war vets guarding the inside of the parliamentary stronghold.

As the sun rose over Moscow on August 21, an architect, an economist, and a historian lay dead, and at least twelve were wounded at the Battle for Kalinin Intersection. Ilya Krichevsky, twenty-eight years old, was shot in the head while attacking a tank with a piece of wood. Dmitri Komar and Vladimir Usov were crushed under steel treads. The liberal former Soviet Foreign Minister Eduard Shevardnadze told Russian Republic deputies that the dead should be buried in the Kremlin Wall. "If there's not enough space for them," he later urged a crowd of over two hundred thousand Muscovites who needed no provocation, "we can remove those who are interred there already."

At one-fifteen P.M., Yeltsin's office verbally ordered all able-bodied men to stop the black Zil limos speeding four of the coup makers out Leninsky Prospekt to the Vnukova airport for a mad dash to the Soviet Republic of Kirghizstan. "Prevent them from escaping. Block the roads," Yeltsin said before taking to the rostrum of a near day-long emergency session of the Russian Republic parliament.

By three P.M., the Red Army had switched its allegiance to the Russian Republic with the help of twenty senior KGB officers who had been in Yeltsin's camp from the beginning of the coup. "It's becoming increasingly clear that the KGB played a key role in trying to topple Gorbachev," read a statement issued by KGB and Red Army officers loyal to Yeltsin. "The junta committed treason because it was backed up by [KGB] officers devoted to the Communist Party *nomenklatura.*"

By three-twenty P.M., the tanks were rolling back to the barracks, and loyalist politicians were organizing a flight south to free Gorbachev, whom they feared had been put under hallucinogenic drugs by Kryuchkov and Yazov in an attempt to make him sign documents. The coup ended with the government back in the hands of its electors, four putschists in the Crimea asking Mikhail Gorbachev for forgiveness, the other four hotly pursued by Yeltsin loyalists and, by six-fifteen P.M., the disclosure that Gorbachev was back "in control" of the U.S.S.R. after sixty hours of plots, suicides, intrigues, and criminal conspiracies that will take much longer than the coup did to unravel.

As liberal Moscow Mayor Gavril Popov sent two mobile cranes to help ten thousand demonstrators remove the twenty-eight-thousand-pound bronze of Soviet secret police founder Feliks Dzerzhinsky from its stumpy base in front of KGB headquarters, there was no shortage on the street of autopsies on the death of the Soviet system. It was the first time in either Russian or Soviet history that a democratically elected leader defeated what Gorbachev described as "reckless adventurers" and "crude and crafty individuals." Yeltsin was less diplomatic: "They are cockroaches in a jar." One man told me that the obstacles to land reform and private property would disappear with Gorbachev's return because the conservative cliques and the fifteen-million-member Communist Party were to be immediately purged. Another said that the failure of the coup repudiated the Bolsheviks and that seventy-four years of centralized bureaucracy had finally ended. Certainly, August 1991 stirred the Soviet people out of the dark alleys of political passivity and cynicism and into the streets to fortify the freedoms Gorbachev's social tinkering had made possible. Democracy persisted, but its survival within the labyrinthine beast that gave birth to the coup was administered by a small group of courageous professional politicians still surrounded by threat, suspicion, and a bureaucracy that nourishes while it neglects.

"We are making a mistake if we think the political situation that emerged as a result of all we have done is over," warned N. Begenkov, a Russian People's Deputy from Novosibirsk, in response to an official motion before the August 22 emergency session of the Russian Supreme Soviet on how to record the sixty-hour coup. "We have to realize that it was a coup d'état! It was not an *attempted* coup d'état! The document here says that on the nights of August 18 and August 19 an *attempt* was made at a coup d'état. Allow me to change this—for my electors and for history."

A much more sinister force is still at work in the Soviet Union, and a coup d'état is but an easily televised manifestation of that creature's continuing ability to confuse and skill to overwhelm. "It would be wrong to think that all the danger is behind us," Mikhail Gorbachev said of the farce that had been played out by his trusted aides, adding later in an aside to close his post-coup press conference: "You are seeing before you a man who is facing a drama." That drama is a tragedy, and the August coup was merely the first action against the characters that Gorbachev's democracy begat. Like the fledgling free-market efforts, the August onslaught was predicated on economic negligence, empowered by political greed, and doomed to failure because it was executed by corrupt, desperate amateurs totally incapable of any long-term strategy.

The *shatoon* still prowls the landscape, but in the euphoria over the failure of the August coup and the backdraft of flames that burned seven decades of secret documents housed inside Communist Party headquarters on Staraya Ploshad, it was all too easy to believe that the least bear had been put down for the winter. A few weeks before the coup, my now ex-Politburo friend Trusishka was pondering—privately, of course—whether any American university might be interested in his becoming a professor of Sovietology. I did not speak with him after the coup, but I'm certain he is still in the job market; there are a lot of people in Moscow's Krushchoba slums these days who would like to see Trusishka's corpse dangling from the Kremlin Bell Tower.

Ibragimov Hajibau Isak Oglu continued to walk in the way of Allah and his fate in the new Azerbaijan is unknown. The president of Azerbaijan had been the first Soviet republic leader to publicly applaud Gorbachev's removal during the coup. "Matters are worse," Hajibau wrote to me before the coup. "And I'm still not allowed to feed the people."

Lorrie Grimes, on the other hand, moved from Seattle to Moscow, where she now arranges American tours for Soviet rock 'n' roll bands. "I'm still hooked," she told me. "But now Russia is only rock 'n' roll."

Michael Mears left the U.S. Commerce Department for a senior position at General Electric. "Very few people understand the reality of the Soviet Union," he said. "It's one of those things that I'm unable to even talk about, let alone explain, with anyone who wasn't there. There's too much naiveté, more than there should be. People don't understand."

Svet Raikov was last seen on a beach in Hawaii, receiving a monthly hard-currency stipend from the Moscow Business Center and trying to marry a Seattle aerobics instructor. Roman Kudriavtsev escaped to Toronto, where he is now living with a cousin as a statistic in the Canadian welfare system and, according to his associates in Moscow, attempting to import Soviet women to dance in topless bars.

Brad Durham returned to Boston to finish his last semester of law school, shaking his head over what might have been, happy that the staff of *Commersant* covered the coup without using "objective experts say" in its copy. "John Reed said it took ten days to shake the world," Durham observed. "This revolution will take over a decade to shake just the Soviets and its cost will be a lot higher."

A few months before the coup, Peter Martin had written a letter to Yakovlev. It read:

> *Thank you for the remittance of the $34,000, which represents payment in full of your obligations to our agency. We deeply enjoyed working with you on this exciting and worthwhile project and hope to continue to capitalize on your success in the U.S. market. We believe that there is a serious potential audience in the U.S. for* Commersant *and look forward to attracting subscribers and media coverage here.*

Yak needed to show the letter to Jean-Louis Servan-Schreiber at *Groupe Expansion* to prove his honesty as a businessman. "*Déjà-vu* is a French word, isn't it?" Martin asked.

Tom Billington spent the weeks before the August coup reviewing reports on the conspiracy, fraud, and copyright infringement laws of France, Germany, Italy, Great Britain, Cyprus, and the Soviet Union. In the United States, he contemplated suing Yakovlev and *Commersant's* new shareholders under the Racketeer Influenced and Corrupt Organization (RICO) statutes unless Yak agreed to a settlement of one million dollars. In the wake of *Groupe Expansion's* public declaration that *Commersant* journalists were an indispensable and innovative addition to the eight hundred "press professionals" who made up the *Eurexpansion* network, Peggy Yott started speculating on what horrors Yak and his staff had in store for Servan-Schreiber's publishing empire. She did not have to reflect for long. A few hours after Yak closed his deal with *Groupe Expansion,* Andrei Vasiliev, *Commersant's* star business reporter, was arrested and jailed for shoplifting women's underwear in Zurich while there on assignment for the paper with political writer Sasha Fadin. Fadin phoned Moscow with the news and asked for someone to call Yak in Paris to see if he could do anything to get Vasiliev out of prison. Fadin said that the Swiss authorities, who later deported Vasiliev, were mystified as to why anyone with over two thousand dollars in his pocket would shoplift. "It's a good question," Yott said. *Commersant* wrote in an issue at about that time that the trend of criminal groups to organize boded well for

Soviet society: "The better managed and more stable organized crime becomes, the less violence it will employ."

Sabina Orudjeva, having deserted her dream to open an art gallery, became a croupier at a hard-currency gambling casino built by German businessmen at the Moscow horserace track. Sabina had both the opportunity and the talent to resettle successfully in America, but she decided to remain in the Soviet Union. Grandfather, she believed, would have wanted it that way. Sabina had told me this on the cold summer day we had driven through a maze of primitive oil refineries to visit Sabit Orudjev's gravestone in a wretched village cemetery near the Caspian. We had spent the morning hauling leaky buckets of water to the grave, using twigs and leaves to scrub off the years of petrochemical filth that had disfigured his headstone. Few people ever came to visit. The former minister and hero of the Great Patriotic War could have been entombed alongside other Soviet heroes in Moscow's Novodevichy Convent cemetery, or enshrined in the Kremlin Wall, where his sepulcher would have been stared at through pine trees by tourists and safeguarded around the clock by the two elite sentinels who defend Lenin's tomb. Instead, the "King of the Bear Hunters" had told the family to bury him atop an anonymous hill. No one was ever really sure why.

"Grandfather never harmed an animal in his life," Sabina explained through the acrid-tasting wind. "That's why it was strange to see him so delighted to receive a gift of such a big knife with which to hunt bears. Now, maybe, it's my turn," said Sabina *Orudjeva*—which in Russian patois means the "woman with weapons."

I had finally left the Soviet Union for good after nearly six years of watching the varying fortunes of *perestroika*. Soviet communism appeared to be nothing but a brutal and inefficient dinosaur. But appearances are deceiving, especially when instantly transmitted into living rooms by satellite and advertised as one of the great phenomena of human history. Soon the curious historians and the next wave of eager Western reporters will arrive in the Soviet Union to search the wake of Gorbachev's ouster for the minutest details of *perestroika*'s success and failure. And they will ask why *perestroika* did nothing but help to cause the civil war that may be inevitable.

The electricity of Boris Yeltsin's courage during the August coup has enchanted the West, which now believes that Russia's free-market revolution can be inspired through democracy. But Yeltsin is a populist. Although populism is a legitimizing and effective weapon to use against coup-makers, populism after the tanks go home is a cartoon bubble that nearly always bursts with the words of negative martyrs rather than the policies of constructive leaders. Simply offering the former Soviet peoples of the fifteen republics an opportunity to vent their frustration through their own ballot boxes, without having leaders able coherently to formulate political policy or the money to pay for their economic strategies, is a recipe for a revolution more lethal than what Yanayev's Gang of Eight unleashed on Moscow's streets. When populism goes nowhere it degenerates into terror, and the collision between dream and reality seen in August 1991 will continue for years to come. This was my *istina*, the sadly ultimate and paradoxical truth with which I watched the green metal of Soviet armor leave Moscow. It was with this conviction that I returned to the West.

The coup was over and I was proud of Volodya Yakovlev's brave decision to risk his life to keep *Commersant* open and independent during what he described as a "mediocre play directed by a producer with no talent." Such courage is rare in life and it deeply touched all of us who had worked alongside Yak to create *Commersant*. The Soviet Army officers assigned to collecting *Commersant's* pages for printing on the Red Star presses never arrived on the evening of the coup, and Yak's plans to turn the paper into a daily newspaper with the help of *L'Expansion* seemed ruined. But a few miles away, in the offices of the Communist Party daily *Pravda*, editor Gennadi Selezvev gladly printed whatever Yanayev's mob pushed across his desk.

"On the whole, we don't regret what we did during the coup," Selezvev said after Gorbachev had been restored to power. "What we do regret is that we *had* to publish the statements of the Committee."

The next morning, a disgraced *Pravda* appeared for the first time in its seventy-nine-year history without the logo "The Organ of the Communist Party of the Soviet Union" inscribed beneath

Lenin's head. *Pravda* instantly converted its logo to "General Political Newspaper," going into free-market competition with *Commersant*'s plans to go daily. By nightfall, both *Pravda* and every journalist who worked for a state publication were doomed: a new national coalition Soviet government had been formed, in which power was to be shared by Gorbachev but with strings pulled and cut by Yeltsin. One of its first acts was to forbid the publication of *Pravda* and to nationalize the hundreds of Communist Party printing plants and publishing houses throughout the republics. On August 24, 1991, Mikhail Gorbachev resigned as the leader of the Communist Party of the Soviet Union and dissolved its Central Committee, effectively dislocating seventy-four years of institutionalized chaos.

Gennadi Selezvev's words and the fate of *Pravda* strangely echoed an evening that Charlie Bausman had spent with Yak before the coup, to try to avoid the ugly legal battle percolating between him and Billington—a battle that would overflow into Western courtrooms where contract disputes were not adjudicated through bribes or emergency decrees contrived to crush the rule of law. The brewing tempest over the Race–Fact/*Commersant* deal was no secret and not even a collapse of communism would stop the legal storm. Such is the reality of capitalism, which was why Bausman went to caution Yak that "It doesn't really matter how successful a person is. If they ruin their reputation, they've lost everything."

"I told Yak how bad his reputation was, on both sides of the political spectrum, in the Moscow foreign community and with Russians he had known for years," Bausman recalled. "We talked about what was going on with Race and the French, and I told him that he had better take immediate steps to repair that situation and improve his image with a lot of other business people. It was tough, because Yak really isn't a bad guy.

"But he just looked at me with that half smirk and started talking about his usual set of *variants*. 'You know, Charlie,' Yak said to me, 'as far as I know my reputation has been shit from the beginning and there's absolutely no reason for me to fix it now.' "

The Yak had just rented a new apartment when I went over

to see him a few weeks after Bausman left Moscow to finish his MBA at Columbia University. The passport wallet in Yak's den contained a multiple-entry French visa stamp and a Societé Générale Visa card, both oblations from his new Paris partner. Through clouds of damp tobacco smoke and endless cups of coffee and Armenian brandy, we talked for a few hours about the mechanics of setting up a foreign staff for the new-look *Commersant,* and then argued long and hard into the night about the situation with Billington. The walls had been lacerated with shurikens; Yak went nowhere without one of the flying stars in his pocket. He tore one of his curved claws from the plaster and placed it atop the desk against the framed letter from Harvard University. Unsheathing a samurai sword as he crossed the room, Yak furiously slashed at his surroundings with the honed steel. No one other than Yakovlev was allowed to touch the blade. An eerie expression of blankness, animation, and frustration passed across his face when I asked why. Yak told me it had something to do with magic and the skill to make people believe in what is not real.

Acknowledgments

BEAR HUNTING would never have been written without the help and support of five very special individuals: William Eaton, the former *Los Angeles Times* correspondent in Moscow; Yelena Kaplan, who nobly suffered my Russian for seven years in both Moscow and Washington; Robert Manoff, who first sent me to Moscow for *Harper's Magazine;* Brian Kelly, who made sure that I stayed there as the *Regardie's* magazine correspondent; and Bob Bender at Simon & Schuster, who was never blinded by Soviet-chic and the hot, pop-politic of *perestroika.* Three others who believed in the hunt, but never made it to Moscow to participate, were Robert Stock and Marylin Bender, my editors at *The New York Times Magazine,* and Ellen Hume Shattuck at Harvard University's John F. Kennedy School of Government. Special thanks go to Frank Bourgholzer, the dean of Moscow correspondents, who came back to the Soviet Union in 1988 after too long an absence and guided me through thirty years of his own Russian and Soviet experience.

Thanks to my Moscow colleagues Bill Keller of *The New York Times* and Anne Imse of the Associated Press for their background briefs on what happened in official Moscow while I was off covering the cooperative movement.

Meg Bortin at the *International Herald Tribune* in Paris, Constance Sayre at Market Partners in New York, and Jack Romanos at Simon &

Schuster were absolutely critical during the final stages of the manuscript during the week of August 19, 1991. Decisive advice and support over exhausted international phone lines also came from Gypsy da Silva and Johanna Li at Simon & Schuster; J. Lanning Aldrich in London; Yelena Schevchenko and Yelena Yeltsina in Moscow; Shaun Conroy-Hargrave in Paris; Marie Stock in New York; Peter Gent in Michigan; and Dr. Hunter S. Thompson at the Owl Farm.

My deepest gratitude goes to Professor Robert Legvold, the director of the W. Averell Harriman Institute for Advanced Study of the Soviet Union at Columbia University. It was the Harriman Institute that allowed me formal historical study of the Soviet Union under their visiting scholar program with Professor John Hazard and, while in Russia, over bowls of soup provided by Sally Onesti in her little green room in the Vampire State Building at Moscow University. In the often foggy world of academic Sovietology, Legvold, Hazard, and Onesti bring a rare clarity that I greatly appreciated.

Essential U.S. government personnel included: Bonnie Glick at the U.S. Commercial Office in Moscow for her wit and hot water; Jeff Glassman at the U.S. State Department, for his unique understanding of Soviet intoxication statutes and his comprehensive Rolodex of Moscow bail bondsmen; and Michael Mears at the U.S. Commerce Department, for daring to serve up the truth even if it meant breaking the rules.

Thank you, Lee Mason, for *always* being at the other end of a bad Moscow–New York phone line with a pencil; Robert Friedman, who worked with me in the coverage of U.S.–Soviet summits for the *Village Voice* and *Newsday,* and Margaret Sagan, who continues to have the time and persistence to deal with her former student.

Three others who deserve particular thanks for their enthusiasm and courage in sorting out Soviet bureaucratic and political matters both large and small are Alexander Avelichev, the director and editor-in-chief of Progress Publishing in Moscow; Vitali Korotich, the editor-in-chief of *Ogonyok* magazine; and Washington attorney Ed Weidenfeld.

Most of all, Artyom Borovik, for always getting me in and never failing to get me out. *Kuda seychas, tovarish?*

Index